Architecture by Moonlight

:~

Writers of fiction generally

must stick to probabilities,

or at least possibilities,

more or less, but in real

life there are no such

limitations. The impossible

happens continually.

W. B. Seabrook
The Magic Island

Architecture by Moonlight

.~

Rebuilding Haiti, Redrafting a Life

Paul E. Fallon

UNIVERSITY OF MISSOURI PRESS

COLUMBIA

Copyright © 2014 by
The Curators of the University of Missouri
University of Missouri Press, Columbia, Missouri 65201
Printed and bound in the United States of America
All rights reserved

5 4 3 2 1   18 17 16 15 14

Cataloging-in-Publication data available from the Library of Congress.
ISBN 978-0-8262-2039-4

♾™ This paper meets the requirements of the
American National Standard for Permanence of Paper
for Printed Library Materials, Z39.48, 1984.

Jacket design: Mindy Basinger Hill
Design and composition: K. Lee Design & Graphics
Typefaces: Palatino and Gabriola

Contents

Architecture by Moonlight

✌

Demolition

January 12, 2010

Renee Edme works alone in a windowless room at Mission of Hope in Grand Goave, Haiti. She hears a truck outside. It's unusual to hear traffic noise within the concrete building that's both Mission of Hope's office and her family's home, even though it sits tight to Rue St. Jerome, a main street that connects National Route 2 to the Bay of Gonave. Her mind flicks back to the wayward jeep that rammed into the corner of their house a few years ago. Trucks often drive too fast along Route 2, though they ought to slow down along the market. But it would be hard for one to gather enough speed on St. Jerome to make such a ruckus. The noise distracts her from the report she's writing about Mission of Hope's evangelical activities. She tries to rationalize it away. The jeep struck at night, and she's in the back of the building, next to the courtyard where Marieve is preparing dinner. The truck can't harm her. But it keeps coming. It grows louder. It pierces her ears. She grips the edge of her desk. The lights go out. Power is so unreliable in Haiti. She needs to switch over to the generator. But the racket increases. It defies geographic logic. The truck is coming right for her.

For a few seconds, a lifetime of seconds, she cannot move. She sits in the dark, unable to reach the generator, unable to counter what God has ordained, resigned to the truck crashing through the wall, crushing her. The din reaches a grueling decibel. Renee jumps from her chair, stumbles to the door and down the narrow passage to the courtyard. The menace is upon her, pounding her eardrums.

A roaring wave claps her from behind. Renee is a big woman, not tall but stout, with long brown hair pulled in a taut line down her back and a mouth prone to descend at the corners. She is a creature close to the ground. She weaves. Her legs give out, but so does the earth itself. The courtyard rumbles and shakes, it rumbles and shakes. Her legs are unable to support her. Gravity is confused. The ground pushes and slides when it ought to pull. She doesn't fall; she jellies in place. She has no bearings, no reference plane from which to measure the world. The noise dissipates, it echoes past, a freight train speeding to a distant terminal. The ground settles. Gravity regains the upper hand. Renee goes slack; her body slumps against the doorway.

The moment her back rests against the hard frame Renee jolts it back to attention. Where's AJ? Alexis? Lex? She calls for her children, her husband, but hers is just one more voice in the agonized chorus that rises from the rumbling. She steps out of the doorway; it doesn't feel safe. She scans the courtyard. Marieve stands not more than twenty feet away, wailing. The earth turns solid once again. For a moment Renee wonders if perhaps she dreamed, but the screams rising all around confirm grim reality.

Renee and Marieve walk toward Route 2. Mission of Hope's church and school are at the edge of town; people will congregate there. Instinct guides them, as nothing is recognizable. Renee has lived in Grand Goave for ten years, but her town has turned into a foreign landscape. Buildings are racked, some fallen. They pick their way through an obstacle course of vehicles, toppled concrete, and intimate belongings. Others pick their way through the chaos, seeking their community of refuge.

By the time Marieve and Renee reach Route 2, a mob has formed along Grand Goave's umbilical cord to the world. The sound starts up again. The wind rises from the east, propelling the noise. This time Renee knows it's not a truck. She stands on the road's white line, far from anything that might fall, yet packed tight to others. The noise deafens. The crowd braces against each other. The earth gives way beneath them. It's more difficult to bear the second time, knowing what's coming, knowing that time will stop as waves ripple through her town, her loved ones, her bones. The tremor passes, undulating west toward Petit Goave. Roofs and walls that precariously survived the first tremor topple to the ground. The

crowd wails in the tremor's wake. They have survived an earthquake and its first aftershock.

Renee and Marieve arrive at Mission of Hope's church and
school before the next tremor. They find AJ and Alexis, safe, but
Renee's husband, Lex, is in Leogone, ten miles to the east. God
alone knows when she might see him. Renee organizes the gathered. Yet each time she tries to pair parents with children or safety
check the filtered water system, the noise picks up, accompanied
by the wind, followed by the tidal earth.

For days everyone stays outdoors, fearful of roofs overhead.
News reports from Port-au-Prince itemizing eight or ten aftershocks are laughable; the aftershocks come in a continuous stream.
The people clustered at Mission of Hope learn to ride them out.
Just before the earth shakes, before the deafening noise wells out
of the east, they hear cries of *Bondye Jezi*, Holy Jesus, warning them
what is approaching, exclaiming to God that they have weathered
yet another wave. Renee and her family hear the screams coming
toward them, followed by the clatter and the wind and the shaking.
Then they let out their own screams. Screams to alert those farther
along the earth's unstable flow. We have witnessed this trauma,
and we are still alive.

I am far from Haiti during the earthquake. I barely even know
Renee. I remember her husband, Lex, Mission of Hope's pastor,
who chaperoned our group last summer and took a keen interest
in the clinic construction. But Renee and I met only once, briefly,
before the quake. More than a year will pass before Renee recounts
her story of that day. By then we will know each other very well.

January 12, 2010, is a cold, short winter day in Boston. I wear
double gloves to keep my fingers from freezing stiff when I bicycle through the dark to my morning yoga class. Afterward I eat
breakfast at my desk, leftover chicken and rice washed down with
a Diet Coke—make that two. I spend the morning coordinating
equipment for Albany Medical Center's new operating rooms,
tedious work that is aggravated by all the compromises the project suffered; I cannot dispel the notion that the building could be
better. I warm up meatloaf and carrots for lunch—my housemate
Paul is a prodigious cook, and our refrigerator is full of Tupper-
wared leftovers. I cap my meal with a handful of cookies. In the

afternoon I revise the plan for the Newton-Wellesley Hospital Cancer Center, which sparks enough creative juice to remind me why, after thirty years, I still like being an architect. It's long since dark by the time I ride home to Cambridge along the Charles River. The city lights reflect on the water. I skip dinner, still full from all those cookies.

About 8:00 p.m. my sister calls with news of Haiti's earthquake. "As soon as I heard, I had to call you; I'm glad that you're here, that you're safe." Pat has a flair for drama that I lack. It's been months since I was in Haiti; I am in no danger. As she relates the tragedy, the magnitude sinks in. I realize she's not calling out of any legitimate fear; she's simply seeking the community we all crave in crisis. We are thousands of miles from the shaking, but because I once walked over the same ground that is now so treacherous, I am the person she connects with the disaster. She needs the reassurance that someone she loves is safe. We are simultaneously in sympathy with the people of Haiti and relieved to be far away.

After we hang up I Internet search the quake and field half a dozen calls from concerned friends and family. *Yes, I passed through the location of the epicenter. No, I don't know if the clinic is damaged.* Everyone expresses gratitude that I am safe and offers personal sympathy, since, as they say to a person: *Haiti means so much to you.*

I am surprised by this collective impression that Haiti is central to my life. True, I volunteered to design a clinic there for Forward in Health, a nonprofit medical group from Gardner, Massachusetts, and I visited Haiti last summer to review the construction. But I do lots of volunteer work. As a long-divorced middle-aged man with grown children, I have ample time and prefer to spend vacations getting my hands dirty. I'd rather build houses in New Orleans post-Katrina or clear out trees for Smokey House Center in Vermont than sit on a beach or ride a tour bus. It's more practical than noble. A man alone benefits from structure and purpose when he travels, and fellow volunteers offer interesting company. Yet so many people describe the taut connection between Haiti and me, there must be something to it.

When it comes to acknowledging feelings, I am as opaque as any guy; emotions have to whack me on the head. The evening my high-school girlfriend first said she loved me I was caught off guard. I had to process the ramifications. My emotional compass oscillates between ambivalent and unreliable; it was years before I returned the sentiment and years more before I proposed. Add thirteen years more until I finally understood my feelings toward other men. As a married man with children, I considered being gay an odd inconvenience; she was the one who understood it was a deal breaker.

Now, as this earthquake pushes Haiti into the world's attention, my own feelings surface. I begin to understand what others already know: Haiti dwells deep in my psyche. They know how quick I am to regurgitate my adventures there; how my ordered and rational mind grapples to extract sense from that irrational yet beguiling place.

I set the phone down after talking with my nephew Jeff and stare outside. Ice clings to the naked branches of the pear tree beyond my window. Frost collects along the edges of the storm pane. But I feel hot, sweaty, and dirty. The six months since my visit dissolve. Recollections race through my head; images of Haiti throbbing with present tense immediacy. The pill man, who mesmerized me on my first day, leads the cacophony. I sometimes wonder whether he is the key. If I can make sense of him, can I make any sense out of the rest?

I am three hours in Haiti when the guy with pills sticking out of his hat drifts into my field of vision. I stare at him through the sooty school bus window that separates me from Port-au-Prince's street market. He struts through the crowd balancing a metal bucket on his head, its base hammered to fit his skull. The bucket is filled with row upon row of colorful tablets and capsules shrink-wrapped to cardboard. Each packet nestles into the one below and is held in place by the one above. The rows rise to create a headdress that spirals high above his head. The pill man towers over women squatting before baskets of mangos, bananas, and sugar cane, trays of American surplus toiletries, skillets sizzling with fried dough, and pots full of percolating stew. He is a peacock, a Dr. Seuss character; thousands of bright dots pulse above his bucketed head as he wends his way.

The market extends as far as I can see. Through the dirty bus window I search for pattern or purpose among the black heads that shift in a slow current over the dry, dusty earth. Individual faces merge like an oil spill oozing over the landscape. I have never seen so many people so unlike me. I cannot discern the crowd's underlying structure. The logician in me is unsettled; yet, I am also intrigued, energized, by the precarious life I observe beyond.

Who would buy unmarked drugs from a street vendor? Does this walking pharmacy have regular customers who know what they need? Is there a local understanding as to which color addresses what malady? Does he offer advice like the articulate woman who wears a white coat and a "registered pharmacist" badge at my CVS back home? Or does the pill man simply gauge a customer's pain, pull a colored packet from his hat, and whisper, "Here, man, this will make you feel good." I will never know; he makes no sales while our bus crawls through the mob. His glorious headdress recedes into the marketplace.

Earlier images of that trip fill my head: the gauntlet of beggars at the airport and the grabby little men in red shirts who keep trying to wrestle my bags away from me. Hot and sweaty, breathing hard from luggage battles, I am barely settled into my lumpy bus seat when we drive away from the airport and pull on to the main road. A truck in the oncoming lane rams against a jeep and spontaneously combusts. Orange flames erupt. Vehicles skid. Fenders bang in the pile-up. People stream out of cars and trucks. I gasp for air. *What have I gotten myself into?* But the flames shock me like a defibrillator. They recalibrate my pulse. I stop my heavy breathing; I cease trembling. Whatever coping mechanisms fifty-four years of American comfort have taught me are useless in the face of Haiti. I abandon all pretense of controlling my fate and give myself over to this alien landscape. I taste its polluted grit, hear its foreign tongues, inhale its noxious fumes.

Initial impressions of Haiti confirm my preconceptions. It is crowded, noisy, dirty, smelly, and poor. There is no end to the line of people who shuffle along the sides of the road or jam into *tap-taps*, covered pickup trucks and ancient buses painted with iconography exalting Jesus as well as J Lo. We Americans are preconditioned for the blight. We have seen it on TV; we think we know it. But my certainty wavers the first time I distinguish a specific face among the crowd, and the human soup bubbles into a kaleidoscope of unique individuals. It shatters completely the moment a hand reaches into my seat, clutches my arm, and I feel the pressure of another person upon me. I am not in a movie; these are not extras in *The Constant Gardener*. These are individuals; thousands, millions of them. They share my own aspirations and fears; each striving to cope in a place stacked against survival. Stripped of my preconceptions, Haiti ceases to be a forty-two-inch image animating my den. It is a reality I must confront right here, right now. I nearly collapse in its exotic stupor, yet I cannot turn my eyes from the sights beyond my dusty bus window. Sights still vivid six months later through the frosty, winter glass.

We leave the pill man and the market behind. We crawl through Port-au-Prince's squalor toward Les Cayes. Tight-packed houses give way to open countryside. Land that is mostly depleted retains welcome patches of lush vegetation. I recall the shiny clean little girls at clinic in Sunday dresses with the lacy tops of their anklets turned down over their patent leather shoes, hiding behind their mothers' long skirts until we hold forth lollipops, and they rush up to be examined. I see the crowds that surge at night after the sun vanishes, when the breeze tickles and the street swelter lifts. There are nine million people in Haiti; the most densely populated country in the Western hemisphere. Over ten days I reckon I see half of them. The flow of people along the side of the road never ceases.

I even see people who try not to be seen. Our bus hits a pothole; we get a flat. We hobble to a corrugated metal shed along the highway that has tires hanging off its sides. After greetings, negotiations, gesticulations, and handing over gourdes (Haitian currency) we disembark while three Haitians jerry rig a replacement from their meager inventory. A group of us drift toward a clump of trees, seeking shade. The whites of six eyes puncture the shadows. Three children, the oldest no more than ten, observe us in silence. How they got here, where they came from, or why they stand so quiet, without house or cart or food or adult in sight, we do not know. We nod. They nod in return. But they do not move. I want to shelter them under my shoulder, give them a Power Bar from my pack, and bring them with us until we can find their parents. But they scare me, standing so silent, so somber, so arbitrary. Hardly children at all. They remain still, barely breathing, until we reboard the bus. I castigate myself for doing nothing, yet I have no idea what we might have done.

We continue. The ride is bumpier due to our makeshift spare. Along the blacktop, streams of people flow by on either side. We pass a scattering of shacks; the distant hills appear uninhabited. Yet I know that beyond every bend, every tree, Haiti is packed with people who occupy a tiny footprint. The children in the shade have thousands of brothers and sisters, all lurking in silence.

Those six eyes watch me; they implore me for the rest of the trip. They motivate my work on the new clinic building, which is not as far along as I supposed and less well built than I hoped. They stare back at me from the feverish, scabbed faces of children seeking care. They populate the painted tin *tap-tap* I buy from a vendor the last night of our trip.

On the night the earthquake strikes, memories of my ten days in Haiti ricochet around my brain without hierarchy or order. The recollections fill me with energy; I want to do something—right now—to alleviate the disaster. I send an email to John Mulqueen of Forward in Health, complete online applications to Habitat for Humanity, Architects for Humanity, and the Red Cross; I send money through cyberspace. But none of that assuages my need. Haiti demands active engagement. I have something to offer: permanent concrete and steel. And though I don't know exactly what it is, I intuit that Haiti has something to offer me. Something to nourish my soul, soften my nature, and stir compassion long lost.

On January 12, 2010, I do not yet know the depth of Haiti's grip on me, how I will return again and again, how I'll be compelled to document my experiences in a quest to shape a clear narrative until I finally understand that clear narratives about Haiti are misleading. The true spirit of the country lies in the interstices of its inconsistency, its opposition to the rest of the world. The pill man floats back into my mind. He wears Haiti's duality lightly on his head, casually offering the peril and promise of unmarked drugs. I imagine his business flourishes amid desperation. I have no pills—magic, labeled, or otherwise—to offer Haiti in the face of this great tragedy. I can only offer my knowledge, discipline, and logic to a land that captivates me by flouting them all.

Plastic Sheathing

August 2010

Haiti, the second time around, is surreal—not just because of the earthquake's detritus, the unexpected crack in the road that makes my stomach lurch, the random collapsed house marked with a deadly X, or the zombie eyes of the women in their market stalls who have seen so much pain they no longer see anything. It is also surreal because we are such a diffuse band of seekers. Last year's euphoria of twenty-five volunteers buoyed by the opportunity to raise a simple smile upon this troubled land is replaced by eight discordant souls with imperfectly aligned agendas.

We hatched this trip two months earlier over steak and beer on John and Paula Mulqueen's patio. There I met Len Gengel, a guy from neighboring Rutland who found out about Forward in Health's work in Haiti after his daughter, Britney, died in the earthquake. Britney, along with seven other students and six faculty members from Lynn University, was on a service trip to Haiti. She was dark, vivacious, and as scattered about her future as any college sophomore. People called her a pampered princess, a solid friend, a party beast, and a caring soul. I'm sure they were all correct. On the afternoon of January 12, the Lynn group visited an orphanage. Britney texted her parents back in Massachusetts: *They love us so much and everyone is so happy. They love what they have and they work so hard to get nowhere, yet they are all so appreciative. I want to move here and start an orphanage myself.*

When the group arrived back at the Hotel Montana that afternoon, Britney's roommate trotted off to the pool while Britney headed for the shower. Who lives and who dies can be as arbitrary as that. With the water rushing over her, Britney must not have heard the truck coming her way.

Britney was but one of the 250,000 people who died in the 2010 Haiti earthquake: 250,000 dead is a horrific statistic; a number that invokes sympathy, even provokes rage. But 250,000 deaths numb our capacity for empathy. Empathy requires a personal connection; something to link our comfort to the horror. We cannot empathize thousands of times over. Yet empathy's required to fuel compassion; it propels us beyond our immediate interests and drives us to act. When we can envision ourselves in the wreckage and extend our hands to others, we raise not only the victims; we raise ourselves as well. For many Americans, Britney Gengel became the face of the Haiti earthquake.

After the ground settled, Britney could not be found. The media picked up her story. Her father, Len, is a bear of a man whose emotions pop off his face. The cameras loved his palpable grief, and he wielded the exposure they provided to help find his daughter. He demanded to know what was being done to find Americans missing in Haiti; he challenged President Obama to do more. Three days after the quake, the Gengels were told that Britney had been found alive. Len and his wife, Cherylann, flew to Florida to meet their daughter, reporters in tow, only to encounter a case of mistaken identity. Ten days after the disaster Len collaborated with the US State Department as well as the media; he visited Haiti with US Representative James McGovern to monitor the search for Britney and other missing Americans. He received national attention and ensured the search for bodies continued, at least at the Hotel Montana.

Len is a man of charisma and connections, energy and drive. If every family member of every victim had acted as he did, the result would have been utter chaos. Yet he helped propel the rescue effort. No protocol bound him. He bent any rules necessary to serve the agenda of finding his daughter. Thirty-three days after the earthquake, Britney's remains were found deep in the rubble of the Hotel Montana. She was the last person accounted for from Lynn University.

As he told this story in the Mulqueens' backyard, Len's grief was still palpable. His pain washed over me, pressed against my skin, and stifled me. His puppy dog eyes, those wide and innocent whites swimming frantically in his big head, revealed unfathomable loss. Len recounted Britney's story so succinctly I knew he had told it a hundred times before. Yet he spoke with such angst he could tell it a thousand more times without finding resolution, a million more times without finding peace. For Britney's death defies reason.

Len's grief was coupled with a fierce determination. "My daughter's text is my mission. I want to open the orphanage on the first anniversary of the earthquake." I knew a seven-month target was laughable, but I held my tongue in deference to his noble intention. We agreed to visit Haiti together, to evaluate Forward in Health's site as a possible location for the Gengels' orphanage, and tour other orphanages to learn how they work. We would design and build a memorial to Brit; we would channel the family's grief; we would benefit the children of Haiti. The order of importance for these competing demands was not obvious to me. What was clear, however, was how desperately each need cried out for attention.

As I walked to my car that night, I considered my first impressions of Len Gengel. I couldn't say I liked the man; we certainly didn't have much in common. I surmised that Len could be a fierce ally, but if he felt crossed he would be a crushing foe. I acknowledged my reservations and then tossed them aside. I was itching to get back to Haiti, and one meal convinced me that Len Gengel, his passion seared in pain, was going to do something big and meaningful. I wanted to be a part of it. I feared we would clash, but rationalized that if we weren't an easy team, perhaps we'd be an effective one.

The trip resulting from that meal is our somber group on this peculiar mission, bypassing the heart of destruction in Port-au-Prince, Carrefour, Leogone, and Grand Goave to come to Les Cayes, which was spared direct earthquake damage but is overrun with refugees. Our purpose is not one of temporary aid or shelter, but to conceptualize something permanent. Cherylann Gengel is here with her son Bernie and her sister Jodie, along with John and Paula Mulqueen; Robert Travis, a philanthropist interested in Forward in Health; my son Andy, and me.

John and Paula are stalled. They want to build their clinic, to provide permanent roots for their medical mission. But the earthquake put a halt to construction and diverted their energy to emergency trips throughout Haiti. They are no closer to a completed building than when we visited last year. Actually, they're further away. Although Les Cayes was spared much damage, it lies on the same fault line. I have enlisted the help of structural engineers at Simpson Gumpertz & Heger (SGH) to make the clinic design earthquake-resistant. When construction finally resumes, it will be more complex and more expensive

Cherylann's flat affect reveals nothing as we motor through our agenda. Her eyes betray the same loss I see in Haitian women, but her grief is sharpened by its loneliness. Unlike the people here, all of whose lives have been shattered, Cherylann suffers alone. Friends and neighbors back in Rutland can offer condolences and sympathy, but they cannot share her bizarre reality. Her daughter was swallowed by the earth. Affluent Americans expect prosperity to buffer against such arbitrary tragedy. Cherylann hates it here, I can feel it; it seems only right that she should hate such an unstable land. She is reserved, especially compared to Len, and if she has the passion required to make this orphanage a reality, it will have to emerge from energy she's yet to reveal. But she goes through the motions, because doing something, anything, is preferable to the paralytic horror of standing still.

Len could not come on the trip, for reasons undisclosed. Jodie is here instead, her obvious role to prop up Cherylann when she tumbles. Jodie is perky, fun, full of stories about when they were kids, and quick to fill awkward gaps in conversation with tales of her four-year-old daughter.

Bernie is also here to help out his mom, but he has his own agenda. He may be the oldest-looking high-school senior on earth, with a full beard, dark brows, and flesh on his bones. He smokes and scowls and passes hours without a word, then he utters fragments that are quiet and too mature. Bernie is reverent toward his sister, my first clue to how Brit's beatification is going to influence this endeavor. Unlike his mother, Bernie finds solace here. Haiti is not only the place where Britney died; it contains the essence of her last breath.

Then there are the other three guys. Robert Travis is a jocular middle-aged man, the shepherd of a Rotary fund charged with investing in clean-water systems. He's considering underwriting the well at Forward in Health.

Andy, my nineteen-year-old son, is wrapping up a year off from college during which he started a handyman business, made some bucks, and then hiked the Appalachian Trial with two buddies. Andy has little agenda beyond finding a bit more adventure before returning to academics.

Finally, there's me. What do I want? My objective is more diffuse than anyone's; a dull sense that something is missing in my life with only shadow notions of how to fill the void. I would like to save the world, or, at least, being an architect, make it more commodious. My life has grown stale. I want to build something durable, shape it with my own hands in a more direct way than I can by sitting in my Boston office. I am a seeker in tune with Cinderella's refrain from Sondheim's *Into the Woods*: I won't know what I want until I have it and see if I like it. For now, I must be patient that these vague motivations pulling me back to Haiti will, in time, reveal good reason.

We spend four days together. We visit the Forward in Health site, five orphanages, Mother Teresa's compound in Les Cayes, and the public hospital there. Orphans sing for us, march for us, and recite for us. Some live in clean, if empty, houses. Others live in cracked ruins. In one place seventy boys sleep in one room, three to a bed. In another, the six hundred orphans are kept out of sight; our tour never gets beyond a guesthouse courtyard. We learn things that surprise us. Haiti does not adopt children out to other countries; children remain in orphanages until they are grown. Orphans have better opportunities for health and education than most other children. Parents place their children in orphanages as a route to a better life and often visit on Sundays. Although children are supposed to move out at eighteen, many remain well past age twenty, as there is little opportunity beyond the orphanage walls calling them to adulthood. The more we learn, the more questions we have.

We part in Grand Goave. Andy and I will remain at Mission of Hope to help with reconstruction; the other six will return to

Port-au-Prince and fly back to the States. Conversation is light at our last group meal; each of us absorbed in private reflection. I pull Cherylann aside and give her a gestural hug; mutual warmth between us is incubating. I tell her that wherever the Gengels decide to build, they can count on me. She thanks me and says she will be in touch.

Andy and I arrive at Mirlitone, the guesthouse for missionaries that Lex and Renee Edme run in Grand Goave. At least that's what it was last year. Now it's just an expanse of beach along the Bay of Gonave with a congregate bathroom, a lean-to kitchen, and a field of tents. It's almost dark when we arrive but Andy is careful about tents. Fresh from living out of doors from Georgia to Maine in rain, heat, and snow, he takes his time finding level ground, digging a trench around our perimeter, and ramming the tent stakes deep. It is past dark when he announces our accommodations fit for sleeping. I crawl into my canvas abode, exhausted. About midnight the wind comes fast off the bay, rains pummel the earth, and I find new appreciation for my son. All around us tents collapse and people scramble for cover in the deluge. We sleep high and dry.

The next morning we strap on tool belts and discover that nothing is more satisfying than building a house for a family in two hours, right before their eyes. Here's how it works. Samaritan's Purse, an international aid organization based in South Carolina, provides precut materials, which include a wooden frame for a twelve-foot-square structure, metal roofing, a gutter, built-in bunk beds, and a portable table/parents' bed. The kit includes a roll of reinforced blue plastic sheathing, hundreds of siding nails with fat concave washers, four foundation straps, and galvanized roofing nails. The materials come prepackaged; five kits fit in a standard box truck.

A Haitian crew carries the kit to the site, whether along a city street, a jungle path, or high in the mountains. They create a flat area about fourteen feet square. At urban sites this usually involves clearing debris from a damaged house; on hillsides it entails digging and tamping, known in construction as "cut and fill." When the erection crew arrives the next day, the building pad is already prepared and the building components at hand.

We are a team of fourteen Haitians and Americans. Boss Pepe is our supervisor, a heavyset local with a weary affect, an easy smile, and a Texas Longhorns baseball hat. His sole responsibility appears to be getting us to the site. Once we arrive, he seeks shade and takes a snooze. Manuel, Johnson, and Frederick, the other Haitian men on the crew, are wiry and tireless. Then there is Michelle, the only woman I ever meet in Haiti who crosses society's strict gender lines. She is beautiful, with luminous skin and sparkling eyes. She is also an expert carpenter. The quality of the American workers varies. Andy and I join seven volunteers from the World Race—evangelical missionaries who circle the globe, eleven countries in eleven months, to witness for Christ. Our World Racers include Craig, a Texas Aggie who bristles at Boss Pepe's hat; Tommy, a silent cowboy from Wyoming who resembles Heath Ledger in *Brokeback Mountain*, though I do not imagine he would favor the comparison; and five girls: Shannon, Woody, Melissa, Natalie, and Alicia.

Andy and I learn fast. Manuel and Johnson lay out the four sill plates. Craig and Tommy dig a hole at each corner, fasten metal strapping tape to a pressure-treated two by four, bury the wood in the ground, and fill the hole with the metal extending above the surface. Michelle and Frederick lay each wall out on the ground and nail the studs in place. Two walls have identical raked sides. The front is tall with a door while the back wall is shorter with a window for cross-ventilation. All the studs are precut; no saws necessary. Andy and I help frame the walls. Among the five World Race girls, Melissa wields a strong hammer. Shannon and Woody are great storytellers who entertain the crowd that inevitably gathers. Natalie takes one or two children aside to play. And Alicia, well, she stays back at camp pretty much every day.

Raising the walls takes all of us working together. We level, square, attach, and bind the frame to the foundation straps. In less than ten minutes, the three-dimensional form takes shape. The crowd applauds when it's in place. Once the walls are upright, the Haitians scramble onto the top sill to install the joists. On day one Tommy is the only American allowed on the roof, by the end of our trip Andy is banging away up there as well. I am never deemed capable, and rightly so; my desire to be handy exceeds my ability. There is still plenty to do from the ground: nailing the hurricane clips along the top sill or hoisting up sheets of corrugated tin to cover the roof. I install the triple-bunk beds and ladder that line one side of the house and provide lateral support. Melissa assembles the double-bed frame, the only freestanding piece of the building.

It takes an hour to erect the frame; the sheathing takes another hour. The key to successful siding is to make it tight, tight, tight. We start at the high corner, near the front door, make sure it's square to the frame, and nail it every eight inches vertically. Two people stretch the roll across the first wall. Three Haitians gesture ferociously and yank it tight around the corner while the rest of us nail at every stud. The plastic washers create a watertight seal. It is a sweet system until we get sloppy and miss a stud, in which case we've just put a hole in someone's new house. Installing sheathing involves greater teamwork. We learn a few Creole words; the Haitians sing songs. It takes hundreds of nails, but the old adage of many hands rings true. We hang the gutter off the low end of the roof, screw on the downspout, utility knife an X at the window opening, fold the plastic back, tack it in place, cut a flap at the door, and we're done. We build two houses in the morning, return to Mission of Hope for a lunch of rice and beans, build a third house in the afternoon, and ride back to Mirlitone by four, in time for a swim before dinner.

By day three Andy and I are experts. We tramp along the narrow paths and play with the children; it's more fun than disaster relief ought to be. Which raises the nagging question: Why do Haitians need us here? Erecting the houses is easy, and with more people watching than building, there is no shortage of manpower. Yet houses are built only when volunteers pitch in. Mission of Hope has constructed three hundred structures so far and has hundreds more kits, but nothing gets built without *blan* (Creole for foreigner).

I develop a theory, a Haitian variation on the Arkansas Traveler fable that insists there is no need to fix a roof when it is sunny, and impossible to do it in the rain. The Haitians we meet all seem appreciative of our presence; when the *blan* show up they build with gusto. Yet when we are gone they are not much disposed to action. It makes no sense to me; the Samaritan's Purse houses are far better than the tents so many survivors inhabit. But I'm not going to make sense of Haiti in a week, and I don't pretend to understand Haitian motivation, except to acknowledge it is very different from our own. I could be frustrated by their indifference; I could call them lazy, but having worked alongside them, I know better. I land here bubbling with energy and a zest for putting the world right. The people greet me with yawning complacence. Their life was difficult before the earthquake and it is difficult now, albeit in different ways; weighing the relative levels of difficulty would simply breed pointless frustration.

On our fourth day in Grand Goave we erect a house midway up the mountain for a thin, pregnant woman, her jaundiced husband, and a swarm of children. As we nail the frame in place Andy mentions that you know you've been here awhile when you start to differentiate the gradations of poverty. These people are very poor; the children's bellies are distended, their eyes listless from lack of everything.

I stand on a ladder as we unroll the plastic sheathing. When I reach down to my bucket of nails, a small black hand holds up three. I have not seen this boy before; it's hard to believe he belongs to this family. He's small, like most Haitian children, but his smile is quick, his skin shiny, and his proportions suggest regular meals. *"Meci."* I take the nails, reach up to bang them into place, and find another handful ready the next time I lean over.

"Que ou rele?" I ask his name on the third round, when it's clear that I've acquired a helper. "Jenison," he calls up at me with an eager smile. I nail my way along the top of the wall and double-fold the tarp as Manuel has demonstrated. If I drop a nail Jenison picks it up and puts in my bucket; he's always ready with the next handful when I need them. We communicate in perfect pidgin—a bit of English, a bit of French, a touch of Creole, lots of hand gestures, and many smiles. I discover that Jenison is nine, though he looks no more than six. When I ask where he lives, he points to the valley. He says he goes to school. Every Haitian child tells every white person that he attends school, whether he does or not, but I believe Jenison. He possesses a confidence and authority that suggest experience beyond a simple shack and a charcoal fire. Following his example, other children try to help me, but Jenison nudges them aside. They shuffle off to other *blan*. We finish

a house, and he tags along to the next. We chat along the path, a conversation more convivial than informative. I carry the bucket of nails; he grips the handle as well, sharing the burden.

When we return to Mission of Hope for lunch, Jenison disappears; he is not allowed inside except for class or church services. He finds our afternoon location—I have no idea how—and continues as my helper. Every day thereafter, whether we build in the flats near the bay or on the hillside beyond the highway, Jenison spends his day in my shadow. It is a sort of inverse adoption. Jenison chose me; he is my Haitian.

We work six days a week; Sunday is our day of rest. I attended church service when I visited Haiti before the earthquake, and look forward to going again. There's nothing religious for me in going to church; it's an anthropological experience. Lex Edme's a master of satisfying competing agendas. His strong voice alternates between Creole and English, simultaneously accommodating the many American missionaries who've come to rebuild while exposing his local congregation to the world's power language. I get the added benefit of picking up some Creole.

The church is a shallow-pitched tin roof supported by wooden posts crafted from small trees that shades a few hundred people on packed dirt. There's a raised platform at one end, a few suspended lights, and an audio shed at the back. Rows of wooden benches with angled backs that serve as school desks during the week flip around to become Sunday pews. Mission of Hope's main structure, a concrete pavilion with a proper roof, was damaged in the earthquake. But it would be too small now; church attendance spikes after disaster. Alexis, Lex and Renee's thirteen-year-old daughter, blessed with stunning beauty, leads a chorus of five young women, who clap and sway across the back of the platform. The congregation joins in, arms outstretched, torsos rocking, heads flung back in praise. I tap my foot to the beat but am too self-conscious to join in. It would be disrespectful to act as if the spectacle signifies anything beyond theater to me.

At some point during last year's tumult, thirty-three orphans came to live at Mission of Hope. There is no formal orphanage and no staff to tend them. Lex and Renee built a two-room shed, lined with bunks, where children crash when they're tired. Otherwise they chase each other about Mission of Hope's yard, devour giant plates of rice and beans, and master the art of captivating missionary hearts to secure the sweets so many foreigners keep in their pockets. The orphans lead a far better life than many of their peers.

On Sunday mornings the orphans drift between wooden benches until they get scooped into empty laps, where they sleep in greater peace than their bunkhouse affords. This morning I have a chubby boy's dead weight on one shoulder and a skinny fellow propped on my thigh. One of the older orphans sidles up to Andy and dozes against his hip. They cling to us like glue in the dense heat, humidity, and salvation. Worship escalates into delirium, clapping and singing and whooping praise. The crowd abandons English; everything is now Creole, percussive, and fast. I don't understand a word and wouldn't subscribe to its meaning even if I did, but I find solace in the frenzy, and contentment in this crowded space.

By our second week, Andy and I take daily swims in the Bay of Gonave. The water is refreshing though we tread lightly; the bottom is murky and we have to dodge floating debris. A pronounced green line toward the horizon marks the extent of runoff from the Grand Goave River, and all the garbage tossed into it. Beyond that line, the sea is clear blue. One afternoon we swim far out to experience water free of silt and trash. Another afternoon we float in the shallows, and a trio of tall boys wades toward us with a soccer ball. We toss it about, dive after it, laugh, and generally show off. I cannot recall adult strangers in the United States joining in spontaneous play, but no one seems much of a stranger here. Everyone is equally poor in possessions yet equally rich in spirit. Everyone is related to everyone else, and if good fortune blesses someone with a soccer ball, it's more fun shared with a wide circle.

There are more than fifty people camping at Mirlitone, all evangelical Christians except for us. Their prayers grow particularly loud before dinner, so Andy and I escape the throng to enjoy cocktails on the cruise deck. Cocktails consist of fresh water from our Nalgene bottles. Our lounge chairs are plastic folding numbers that we prop into the sand and lean against the chain-link frames filled with boulders that form Mirlitone's breakwater. The particulars may be improvised, but the scenery is worthy of any travel brochure. The cliffs of Petit Goave cascade into the sea, the dugout canoes float serenely over the surface, and buoys made from clusters of plastic bottles reflect light like crystal. The Isle de Gonave rises from the bay in a Bali Hai mist. The sea shimmers in blues and grays and greens, highlighted by the dazzling orange sun whose brilliant tentacles reach out and touch us.

This is our *sabasana*, time to digest our adventure. Andy is quiet by nature, with a systematic, scientific mind. He considers how the aid flooding into Haiti can be used in a comprehensive way. "Take the garbage; it's everywhere. Why don't we build power plants that run on solid waste, pay people twenty-five cents a bag for trash, and use it to create electricity? People will get income, they'll get power; and the countryside will be cleaned up in no time." He's also a master of dry humor. "Being in Haiti is just like hiking the Appalachian Trail; life is reduced to its essentials. You wake up every day and spend your time finding food and clean water and figuring out how to get from A to B. On the Trail, A to B is twenty miles; in Haiti it's sunrise to sunset." We look out over the water, at that green line that defines Haiti's enduring challenges of erosion and sanitation. As light fades, the green dissipates until it finally merges with the blue beyond. "The weird thing is, the whole time you are focusing on the basics, your mind wanders; you think about stuff you never think about in your regular life. Everything here is simple and complex at the same time."

We sit quietly during the few moments it takes for the sun to draw itself into a white ball and drop into the sea. The moment the orb hits the horizon, light flashes across the edge of the earth and is extinguished. In the sun's final flash a young man silhouetted along the beach thrusts his arm into the violet sky and shouts, *"Ayaiti!,"* the Creole name for this magical land. His proclamation is directed at no one in particular, yet for everyone to hear. His exuberance cements a truth I have considered for some time. Happiness arises not from having things, but from having hope.

Machetes

September 2010

My cell phone rings. "Where are you?" "On the Silver Line; I'll be at the airport in twenty minutes." "Get here as fast as you can, we're in Terminal C. The reporter is already here." Len hangs up. The word *reporter* echoes in my ear.

I stare at my phone, wishing it would explain more.

Terminal C is Logan Airport's futuristic remnant of the 1960s with a cavernous roof that swoops in a dramatic curve over a sea of check-in counters. It is cousin to Eero Saarinen's famous TWA Terminal in New York. Although Terminal C has been expanded many times to accommodate the long concourses and repetitive departing gates that define contemporary airports, it still has a center, a heart. Len and Bernie are easy to find in the middle of the huge space, wearing "Be Like Brit" T-shirts and standing alongside a reporter with a mic and a cameraman.

"Here, put this on," Len says, tossing a T-shirt at me. I scan the crowd. I will look ridiculous if I slip it over my button-down oxford. I shrug, remove my shirt and undershirt, tuck them in my carry-on, and pull the T-shirt over my head. I sidle up to Bernie and focus on the reporter, ignoring the burn of hundreds of eyes that watched me undress.

The reporter tosses me a few questions, though I can tell from his flat delivery I'm destined for the cutting-room floor. Len is the story. Len would say Brit's the story, of course, but that's not really true. It's Len's lovable, if unattractive, mug that plucks at the bulldog strings of our hearts. "We are going to Haiti to build an orphanage out of the destruction. We are going to honor our daughter, Brit. We are going to help the millions of people who suffered in the earthquake." Len's anime eyes glisten; he wraps his arm around Bernie and pulls him close. "My son, Bernie, here is committed to preserving his sister's memory." I watch the man. I listen. He's not profound or even all that articulate. But he sure is good.

The interview is a wrap. Len and Bernie have already checked their luggage. They give me a pair of hockey bags to check, stuffed with T-shirts, lollipops, and medicine. The custom for missionaries flying to Haiti is to carry on personal items and check supplies. I wonder what other countries do so much importing via duffle. My own carry-on is a purple nylon number with a shoulder strap. I've learned that rolling suitcases are worthless in Haiti. The rollies' wheels break on the bumpy pavement at Port-au-Prince airport, which we refer to by its PAP code. Besides, I need two free hands to drag my hockey bags. It's easier to have additional weight hanging from my shoulder, and if it happens to be bright purple, so much less the chance of its getting lost.

I hand the agent my passport; she weighs the bags, tags them, hands me my boarding pass, and then tosses me a wink. "You were looking pretty good there with your shirt off." I am embarrassed and pleased. It's been years since I turned a woman's head.

Traveling to Haiti with Len Gengel is unlike going with other Samaritans because Len interprets the guiding dictum—avoid Port-au-Prince after dark—differently than anyone else. The usual strategy is to rise at 3:30 a.m., catch the first flight to Miami, arrive PAP early afternoon, and head straight for Grand Goave. But Len leaves Boston at 2 p.m., flies to Fort Lauderdale, enjoys dinner, stays overnight in a hotel, and then takes the next morning's flight to Haiti. He arrives in Grand Goave before noon.

Len's connections yield creature comforts every step of the way. A black Escalade awaits us at the Fort Lauderdale airport. Norberto Cintron, Command Engineer for United States Southern Command, a dashing army colonel in fatigues and a crisp hat, takes our carry-ons and opens our doors before gliding us through airport traffic in the cushioned comfort that only Cadillac can afford. Colonel Cintron is the kind of soldier who gives the army a good name. He is articulate and considerate, a great storyteller and a good listener, and he does work that even the most passionate pacifist can appreciate. He's responsible for all disaster response, humanitarian missions, demining, and environmental programs in the Southern Hemisphere (the army's geography is a little loose; Haiti actually lies at 19 degrees north latitude). Colonel Cintron oversees a nine-figure budget and works with NGOs all over the Caribbean and South America. He was in charge of US relief efforts after the earthquake. Len credits the colonel's tireless efforts for unearthing Britney's remains; and Colonel Cintron appears to hold Len in equally high esteem.

We drive a few miles to The Tropics, a low-slung roadside restaurant frozen circa 1963 that's become Sunshine State retro chic. I picture a *Life* magazine cover: a pair of svelte women in starched shirtwaist dresses and two pompadoured men in pleated gabardines emerging from a Chevy Impala parked under the immense porte-cochere. Unfortunately, our dinner party is not so buoyantly innocent. Four students from Lynn University join us at a sprawling table in the back. We enjoy drinks and appetizers. When I order a salad for dinner, Len overrides. "That's not enough. You're going to Haiti fella, you better eat up." He orders me a steak on the side.

Before I met the Gengels, I'd never heard of Lynn University. Judging from PJ and Alec, Deidre and Lindsey, it is a different place from my alma mater. All four are fresh, magazine-cover attractive, well spoken and well heeled. Alec arrives in a Hummer. They hail from affluent East Coast suburbs like Rumson, New Jersey, and Madison, Connecticut. Carefree, smart, and beautiful, they exemplify the young adults our society strives to produce. Except that they're not, as each has been scorched by a tragedy few twenty-year-olds endure. Nine months have passed since the earthquake; they are back in school, and most of the conversation revolves around their courses, concerts, and dating. But death weaves through their conversation too easily. Mortality lingers near the front of their psyche, and I can understand why they enjoy spending time with the Gengels. The survivors are a select group, and their bond is deeply forged.

The next morning we arrive in PAP on time. Lieutenant Pierce, another one of Len's connections, meets us on the tarmac and expedites us through customs. Port-au-Prince looks measurably better than it did six weeks ago. The roads are fully passable. The tent cities are still squalid, but there's more energy in the street bustle.

People's crisp white clothes stand out against the drab tents. I will never understand how Haitians stay so clean; I'm shrouded in dust the moment I emerge from the airport terminal.

We are on a reconnaissance mission; perhaps that's why the military tone seems appropriate. We will be here less than forty-eight hours with the sole purpose of evaluating a property Lex Edme has discovered for the orphanage. Our Google Earth analysis displayed a broad plot on a hill. I am concerned that the site is too far from a road while Len is unwilling to buy land based on Internet data alone. Since Lex is convinced the site is a prize, we're making a personal visit. When we arrive at Mission of Hope, Lex is waiting for us in the yard, visibly excited.

Lex and I met when he was Forward in Health's man on the ground during my first trip to Haiti. We didn't spend a lot of time together, as he chauffeured the doctors in the air-conditioned Mitsubishi while I rode in the short bus. However, one afternoon when we were at the site of the clinic construction he sought me out. Lex is the blackest man I've ever seen. He has a running back's broad shoulders and thick thighs. His head is a perfect orb; his shiny eyes and thumbprint nose are too small for his face, and his teeth pop out so bright against his skin they conjure the Cheshire cat. "Let me show you this, Paul." Lex walked me though the clinic's rudimentary construction. "This is strong": he yanked on the vertical rebar jutting out of the mortar. I couldn't help but notice the dimples in his forearms.

There were many problems with Forward in Health's construction. The foundation was too high; the column spacing was irregular and the footprint didn't match the drawings. I could hardly inspect the work with the thoroughness required in the United States nor did I want to dampen Lex's enthusiasm. I could have argued when he boasted, "It is built exactly to plan." Instead, I apologized that we had made some changes, and explained the variations between the proposed design and reality. His face fell. I realized the drawings I brought from the United States were meaningless, so I changed tack and devised a functional clinic layout that accommodated what was already in place. "I knew you would like it, it is very good construction." Lex put an arm around me and pulled me into his shoulder to seal the bond between us. "You can make the plans fit what is built."

After that first encounter Lex took a shine to me. He was an engaging talker and I've always been a sucker for confident visionaries. The following afternoon we left the clinicians to their tasks and he drove me through Les Cayes. Lex pointed out buildings he liked. I enjoyed bouncing along the dirt roads while he described his preferred profiles for column capitals and plaster finishes. Lex had lived in Gardner, Massachusetts, for ten years, which was how he developed so many contacts from that area. His English was fluid, though I found myself leaning in close to filter his accent. Lex recounted how he grew up on La Gonave, the island in the middle of Haiti's main bay. After being sponsored by an American woman through Save the Children, he received regular meals and education and later moved to the United States. He returned to his homeland in 2000 to start Mission of Hope with his American wife, Renee, and their two babies. Through Lex's eyes, Haiti's half-built structures were not evidence of construction stalled but harbingers of a brighter future. The guy's confidence registered a millimeter shy of cocky; his exuberance made me a tad nervous, but I was won over by his transparent, infectious love of country.

The enthusiasm Lex showered on me that day last year now extends to everyone in the truck cab as he climbs in and directs us toward the site. We turn off the pavement and drive through a small tent city. When the road gives out, we park and continue on foot. We pass a group of men building a bank of outhouses courtesy of Oxfam. We bear right and come upon a steep incline. At least forty men, women, and children toil ahead with hand shovels, rakes, and hoes. They scrape the earth and move rocks, widening the footpath. I admire Lex's strategy, staging a demonstration of road construction to allay my accessibility concerns. I wonder what incentives he used to turn workers out today; money, the promise of construction, or the fear of God. Regardless, everyone digs with fervor until Len pulls out his lollipops, and the children abandon their hoes.

The site is beautiful, everything Lex advertised and more: four acres on a bluff overlooking the sea about a quarter mile off Route 2, with a sizable area flat enough for the orphanage. A prominent mango tree, visible from the highway, is a distinctive landmark. We discuss the site's features, take in the view, and after an hour or so descend to Mirlitone. The missionary camp has benefited from many improvements since Andy and I stayed here. The chaconne is complete, a giant circle of columns sixty feet wide with a picturesque thatched roof. Lex leaves us to enjoy a gentle breeze and a pitcher of passion fruit juice while he goes off to negotiate with the property owner: "If the big white guy shows up, the cost will double." Two hours later Lex returns. The deal is done.

Len is not a tent kind of guy, so we stay at a hotel over the mountain in Petit Goave; Grand Goave has no hotel. The place is an odd mix of rudimentary accommodation and luxury appointments. My room is immense; evening light plays off the cathedral ceiling. The bathroom features an oversize tub with a view of a lush garden. I hear birds sing. The idea of a bath thrills me. I strip off my dusty clothes, climb three tiled steps to the platform, kneel at the tub fill, and turn on the faucet. Nothing happens. I open the valve all the way. Nothing. Finally, a thin drizzle of cold water drips from the showerhead above. I laugh. Silly me for harboring expectations. I take travel soap from my nylon bag; there is none in the bathroom. I teeter on the edge of the tub, cup a washcloth under the drip, soak it, soap up, and repeat the process to rinse. I get clean, if not refreshed, and the birdsong is pleasant.

On Saturday morning Len, Bernie, and I return to the site with a three-hundred-foot measuring tape and a detachment of Haitians Lex appointed to help. Pastor Beauvais, an ancient, wiry preacher for whom Andy and I built a house in August trots all over the site, proclaiming the land's virtues in such energetic Creole I cannot make out a word. Two teenage boys hold the tape while two guys in thick pants hack around the site perimeter with machetes. We communicate in rough Creole and hand gestures until Winkinson comes along. Winkinson is a tall, thin Haitian who brags of being a graduate of the University of Kansas, though his King's English is more Oxford don than middle-America. Andy and I built a tarp house for Winkinson last summer high up the mountain. There is little Winkinson enjoys more than showing off his English, so he lingers and translates while we measure the site.

One thing I love about Haiti is how people show up from nowhere, hang around, and then disappear. I have no idea why Winkinson arrives when he does or where he might have been going, but he decides we are interesting, so he stays for a few hours. I'm hard-pressed to recall when a spontaneous diversion interrupted my day back home. I am too bound by commitments and schedule.

We track the underbrush along the site's boundaries. I traipse behind a machete guy. I cannot understand a word he says, but our bodies move to the rhythm of his giant knife as it carves our path. One kid stays back, holding the dumb end of the tape, while the other walks beside me, unspooling the measure of the property.

There is nothing but the rustle of fallen leaves, the whisk of the blade, the buzz of gnats attracted to my sweaty neck. The three of us move through space: the machete man, the tape-measure boy, and me, creating this arbitrary path binding an arbitrary set of corner posts. We are in no hurry. The land—the rocks and the vines and the steep grade—sets the pace of our exploration. It reveals itself as we cut and walk, stake and measure. Our understanding of the site is both empirical and intuitive. We spend hours at our task. Neighbors stare at us from behind trees; some come right out and question the trailblazer. I do not know if he satisfies them with his responses or his knife, but they accept our presence.

I want to explore more, to cover the ground from a different angle, but the sun is high and Len is tired. I return to the middle of the site and make a 360-degree video, narrating my site observations. The view toward the sea stops my breath; it's that beautiful. The late summer breeze is a gift. I want to document the magic, to digitally capture my challenge: to shape this particular Caribbean slope into a monument to life cut short at its idealistic peak. It must be a place of both aspiration and innocence.

Pastor Beauvais huddles us together to give his blessing; a long, low, thunderous oration, replete with upraised hands and loud whoops more akin to a Native American chant than a Christian prayer. Intense, raw, and primitive, his passion feels right for this land. We head down the hill, off to a good start.

Before we reach the highway my friend Jenison pops out of a side path, another bit of Haitian serendipity. He runs over and latches against my waist. I wrap my arm around his shoulder, and we walk in step to the road, where he detaches himself and dashes off to the flats.

On Saturday afternoon I draft a site plan based on our measurements of perimeter and landmarks. It's not survey accurate but is enough to start making sketches. The Gengels have very specific design requirements, each of which represents some aspect of Britney they wish to commemorate. The orphanage needs to house sixty-six children, thirty-three boys and thirty-three girls, because Brit was missing for thirty-three days. They insist the building take the shape of a *B*. Such obvious symbolism puts me off. I counsel to let the site inform the building's mass, but I get nowhere. I'm good at reading my clients and realize there is no arguing against the *B*. So I embrace it. I test its opportunities. I develop quick ideas and explore their strengths. A *B* has strict symmetry; it can incorporate curves, possibly even a pair of courtyards. I draw the shape in relation to the predominant site features. A solid concept emerges. I locate the building's axis along the mango tree. This optimizes solar access, creates a clear vehicle area, and defines the play space. I separate the well from the septic. I develop five variations. Each incorporates specific approaches to separating the children by gender, making space for the manager's apartment, and accommodating visitors, the kitchen, the laundry, the water filters, and the generators. I lose myself in my work until Len demands to see what I've done. I feel good about the *B*. A thought whizzes through my mind. *Thank god her name wasn't Wendy.* I laugh to myself as my imagination spins the challenges of creating a building shaped like a *W*, *Q* or an *R*. I don't say it out loud though; it feels irreverent. I don't know Len that well, yet.

On Saturday night we attend a celebration at Mission of Hope in honor of the students who recently passed their national exams. The school takes pride in its 100 percent success rate. This is my first experience of Haitians in party mode, and I'm struck by their exuberance, released from lives filled with trial. There is an eight-piece band, individual talent spots, and speeches by Lex and the mayor. The men are neat and clean; the women are dressed for WOW! I marvel how such elegant black silk, sequins, and sheer stockings can emerge from dirt-floored tents. There's singing and dancing and jokes and wild applause for the graduates. The electricity goes off at least ten times. Singers simply stop mid-song, audience members flick cell phones to cast a glow, and we all wait patiently until power returns. When the bare bulbs spark back to life, we pick up right where we left off. Nothing can thwart the good time.

The next morning we drive to PAP and fly to Fort Lauderdale. Since we have a four-hour layover, Len decides we'll leave the airport to get some real food. Just as Haiti's crowded, dusty squalor seems more intense than I remember every time I land in Port-au-Prince, I am equally struck by the United States' antiseptic emptiness when I return home. People move so fast and purposefully, encased in their cars. Sunlight turns hard on so much concrete.

We accept the cabbie's suggestion to eat at The Rustic Inn, a seafood shack along a channel near the airport. Len tells him about our trip, the orphanage, Brit; he never loses an opportunity to recount the tale. The cabbie listens respectfully. Then he tells us his wife died in the earthquake, his baby daughter, too. He recites his story in a voice so calm, so quiet, as if the horror drained his emotions long ago.

The Rustic Inn is nearly empty in the long hours between lunch and dinner. We sit at a picnic table with a view of the water, order local specialties, and Len gets to work. He calls the Boston TV stations as well as the *Globe* and the *Worcester Telegram*. He calls Colonel Cintron, Representative McGovern, and Susan Wornick, a personality on WCVB Boston. He recounts our trip to each of them; he raves about the site; he reiterates our return flight time.

Hours later, when we step from the jetway in Boston, every network is there, cameras glaring, microphones pressed in Len's face. I get home in time for the ten o'clock news. There's Len, on every channel, with Bernie beside him. I stand, smiling, in their shadow.

Bulldozers

January 2011

Len's goal to open the orphanage on the first anniversary of the earthquake evolved into the more modest objective of starting construction before that date. Since September, a working group that included Len's family, his construction buddies, architects, and electrical designers from my firm, TRO JB, and structural engineers from SGH met at our office every other Monday to refine the design. My job was to move the project forward and keep everyone happy.

Every building project suffers scope creep—clients always want more than they can afford—but altruistic projects often develop agendas that approach fantasy. *We should install geothermal. Haiti would be great for wind power. We must have composting toilets and recycle gray water. Hydrogen cells.* I have little patience with Americans keen to impose on others technologies that the richest nation on earth is slow to embrace itself, but I allowed each idea to bounce around the room long enough for people to feel heard and then steered us back to our main objective: building an orphanage.

Happily, the letter *B*, which derived from the Egyptian hieroglyphic for the floor plan of a house, serves our needs well. We keep our *B* simple, the same Varsity font as the Boston Bruins logo, with forty-five-degree angles instead of curved top and bottom loops; we don't want the challenge of forming curved concrete in Haiti. The *B* spreads across the site in an east–west direction, the straight-line back of the building faces uphill to the south, the crenulated front faces north to the sea. The main entrance sits where the letter's two bulbous portions come together, on axis with the site's beautiful mango tree. This creates a formal site arrangement that enhances the monumentality of our memorial. Unfortunately, our site has a single access point—the northeast corner. Everyone, public and service, arrives at this low spot. We cannot create a grand, axial progression to the entrance.

The interior is organized around two courtyards. We create four neighborhoods, designed for sixteen orphans each, in the southeast and southwest corners along the straight side of the *B*; two upstairs and two down. Each neighborhood includes four orphan rooms, a matron suite, a shared bath, and a common room. The building's infrastructure—generator, battery storage, water filtration, laundry, kitchen, and supplies—occupies the northeast corner of the first floor, closest to the driveway, while the northwest corner contains the administrative office and manager's apartment. The entire front of the second floor houses visitor accommodations: six suites plus a large common room overlooking the bay. The crossbar running between the two courtyards contains the main dining room on the first floor and a large library/computer room for the children on the second floor.

Everything we learned from our survey of orphanages in Haiti gets discussed during our Monday evening meetings. We debate what features we want to replicate and where we want to "raise the bar" by introducing America standards.

The most critical aspect of the design is the structural system. The orphanage must be able to withstand another earthquake. The American approach to seismic design is to make buildings flexible; when the earth rumbles wood and steel structures bend to the lateral force. But Haiti has little wood, less steel, and a long tradition of concrete construction. Concrete is inherently brittle and crumbles when shaken. SGH understands that the American approach to seismic design is inappropriate in Grand Goave and develops a structural system known as constrained concrete. Instead of flexing with the earthquake, a constrained concrete building bucks tremors by being heavy and rigid. Our foundation is wide and dense, with a low center of gravity. The columns, beams, and walls are tied together, so that when the earthquake hits, the structure moves as one entity, like a boat with heavy ballast riding out the waves. It's a simple concept but one that causes ongoing challenges for Len and me, guys used to building systems that allow us to poke holes wherever we want. In a constrained concrete building, a hole becomes a weak spot in a quake.

One afternoon, during a session at SGH's office, John Thomsen, the lead engineer, explains the orphanage's matrix of grade beams, the large concrete elements reinforced with steel that will form a giant grid underneath the building. "The foundation locks all the columns in place, and after the grade beams are poured we'll back-fill between and above them with compacted sand; that will be the ballast for our boat." I study his sketches of intricately reinforced concrete entombed in the earth. I stifle a laugh, but it will not subside. "What's so funny?" Len's despondent; his contractor eyes see only dollar signs in so much concrete. "I just want to be there," I'm laughing very hard now, though still laughing alone, "after we've dug up the site and poured all of this concrete, and then we shovel sand back on top of it." I envision the local audience, fresh from their tin shacks and canvas tents, watching us pour precious concrete into the ground only to bury it. My chest heaves. "The Haitians already think *blan* are nuts. This will confirm all of their suspicions." The rest of the group stares at me as if I am the nut. But in that moment, the idea of translating these elegant, complex drawings into steel, cement, and gravel on a mountainside in Haiti seems ludicrous to me.

Which is now the challenge before us. It is time to transform our drawings into three dimensions. Unfortunately, we have much work to do before we even get to the point of covering the foundations in front of bewildered Haitians. Our task for this trip is straightforward: to excavate the site, stake the building, dig enough to stage a media event, and get out of Haiti before the anniversary of the earthquake. We don't know whether January 12 will prove to be a day of national rejoicing for those spared or a day of national chaos to protest lagging reconstruction efforts, and we don't intend to be around to find out.

Len, Bernie, and Ross, Len's nephew, arrived December 24, along with Gama, a Haitian American who's agreed to coordinate daily construction as clerk of the works. Gama will remain in Haiti for the duration. I told Len there was no reason for me to arrive before the new year since the first week would be lost in setting up.

"No, no, I am going to need you right away," he protested. But I partied on New Year's Eve in Boston and arrived in Haiti with my daughter Abby, her boyfriend, Khalid, and Len's excavator, Duke, on January 2, before a single shovelful of dirt was turned over.

All we missed during week one was a flurry of hurry up and wait. Bernie and Ross organized the truck that had arrived by freighter from Miami loaded with power tools, a generator, a Mule (Kawasaki off-road vehicle), picks, shovels, hammers, screws, stakes, orange paint, tampers, lumber for an outhouse, an eight-foot propane grill for Mirlitone, and the usual carton of lollipops. Len spent the week on his cell phone chasing the rented bulldozer, chasing the soil-testing firm, chasing the surveyor but never finding any of them. Instead he found three Haitians loitering on his land in matching shirts and ID tags. Len dubbed them the Neighborhood Association, though it's not clear whom they represent beyond themselves.

The day we arrive there is still no bulldozer and the site boundaries are still vague, but we have a beautiful letter penned by the mayor of Grand Goave proclaiming our intention to build. This is as close to a building permit as we are going to get.

On my first afternoon back in Haiti, Jenison finds me. The boy has an internal compass that points straight to my heart. He is taller and thinner, though still more robust than most children here. He jumps into my arms, and Abby takes our picture. He smells of damp earth; his scalp is covered with knots from lice or some other tropical delicacy; his bare feet are a Kandinsky collage of cuts and scrapes caked with mud. His eyes, which I recall being pure white around the iris, show that trace of yellow common among Haitians. But his smile is as wide as I remember. We march up the hill to the orphanage site, his arms around my neck, his hips and ankles locked around my waist.

Haiti is full of children; almost 40 percent of the population is under fifteen. Although the infant mortality rate has been cut in half in the past twenty years, (48.8 deaths per thousand, making Haiti 135th in the world, per UN World Population Prospects), and the fertility rate is dropping, 3.17 births per woman means that Haiti will still be full of children for a very long time. By most measures the lives of Haitian children are improving. More children are in school, more are immunized (75 percent), and fewer are officially malnourished. Still, compared to their American counter-parts, Haitian children are small, quiet, and subdued.

Except, of course, Jenison. He has boundless energy; he engages other children in his hijinks and then rebuffs them with elastic abandon. My first day back he has mud caked to his shins; the next day he shows up at the site in clean shorts and a button-down shirt; the third day he wears rags; on the fourth he is scrubbed shiny and proclaims he's going to the carnival with his mother. Just as his appearance changes, so, too, does his demeanor. He's alternately solicitous then bullying then taciturn. He doesn't have a cohort of friends or move in a singular mob as most children do here, yet every child is keenly aware of him. He is a cunning pint-sized figure who triggers suspicion and commands respect.

Haitians rarely drink water and never between meals. To them, the water bottles we Americans strap to our belts are just another curious habit of *blan*. After the earthquake, one survivor was re-portedly found after 21 days without fluids. I cannot attest to the truth of that tale, but I have witnessed Haitians working for hours under full sun without drinking anything. Jenison, being bold, asks for a drink from my water bottle. I give him one. "Thank you, Jesus!" he shouts as he hands it back to me, a standard bit of English that Haitians parrot to win favor with missionaries. I tell him that Jesus has nothing to do it, and, being a quick study, the boy never utters the name Jesus in front of me again. Later on he asks me for one dollar. I tell him no, and he shrugs. A Haitian who doesn't at least ask a *blan* for money isn't worth his salt, but my rejection doesn't dampen our camaraderie one bit.

My niece and her three boys have sent a packet of children's books, which I carry to the orphanage site because I know people will congregate there. Jenison and I stack them under a tree. *Ferdinand the Bull* seems right for him. We read it together. He likes the pictures. When we're finished I gesture that it's his to keep, but he leaves it with the others. Over the course of our week that patch of shade beneath the tree turns into a small lending library. If a child picks up a book, his right of use is fiercely guarded, and a clawing fight breaks out if another child tries to snatch it. But once finished, the book returns to the pile, available to whoever might want it next. Because Haitian children have so few possessions of their own, I thought these books would be precious, but the opposite seems to be the case. The children own nothing; things that fall their way are welcome, but they don't become attached.

Our bulldozer arrives in Grand Goave on Monday morning but is delivered to the wrong site, so we negotiate its release from a group constructing a local elementary school that claims the machine as manna from the heavens. By noon it appears along Route 2; by 1:00 it's at the base of our future road, and by 2:00 we are moving earth. At 3:00 the Neighborhood Association mobilizes a contingent demanding that construction halt. At 4:00 Lex negotiates with the Neighborhood Association the exact path of the road: the Americans advocate an S-shape that works with the grade; the Haitians insist on going straight up the hill. By 5:00 resolution is achieved, though of course by that time it's too late to do any actual work.

Tuesday morning brings an aftershock of Neighborhood Association activity—new abutters to be placated—but by noon there are hearty handshakes all around, and the bulldozer pushes dirt straight up the mountain. One stretch of the road approaches a twenty-five-degree grade. At the first heavy rain, it will become a class-five rapid.

Back at Mirlitone, Abby, Khalid, and I assemble the outhouse. Len is intent on having this for job-site sanitation. We're convinced he's the only person who will use it. We make sure there are no splinters in the seat, and I insist we carve a half-moon in the door. No outhouse worth its scent should be without one.

By Wednesday the dozer is moving dirt on the site. The box truck makes it up the steep grade; we unload and assemble the latrine. We have a regular audience of baffled neighbors. A dozen children horse around the site, hovering for lollipops; silent men nap in the shade, hoping to get hired for day labor; a few women sit on low stools and watch the dozer scratch across the land. Whenever it unearths a sizable root the women scamper across the site and collect the snarled wood. By the end of the day they have large piles of roots, which they haul off to turn into charcoal.

Len hires two men to dig the latrine pit and Baptiste, a young bilingual Haitian, to sit the site all day and ensure that tools do not walk. Four dollars a day is the going rate. By Wednesday afternoon Duke and I lay out the building perimeter in relation to the magnificent mango tree. Our preferred orientation lands the building too close to one property line, we pivot everything ten degrees off direct north but maintain the axis of the tree. The grade is steeper than we eyeballed back in September; we need more excavation.

Thursday is more of the same except for a foreboding that the more earth we move, the more earth needs to be moved. The machine operators are more interested in watching the clock than completing their task. They don't start until 8 a.m., take a break at 10, sit on their machines during lunch hour, and quit by 4 p.m. With that schedule, we'll never have foundation grades by Saturday. Len calls the machine guy in Port-au-Prince to rent an excavator to work alongside the dozer.

Miracle of miracles, the excavator shows up, and on Friday we have two machines, which means twice the opportunity for delay. The bulldozer has a bum battery; it takes about thirty minutes to caress it back into action every time it stalls. At one point, both machines run beautifully for about fifteen minutes, but then it's noon, time for break. After lunch the machines chug and heave due to impure oil and dirty gasoline. Directions involve English and Creole and arm waving; some Haitians work in feet and inches, others in meters. The bulldozer operator is taciturn and scowling; the rail-thin excavator wears a heavy wool hat and amused detachment. Duke and I run transit lines. Finally, we excavate one corner to its proper depth. The soil is good, very good, but we won't be able to level the entire site before our group leaves in two days.

An ancient man arrives with four mules, each saddled with a pair of woven baskets. He begins to pick some of the smooth unearthed stones and burden his animals. One of the root-collecting ladies jumps up and berates him in a torrent of Creole. He replaces all the rocks and leaves empty-handed. A translator tells us that Lex has given approval to remove roots but not rocks. It's good to know the woman is part of our team.

On Saturday we continue to set temporary stakes whenever the machines work. There are pristine moments when their growling engines sing a duet of productivity. I peer across the carpet of treetops to the blue, blue water beyond. The sea is a vast, smooth plain. Subtle shifts in color mirror the shallow sand formations beneath the surface. White sails, tiny as confetti, hover over the expanse. The horizon blurs as the Isle de Gonave rises in a misty sky. Beyond the poverty, Haiti's beauty is breathtaking.

The picture books I brought for the children prove equally interesting to adults hanging about the site. I spend an hour with Baptiste carefully wording through a book on Antarctic penguins. His pronunciation is good, but his comprehension sketchy. I wonder what reference he can possibly have for the Antarctic. He's never seen snow, perhaps not even ice.

I spend two hours reviewing the drawings with Gama, who will remain when we leave. I outline how to do the final layout, how to understand column lines and detail references. I make a diagram showing all key measuring points and relate them to our benchmark mango tree. He is shocked that we actually lay out the building using those triangle theorems he avoided in high school geometry.

We get as far as we can. About one-third of the site is at foundation grade. Gama gets 100 percent when I quiz him on where to find information on the drawings and how to measure the diagonal dimensions I laid out for him. Our benchmark is painted. Two permanent stakes are in place. Len will be back in three weeks. Maybe some progress will have been made. Maybe our building will be square; maybe it will be skew. Most likely the site will look then exactly as it does now. Our work plan is ambitious, but our expectations are realistic. By American standards the two weeks have not been very productive. By Haitian standards, we are making mammoth progress.

The onlookers understand that this week's show is over. I distribute the books to whichever children happen to be around. This time they hold on to them for good. I give *Ferdinand* to Jenison. I want to savor the breeze and the view and my little friend, so we walk down the hill together. When we reach Route 2 I give him a hug and say good-bye. He waves and runs across the highway while I head toward Mission of Hope, where I can catch a ride to Mirlitone. I expect that on my next visit, whenever that may be, Jenison will be taller, stronger, and just as mischievous.

It seems the greatest reconstruction progress in all of Haiti has taken place at Mirlitone. Four months ago we camped in muddy tents. Now we stay in a guesthouse with male and female dormitories on the first floor and private suites facing a large veranda on the upper level. A row of pansies lines the path to the chaconne where we eat our meals. Only one tent remains; Marieve stills sleeps under canvas, though I'm not sure she ever sleeps.

Marieve is up at first rooster brewing coffee and cooking amazingly sweet porridge for breakfast. Then she starts the rice and beans for lunch, which Ricardo delivers wherever volunteers are working that day. As soon as the lunch pots are washed she begins dinner, usually chicken, sometimes goat. When there are fresh volunteers in camp Marieve serves American side dishes like French fries or macaroni and cheese. I prefer the food she prepares for seasoned veterans—dirty rice, spicy lentils, and legume, a savory ragout of braised eggplant and other vegetables. Len jokes that she should cook American food if she wants an American husband, his way of getting more dinners that suit his palate. Marieve laughs and pretends not to understand, though her English comprehension is good. I imagine she does not consider an American husband quite the prize Len implies. After all the day's meals are finished, Marieve sits on the porch outside the women's dorm, chatting with the other staff, chewing sugar cane and drinking coffee. Her laugh is percussive and sharp. She must be rich in stories after spending so much time observing *blan* and our inscrutable ways. Some nights, long after I'm asleep, her cackling punctures my dreams.

Mirlitone is crowded; January is the busy season for missionaries. People from northern climates elect to perform their good works when it's chilly back home. Besides the eight Be Like Brit crew, there is a group of nurses from Worcester running clinics in the surrounding villages. Every night they minister to the young kids—Duke and Ross, Khalid and Abby—who fail to use enough sunscreen or insect repellent. The nurses rub ointments on them and check for lice. There is also a contingent of long-term Mission of Hope supporters who've come to Haiti every January for years. They regale us with tales of how they survived the earthquake.

Maike, a German missionary, remained in Haiti for three months after the quake. The German press picked up her story, and her notoriety helped Mission of Hope obtain a promise grant from the nonprofit group A Heart for Children to rebuild its school. But before the agency delivers $350,000, it wants assurances that Mission of Hope can complete such an ambitious project. One morning Lex and Renee and Maike, Len, me, and a few other volunteers hold a summit on the veranda. We decide that SGH, Len, and I will create a formal proposal for A Heart for Children; our design and construction expertise should persuade the organization to release the funds. Afterward, Lex, Renee, and I spend a few hours outlining the scope of the project, and I start drawing. Before I even have one project out of the ground in Haiti, I am designing another one.

Stakes

May 2011

I know the airport drill by now. American Airlines built its own terminal, very quickly, after the earthquake. It has an air-conditioned gallery that leads to Euro-style shuttle buses that drive us past the cracked and abandoned original building. A lackluster band plays jittery Caribbean music outside the customs barn. The huge metal shelter is teeming with people. Creaky fans on standards offer little relief from the stifling heat; drowsy custom agents offer little speed in processing the crowd. People cut in front of me, but I have neither the energy nor the chutzpah to stand my ground. Eventually I get my passport stamp, shoulder my hockey bags, and push ahead, mumbling *non, meci, non, meci* over and over to the red-shirted ambassadors pawing at my stuff. I would like them to lighten my load, but I can never tell which ones are real and which are fake, and I'm not about to pull out my wallet and fetch a tip in this crowd. They drop away scowling, cheated out of the alms they consider their due.

This is the first time I've arrived in Haiti by myself; I feel acutely alone. Out of doors and under the covered walk that leads to the parking area, the red shirts back off. I inhale the dry, cindery air. It scorches my lungs. I motor myself through the chaos. Actually, it hardly seems like chaos anymore. It's just another day in Port-au-Prince. It's good to be back.

Cherybin, Mission of Hope's number-two driver, waits at the end of the walk. Gone are the days when Lex would smooth a few palms to gain access to the baggage area and escort us through the gauntlet. Now Lex doesn't even come to fetch me. I should be pleased that I'm a veteran, but Cherybin is a letdown. Between his English and my Creole we might manage ten words on the trip to Grand Goave whereas Lex would animate the journey with reminiscences of the route. *This is where drug lords stopped us; this is where we had to push the car through the flood; this is where the police bulldozed a brand new gas station because the owner refused to pay them off.* His enthusiasm would inspire me for our work. *We are going to build a restaurant in the mountains; we are going to build a trade school on the hill; we are going to build houses along the flats.* Lex is the Robert Moses of Grand Goave, and when he proclaims, *Someday we are going to have a university here*, I stare willfully past the dirt paths, the sagging tents, the endless debris, and I believe him.

Since January, the projects have proceeded with bursts of activity interrupted by unpredictable halts: political unrest, lack of materials, and the habitual crawl of Haitian life. The Be Like Brit orphanage site is clear, the excavation dug, and the intricate task of bending, cutting, and tying steel reinforcing for the concrete foundation is under way. Len's nephew Patrick, one of many out-of-work construction guys in the United States, is full-time superintendent. Between Patrick and Gama, the orphanage is in good hands; we hope to pour our first concrete later this month.

Progress at Mission of Hope School is equally impressive. The marketing folks at TRO JB assembled a proposal that we submitted to A Heart for Children in March. We received quick approval of a 255,000-euro grant. Lex immediately demolished the earthquake-damaged structures and began excavating. While Be Like Brit sits on four acres of open land, Mission of Hope occupies a walled urban plot of less than half an acre. The logistics of constructing a three-story building that takes up almost half of the site while preserving the remaining buildings and accommodating hundreds of schoolchildren as well as ongoing church activities are daunting. I worry about injuries; back home, OSHA would close us down in a heartbeat.

Though I've been gone four months, I keep up-to-date through remote communication. Technology moves our effort forward in ways that would have been impossible a decade ago. SGH and I receive daily emails from Haiti, study photos of work in progress, and observe real-time YouTube clips. We provide immediate direction by overlaying comments and Photoshop sketches on the images. Thanks to satellite Internet, it's easy to manage our functional progress from a distance. But remote participation fails to stimulate my spirit. I can't smell the acrid charcoal through cyberspace; I don't have a skinny dog scampering underfoot at my desk in Boston. Working in Haiti revitalizes me, but when the magic island is not tangible, Be Like Brit and Mission of Hope become just two more obligations in my day.

Commitments back home limit this trip to five days. Mission of Hope is at their nadir: they have nothing; demolition is over, and construction's yet to begin. Lex has torn down most of what took ten years to build and has only a giant hole for his effort. The stated purpose of my trip is to set the stakes for the school, but just as important, I need to walk the site with Lex, envision the building with him, and bolster his enthusiasm. I'll also spend time at Be Like Brit and make a day trip to Forward in Health, where construction has resumed, but similar cheerleading will be in order.

It's late afternoon when we arrive in Grand Goave; Cherybin takes me right to Mission of Hope. We drive through the gate. The open church with its tin roof remains, as does Renee's wood-framed office shack and the lean-to roof that shades a half dozen picnic tables. A precarious row of temporary plywood classrooms sits on the roofs of the concrete structures that line the west side of the site—the only buildings to survive the earthquake intact. The rest of the sloped site has been excavated flat. The sides of the hole are only about a foot deep at the shallow end, but over twelve feet high on the south side. I unroll my drawings on a picnic table and compare my taut lines to the ragged reality. Thick black dirt lodges under each fingernail. I chuckle at the too-obvious metaphor that Haiti is already under my skin. But I'm happy to see the dirt, proof that this isn't a virtual visit.

I spend my first two days coordinating efforts at both the school and the orphanage. The progress is heady, exciting. The third morning Pastor Akine drives me to Les Cayes to visit the Forward in Health clinic site, three hours further west. Beyond Grand Goave, Route 2 snakes through the mountains as it shifts from hugging the north coast to skirting the south coast. We traverse crests with inspiring vistas and descend to the Caribbean Sea, which has better surf than the Bay of Gonave and more picturesque beaches. We arrive at the Forward in Health site midmorning. It's been nearly two years since I was here.

Thanks to the earthquake, Forward in Health's site lay dormant throughout 2010. During that time the Mulqueens ended their connection with Lex, though I don't know why. They found an American, Hal, who moved to Les Cayes to supervise renewed construction. His crews laid the first concrete-block walls in February. Hal was slow to share his progress. When he finally sent photos, and we realized the crews had failed to install reinforcing, most of the walls were in place. We salvaged the inferior work but lopped off the second floor, since the structure is compromised. Better, perhaps, than pre-earthquake masonry but well short of our objective. We lost March when rebel forces closed the western peninsula off from the rest of the country; April was eaten up building a storage depot, and now Hal is constructing a tent city on the site to house seventy orphans who were evicted from their last residence.

As I step through the gate I'm pleased to see clinic walls in place, but as I walk closer I experience a disappointment I encounter all too often in Haiti: the details do not measure up to the distant view. The workmanship is terrible; the blocks are poorly supported over the doors; the mortar joints are randomly fat and thin; it will be impossible to grow the building's height evenly. Hal is a lean, agile guy, a few years older than me. We've met a few times in the States, where he boasted of his construction expertise. When I tried to explain the structural system, he cut me off: "I have plenty of experience and know what has to be done."

Facing each other across the terrible work, it's clear that he is not getting it done. We shake hands, warily, and perch on the edge of the construction. I reach over and grab a reinforcing bar projecting from the concrete, necessary to tie the walls and foundation together. The steel comes right out in my hand, and with it comes all of my frustration. "What are you doing here, Hal? This is a mess." Not an auspicious start.

We fire accusations at each other for twenty minutes, and then, to our credit, we proceed to work, albeit from a vantage point of deep distrust. It turns out Hal has no experience in masonry construction and is not employed by Forward in Health; he's a middle-aged adventurer with a motorcycle in Haiti. He cannot read architectur-al drawings, though he never admits to this deficiency. We spend three hours in a tango of mutual suspicion, walking through the work in place, itemizing all the mistakes and negotiating what can be salvaged. I feel Hal misled us; if he had not inflated his skills, if he'd allowed us to mentor him, we could have helped him cre-ate better results. From his perspective I'm an unsympathetic jerk. He adapts the mantra, "I know what you want, but these Haitians won't do it." Blaming his shortcomings on the local crews insults me. I remind him that we are achieving better construction on the orphanage project, but he's not interested in what I say. I've created an enemy.

I'm relieved to get out of there but discouraged. The euphoria, the possibility that permeated my first visit, has turned to poison. Hal is going to build what he wants and deflect his shortcomings onto the Haitians. The clinic I envisioned will never be built.

I doze on the long drive back to Grand Goave, bumpy, unsatis-fying sleep.

The next afternoon, I avoid the heat by working in Mission of Hope's office, the same windowless room Renee escaped on the day of the earthquake. Renee is working at her computer; Lex is fiddling with pad and paper; I am sitting on the chest freezer making sketches for the school, weighing the proportions of jal-ousie windows versus casements. "Paul, we love you, man." Lex says, apropos of nothing. I stop my drawing. I raise my head. I see the knit band of his polo shirt tight against his smooth bicep, the inviting dimple of his sleeve as it climbs toward his perfectly round, broad shoulder. I do not meet his eyes. Nor do I reply. I feel woozy. Something rumbles. Perhaps an aftershock is approach-ing; I am intent on feeling one after hearing Renee describe them so lucidly. But this is not an earthquake; it's just the tremor of my heart.

I am a hard nut, but not entirely unlovable. The usual suspects have uttered *I love you* to me before: my mother, my sister, my wife, even my children. I don't think my father ever said it, and I'm sure I never said it to him. A few guys itching for a husband have tried the phrase out on me, and I've uttered the words my-self to a few inappropriate fellows. But no one ever said it like Lex does, with the declarative ease that makes the phrase at once trite:

for what is not to love about a guy who comes all this way and works for nothing; and profound: as if his love is so solid it can float on the breeze of an afternoon work session. I am numb. My mouth gapes open. The tremor of my heart expands out through my chest; it rattles my extremities. Every surface tingles. I'm embarrassed by his words; I'm soothed by his words. I'm euphoric. My reaction is inappropriate, I know. But Lex is so beautiful; his ebony skin and dancing eyes, the rise of his cheekbones when he smiles, his confident swagger, his sinewy forearms, his inviting hands. Although I never acknowledged it until this moment, I have cataloged every inch of this man.

I am sure Lex and Renee know I'm gay, though we've never mentioned it. Between evangelical missionary beliefs and Haiti's homophobic culture, it's not a topic that flows from natural conversation. But Lex's words, and my reaction to them, spin my head with conjectures I have thus far avoided. Am I so hungry for love that I misconstrue a simple statement of gratitude? Am I in love with Lex? Why does a gay man choose to spend his time among people who consider him sinful, in a country that denies his validity? Why am I not content to stay in Cambridge, where being a gay father is not only accepted but has a certain cachet? Am I internalizing my own homophobia by being here, or am I heroically infiltrating the opposition in a futile crusade against their narrow view?

Eventually my heart settles into a quiet, steady beat. A torrent of question and doubt dampens the initial thrill of Lex's declaration. I redirect attention to my sketch—drawing is always palliative for me—but my hand shakes. I have no idea if I love it here because I belong or if I love it here because it's so far from the life I've made back home. Regardless, I know that I love it here, and that I love Lex in every way that is good and a few less appropriate ways as well. His words force me to acknowledge this beautiful, complicated truth. The details will have to sort themselves out in time.

I regain enough equilibrium to continue with the tasks at hand. I finish my sketches and prepare a quantity takeoff for the steel reinforcing Lex will need for the footings. I avoid looking him straight in the eye when we review what he has to purchase, but I feel every pore of his body near mine. I absorb every breath he inhales as if my own.

It's a relief to help Cherybin load tonight's dinner into the 4x4 and drive it to Mirlitone; being so close to Lex is exhilarating but also exhausting. After dinner I fall into bed and a night of fitful sleep, yet I wake refreshed. Which is fortunate, as my last day of this short trip turns into chaos on steroids.

Our task is simple; we need to place four stakes to define the corners of a rectangular building that sits, more or less, in the middle of a rectangular site. But, oh, the complications. We have no site survey, only a Google Earth photo; the site is overrun with schoolchildren; it slopes more than ten feet toward the north, so that pesky third angle of vertical height must be factored into the calculations. The excavation is not quite complete; a shack remains where one of the new corners has to land, preventing a reliable diagonal check. I have a pair of two-hundred-foot measuring tapes and three World Race assistants who have never worked construction. It is ninety-five degrees without a cloud in the sky or a sliver of shade to be found.

Mission of Hope's property is not really a rectangle, more a series of angled segments, like an accordion bellows open full. Each corner is some unique angle, and due to the structures remaining around the periphery, bearings are devilish to find. I hand the end of the tape to an eager missionary, set her in one location, and check off a series of dimensions. I move her to another spot; take the same data from a different vantage point. Nothing adds. My helpers get hot. I let them hold the tape next to the excavated cliff; it's cooler there. I am in full sun all afternoon. I am so sweaty I pretend to be in a hot yoga class. I embrace the heat; I breathe it in as a way to cope. Finding the square is elusive. We measure and check and plant a stake and a school kid yanks it up. We measure and check, and the excavation slides. We measure and check, and we're four inches long. We measure and check, and we're six inches short. We measure and check until we have something close enough to a rectangle that we proclaim it done, though it's not as square as it ought to be. We cross and recross the site until after 6 p.m., the longest day I've ever worked in Haiti. My three World Racers are hot and grumpy. I have a pounding headache. I slump back in the truck, silent all the way to Mirlitone, and take to my bunk without dinner.

I lie in the half-light of a Haitian evening, shut my eyes, and try to still my throbbing head. I focus on my breathing. My mind races like a pinball that smacks from bumper to bumper; every pulse against my skull is a bright blinker and jarring ding. This trip has been hell accented by a single moment of heaven. Every ounce of energy has been sucked out of me by the giant *ennui* that is Haiti. I arrived wanting to accomplish so much, but I've completed so little.

Eventually I fall into a discomfiting sleep. I rise before the sun, pack my duffle, and take the bumpy ride back to Port-au-Prince. As the plane lifts out of the valley, leaving behind the dusty construction and the green sea, I bid Haiti goodbye. I have created my drawings and inserted a few feeble stakes in the land. The actual construction is beyond me. If Forward in Health's clinic is any indication, I have no reason for cheer. I don't know if, or when, I will come back. I made a good effort, but like so many before me, I am no match for this country of entrenched misery.

Supervision
June–December 2011

I return to the United States with renewed thanks for the blessings in my life. Abby graduates from the University of Massachusetts and lands a job in the Infectious Disease Lab of Massachusetts General Hospital. Andy receives a summer internship studying turtle habitats for NOAH in the Florida Everglades. I do everything required to move the three Haiti projects forward, but given their fitful march, weeks go by without requiring any architectural input. My stateside projects plod along, but after witnessing life's immediacy in Haiti, I find little satisfaction in contributing to America's ever-expanding, often excessive, healthcare system. My last trip was tumultuous; I am in no rush to return to the magic island, yet Haiti etches a craving that my everyday existence cannot satisfy.

My restlessness leads to a personal indulgence. Every summer, I visit my brother and sister in Colorado, and we ride the Courage Classic, a three-day cycling rally through the Rocky Mountains to benefit Children's Hospital Colorado. This year, I decide to use that ride as the starting point for a bicycle odyssey. I negotiate leave from work, fly to Colorado, buy a touring bike, ride over the mountains with my siblings, and then cycle, on my own, all the way home. I cover three thousand miles in seven weeks on a circuitous route that takes me down to Oklahoma City, across the Ozarks, up the Ohio River, diagonal from Cincinnati to Cleveland, around Lake Erie to Buffalo, and alongside the Erie Canal. I savor the two-lane roads and vintage motels. I eat like a teenager; spinning through seventy miles a day lets me indulge in chicken fried steak, barbecue beef on pretzel rolls, and Chinese buffets with abandon. I arrive home a few pounds lighter with shapely legs and a new appreciation for the wonders of America. After Labor Day I return to work and feign interest in my projects, but recollections of Haiti's grit and road cycling render office work tedious. I drift in vague dissatisfaction until fate intervenes in a tragic but potent way.

Architecture is a boom and bust profession; work fluctuates dramatically in step with the economy. The 2008 recession hit TRO JB hard, right after a merger and expansion. My position remained secure—healthcare specialists are always in demand— but when an organization contracts, friction results. I'm oblivious of any discord, a sign of my disengagement, until one Monday morning in early November when an edict from a renegade group of principal stockholders demands a no-confidence vote on our CEO. Everyone must take notice, and take sides. A week of bitter intrigue ensues; tense stockholder meetings and senior-level firings. The protagonists in the drama forge an uneasy truce and restructure the firm in a manner that strikes me as expedient but unsustainable. The office becomes a treacherous place yet, as in any power struggle, it is ripe with opportunity. I decide against stepping into the vacuum. Witnessing people I respect behaving badly and seeing people I value get fired leaves me with a sour taste. I decide to pursue fresh prospects. At Thanksgiving I announce to friends and family that I am looking for new opportunities. The recent bitterness makes me question whether to continue practicing architecture. My mind bends in new and unconsidered directions.

I'm not someone who dwells on the finances of life. I have simple tastes. There's always enough money to do what I want with some left over. I don't follow the stock market or have a financial advisor; my retirement planning consists of depositing the maximum allowed into a 401K. I am as slow to fathom financial realities as emotional ones. But balances accumulate and one morning I acknowledge a new truth—I don't need to work anymore. College tuition is in the rearview mirror; my children's biggest expenses are behind me. I paid off the four-family house I bought twenty years ago; rents from the three units beyond the party wall cover my regular expenses. For four years I've redirected my take home pay to savings and never touched a dime. I must not need that paycheck.

This reality strikes me one autumn morning, but it generates no more excitement than I take in selecting a matching shirt and tie. I don't vet the numbers with a retirement specialist or attend a money seminar; my gut simply confirms that my accounts have adequate digits to support me into a very old age. I attend my usual yoga class, move through my postures, and focus my mind simultaneously on my balance and my newfound security. I'm grateful to be liberated from the search for the almighty dollar; few receive such a gift. But it's a luxury cloaked in responsibility. I'm a healthy fifty-six-year-old man, independent, and thirsty for change. How I decide to spend my time seems all the more important. Since I can do anything, I ought to pursue something vigorous and meaningful.

I could start my own firm; I could ride my bicycle across the United States; or I could join the Peace Corps. I invite my friends to suggest ideas; it's a fun game to play, even vicariously. Some days I'm giddy with possibility. Maybe I will study international development at the Harvard Kennedy School, or enroll in a writing workshop, or become a yoga teacher. Haiti lingers in my mind; I have unfinished buildings and unfinished business there. But I can't live in Haiti; I'm not that kind of saint. I write to Lex and Len and John Mulqueen and ask them for suggestions about my delightful predicament. Len emails back immediately and invites me to lunch.

The two of us settle into a booth at Pedro's in Watertown. The thin December light filters through the tall windows. I haven't seen Len Gengel in months; he looks terrible. He's made sixteen trips to Haiti already this year, with two more to go. Apparently, Pat, the full-time superintendent, returned to the States in October. The guy did great work Monday through Friday, but Haiti offered too many distractions for a single young American with weekends on his hands. Since Pat left, Len has been flying to Haiti every other week, pushing construction there while raising money and managing his business here. I ask if he will hire another superintendent; Len obviously can't keep up what he's doing. "No, I won't put someone in Haiti full time; it's too hard for extended periods." He lifts a forkful of steak; his head hunches over his

plate, more exhausted than hungry. "What I would love is someone to alternate with me; to be down there a few weeks every
month to supervise construction. It's the travel that kills me." The
memory of our first meeting at the Mulqueens flashes through my
mind; I was all in then, I might as well be all in now. "I'll do it,
Len," I blurt out before he finishes another bite. "When do I start?"

The rest of our meal is detail. We will alternate two-week jun-
kets to Haiti in order to maintain a continuous presence. On my
trips I'll supervise Be Like Brit, but also help Mission of Hope and
travel to Les Cayes if Forward in Health wants my assistance. Be
Like Brit will cover airfare; we'll ask Mission of Hope to provide
room and board. I'll start in late December, overlap with Len a few
days, and then be on my own in the new year.

I inform my firm I will be working two weeks a month in Haiti.
Since TRO JB has no precedent for part-time work, this amounts
to quitting, but the new management team asks me to stay on as
part-time consultant. Neither of us knows how that might pan
out, but I agree. The recent tumult's been brutal, but I have lasting
affection for a firm that's been so good to me.

I worry about returning to Haiti; my last trip was grueling. But
the country's grip on my soul throttles reasoned analysis. I am not
finished with Haiti, and I accept that Haiti is not finished with me.

Steel Reinforcing
December 2011–January 2012

There are two routes from Boston to Port-au-Prince. American connects through Miami or Fort Lauderdale; Delta connects through New York. Most flights leave early in the day so the planes can deposit folks in PAP and then hightail it back to the States; airplanes do not layover overnight in Port-au-Prince. Florida connections are preferable; the airports are newer, the on-time stats positive, but I fly whichever is cheapest, and JFK's weathered grit has its peculiar charms. My challenge with flying is that planes move faster than my psyche's ability to process the cultural shift from staid Boston to chaotic Port-au-Prince; routing through New York puts me in a Haitian state of mind.

The gate for PAP throbs with disorder. People press against the check-in counter more than an hour before takeoff. Multiple rollies, backpacks, purses, and shopping bags burden many passengers, but when the clerk suggests checking them they look away in bland detachment. People flying to Port-au-Prince are not average Haitians; average Haitians cannot afford to fly. Still, the crowd ignores the tacit rules of air travel, as if JFK is a buffer zone where American norms and Haitian behaviors collide.

It takes nearly an hour to board the plane. Swaggering guys in embroidered fedoras jive toward the gate; frail old ladies fumble through their purses in search of boarding passes; and elegant men with distinctive goatees, shiny suits, and neon acrylic ties approach the jetway as if processioning to a coronation. Everyone crowds the gate at the first call; the idea of boarding by zones is an affront to the Haitian penchant for disorder.

My flight leaves on time, almost. Flight attendants rasp over the mic: *Take your seats, let others pass; we cannot leave until everyone sits down.* They plead in English, in French, in haste, in anger, and in exasperation. No extra points for customer courtesy—they're simply trying to get us to move. Attendants rip rollies away from end-of-the-line souls; the overhead bins bulge. Eventually we settle in, more in spite of the attendants than in response to them.

The instant the plane lifts off the runway, people pop out of their seats. I'm in the exit row opposite a beautiful French flight attendant who becomes so frustrated she finally tells a young woman: "It is dangerous to be up and walking around, but you'll do whatever you do." These petty improprieties amuse me, the endless itch to thumb one's nose at order and authority, however trivial. Haitian pride of place in this world as the first black republic supersedes any acknowledgment of the tragic battering their country has endured for the past two hundred years. They are simultaneously victims on the world stage and survivors of the highest magnitude. *We will board as we like; we will sit down as we like; and we will get there when we arrive. A few minutes either way won't matter; Port-au-Prince will be the same.*

The first person I see in Grand Goave, of course, is Jenison. He stands outside Mission of Hope's gate as casually as if he had just happened by, as purposefully as if he hadn't moved a muscle since I left him in May. I open the pickup truck's door, reach down, and scoop him up. He was endearing when we first met, pixyish and smart, with a scary facility to mimic English. Now the sores and blisters of a life lived out of doors mark his body, and his rudimentary begging is more insistent. He moans that he's hungry, which he probably is, and pleads *give me one dollar.* Since my heart is more practical than soft, I get him a plate of rice and beans rather than the *peewilly* (that odd Creole term for lollipop) he craves; and I don't even acknowledge his gambit for money.

Mystery surrounds Jenison's circumstances. Word is that his mother died, and Michelle, the female carpenter we built houses with after the quake, adopted him. When I ask Jenison about his mother, he makes a somber face, pantomimes sleep by rolling his head onto a pair of prayer-positioned hands, and whispers *maman dormi.* After a pause that stabs my heart, he flies his hands apart, tosses back his head and yowls like a hyena. I cannot tell if his mother actually died or if Jenison has just mastered another heart tug. The woman's very existence is lost in translation.

Len and I spend a few days reviewing the status of orphanage construction. He's built a twelve-foot-square construction shanty with worktables, electric outlets, satellite Internet, and piles of snacks, even an air conditioner. The orphanage's foundation is complete; we are erecting the first-floor walls. Len explains job procedures, how the crews are organized, and productivity expectations. I have been around enough construction to realize that Len is excellent at running a job site; I have my work cut out for me maintaining his standards. Children come and go all day; he doles out handfuls of *peewillies*. Jenison never shows his face. But the morning after Len leaves and I am the sole *blan*, Jenison appears, looking for shoes. We have a hockey bag full of them for children needing footwear. I can't fathom why Jenison wants shoes; the boy is always barefoot. We rustle through the bag and find a pair of sneakers with room for his feet to grow. I give him a *peewilly* while we're at it. He thanks me with great appreciation and wears his sneakers outside. I turn back to my work. A few minutes later I look up to see Jenison, barefoot, new shoes in hand, racing down the hill. Maybe he'll sell them. Maybe he'll keep them as a prize. Maybe he just wanted them because he could get them. The only thing I know for sure is that the next time I see Jenison he won't be wearing those shoes. Shoes are not his style.

Within a few days of Len leaving, I settle into a routine. Gama knocks on my door at 5:30 a.m. I have fifteen minutes to wash, dress, and get down to the BLB pickup. We leave before anyone else is up, and since it's dry season, we drive along the riverbed as the sun rises over the mountains. Mountains in this part of Haiti are not tall, two thousand feet at most, but they rise straight out of the sea, very steep, which makes them more picturesque than many a ten-thousand-footer.

Gama is Lex's cousin, which is less exclusive than it sounds. Lex has dozens of cousins, maybe hundreds. Many are part of Lex's missionary empire, but Gama is first among cousins. He is an American citizen. Gama spent the last five years with his wife, Angela, in Athol, Massachusetts, where their son, Nathan, was born. Mother and child are still in the States while Gama is here full-time. Although he has no previous construction experience, Gama is a great translator, a patient listener, a hard worker, and a congenial soul. He is a pleasure from morning to night, which I know for a fact because we spend that much time together.

When we arrive at the site seventy workers are already there. Francky, the gofer, locks the gate at 6:00 a.m. sharp; anyone who arrives late does not work, and with jobs hard to come by, especially ones that pay five dollars a day, workers arrive on time. The men are gaunt, their skin pitch black. We exchange *bonjous*; I am beginning to learn a few names.

Gama organizes the work crews while I turn on the computers and check email, our lifeline to Len and the engineers. Once work is under way I walk the site. Gama calls me "eagle eye" because I point out reinforcing bars improperly spaced and electric boxes needing grout. He is a master of flattery in both languages.

When volunteers fantasize about building in a developing country we envision ourselves in shorts and bandannas, laying concrete blocks or shingling a roof under a shady palm tree. The quake shattered that illusion. Be Like Brit is designed to high engineering standards, and my work is supervisory—ensuring quality and teaching local tradesmen improved construction techniques. This sounds noble but is actually tedious. I monitor and observe, anticipate what needs attention and correct mistakes. I walk the site several times a day, make many sketches, and generate a lot of spreadsheets: how many blocks we need to finish the first floor (1,800), how much reinforcing we need for the second-floor slab (1,325 bars, 40 feet long). The only thing that makes my work exotic is that I do it in Haiti.

Three women have set up take-out stands on site. They cook lunch over charcoal grills and sell food to the workers. Gama says a man can eat very well in Haiti on $1.50 a day. Even though Mission of Hope provides lunch for me down the hill as part of my work arrangement, Gama insists on buying me lunch. He considers himself my host, and food is hospitality, so I occasionally accept his offer. Gama refines my Haitian palate. His offerings are more flavorful than the Americanized food at Mission of Hope: cornmeal pellets with beans and a small but pungent fried fish, rice with shredded beef and smoky lentils, and my favorite, legume. My iron stomach enjoys everything Gama serves.

Around noon I walk down the hill to Mission of Hope, which folks refer to as MoHI. The expansive view over the Bay of Gonave never fails to amaze me. I chat with children along the road. They clamor for me to take their picture—every day—and the excitement of seeing their faces appear on my viewfinder never fades. They all know my name and hopefully someday I can reciprocate.

Construction at MoHI is slow; we have neither Len Gengel's resources nor his expertise. We've cobbled together contractors from different parts of the United States who come down to supervise local tradespeople in this new form of construction. Our concrete superstar, John Armour, will be here mid-January for two weeks. In advance of his arrival I determine all the reinforcing we need to finish the foundation and work with a local crew to fabricate 550 U-bars for foundation beams and 30 reinforced column cages. More emails and conference calls, more spreadsheets, inventorying what rebar is on site and determining what we need to order.

On my way back up to BLB I review the stone retaining wall that Len is building along the road, elegant as any found in a tony American subdivision. On my first day here I made a pidgin speech to the laborers saying I would help them build the orphanage if they would help me learn Creole; the masons building the wall always offer up new words and test my phrases. It is the hottest part of the day, the hill is steep, and by the time I reach the orphanage site every inch of my shirt is soaked.

The crew knocks off at 4 p.m., but Gama and I remain, write a daily report, and photograph progress. By 5 p.m., I'm tired. I leave Gama to his paperwork and walk down the hill to catch a ride home. Cherybin drives anyone needing a lift back to Mirlitone. We stop at Lex and Renee's combination house/office/kitchen in town, load pots of rice and chicken and plastic pitchers of juice that Marieve has prepared for the evening's dinner. I enjoy the ride across the dry riverbed with the sun sinking over the bay and the aroma of delicious food rising from the pot on my lap.

By Haitian standards, I live like a prince. BLB rents one of Mirlitone's private suites full-time. The room sleeps five, but since I'm here off-weeks from Len I have the place to myself; BLB volunteers want to be here with the Big Kahuna. When I return from work my bed is made, the bathroom is clean; I shower in the drizzle of cold water, then wash out my microfiber pants and shirt and hang them to dry. I have an alternating set for tomorrow. I change into shorts and a fresh shirt and wander down to the chaconne to see who's around.

Tonight there are only five volunteers, but a group of thirty will arrive from Ohio tomorrow. Night falls, conversation dwindles, and I drift up to my room to read. Within an hour it's dark as midnight. I hear Gama return. His room is next to mine. He turns his TV on, loud. The wall between us is thin. We both fall asleep to the sounds of American popular culture. I sleep long and solid until he knocks on my door again in the morning.

On the Monday morning after New Year's we're running late. Gama drops me off at MoHI. Women and children from the neighborhood stream in to fill five-gallon buckets with filtered water that MoHI provides free for the taking. Leon, the rebar boss, arrives with his crew to fabricate column cages. We review diagrams showing exactly how long to cut each bar and where to make each bend. We need two hundred heavy bars bent into giant *L* shapes. Each column will encase eight of these *L*'s with tall leg upright and short leg buried in the building's footing. We also need four hundred smaller rebar called stirrups, each cut and then bent five times to create a square with overlapping hooks at one corner. We will wrap the stirrups around the eight vertical bars to prevent the verticals from bowing out once we pour concrete around all the steel. Since we need to fabricate so many, it's worth the effort to get the first ones right.

Two hours pass before we make a single cut. First we have to find Renold, MoHI's keeper of supplies, to unlock the tool shed. The saw will not start. A group of Haitians huddles over it, debates the problem, dismantles the saw, oils it, reassembles it, fails to correct the problem, and so repeats the process. I have nothing to contribute to the repair, so I wait around.

I am lousy at waiting, but here I have plenty of diversions. Jenison stops by, dressed for school and wearing shoes, though not the ones I gave him. We draw soccer balls. He shows me how to make an origami boat; I show him how to fold a paper airplane. We get so involved in paper folding that his five-gallon bucket of water overflows; he can barely pick it up and tote it back across the road. Christlove and Mackinlove, two small boys we call the Love brothers, take up folding paper with me. They live with their mother in a shack within MoHI's walls, the only children left on campus since the thirty-three orphans moved to an orphanage run by another evangelical group, Hands and Feet, a mile down the road. We toss gliders everywhere. Mackinlove, age six, draws the letter B all over his wings and sings a little song, "Be like Brit, Be like Brit." Everything is good until both boys want my only red pen. Pulling and crying ensue until Lex, who showed up at some point, laughs. "Trouble always happens when Paul is around." Eventually, the tools are repaired, and we spend the day cutting and bending rebar until we get it right.

The group of missionaries from Akron arrives and focuses their efforts toward improvements at Mirlitone: painting banisters and walls, laying foundations for more guest cottages, and roofing the new kitchen. Marieve is going to move her food operation here since there are more people to feed at Mirlitone than in town. The new kitchen sits at the front corner of Mirlitone's property and incorporates two of the site-boundary walls, which meet at an obtuse angle, along with two recently built walls that sit square to the other buildings on site. The result is a structure with one right angle and three odd ones. In pre-earthquake Haiti this out-of-squareness would hardly be noticed as flat concrete roofs capped most buildings. Since those roofs killed a lot of people; many post-earthquake structures opt for lightweight sloped roofs topped with corrugated metal. A wood and metal roof will not last as long as concrete in a country where wood is susceptible to decay, but it won't crush people if it falls.

Four guys built the new roof in three days. When it is finished, one of them explains their logic to me. "We knew the metal roof needed to have between *2 in 12* and *3 in 12* slope" (slope is the ratio of vertical rise to horizontal run; a *3 in 12* roof rises three feet vertically for every twelve feet of horizontal distance). "We set the ridge 4 feet above the dividing wall in the kitchen, so it could be sheathed in full pieces of plywood. This put the slope in the correct range. We had to sister the joists, which were only 16 feet long, but set the longest rafter perpendicular to the ridge and extended it to the top of the wall. From there, we laid out the other rafters, some parallel, some not, to achieve a consistent slope, and then built up the angled walls as high as needed to meet the rafters." The result is a roof of consistent pitch sitting atop a skewed box.

I ask how they made hurricane clips, necessary to hold roofs down in a tropical storm. "We couldn't find any anchors to drill in the concrete-block walls, but we found a spool of metal tape and some through bolts (threaded rod that can be secured at either end by nuts). We epoxied the bolts into the top course of masonry, anchored one end of the metal tape to the bolt's threads, wrapped the tape over the rafter, pulled the other end of the tape over the bolt, and tightened the nut on everything."

The details of this construction demonstrate fundamental differences between American and Haitian culture. Take four guys from Ohio, throw them in Haiti, give them an assortment of tools and materials and a jumbled problem, and in three days they concoct a rather elegant solution. Americans' ability to problem-solve is great, and we relish the challenge.

At Be Like Brit, we are building a larger yet more regular building. Still we must repeat every direction over and over. The crew can trowel grout into ten courses of concrete block, but unless we tell them to grout the eleventh, they might not. This lapse is not due to laziness; Haitians work hard. Nor do I think it's entirely explicable by education. Haitians think differently than we do. Americans seek pattern and logic; we apply order wherever we can. Haitians experience events as isolated and idiosyncratic; they are disinclined to relate effect to cause.

When the earth shakes and buildings fall, Americans say *let's build our buildings better,* while in a land where mysticism runs strong and Voodoo runs deep, Haitians are just as apt to say *the spirits are angry.* We strive to affect the world around us; they are inclined to accept the world they know. We put our faith in physics, they are more comfortable with magic. The more time I spend here, the more balance I seek. There is truth in magic as well as physics. Logic is not always valid. Haiti confounds my definition of rational.

One magical aspect I've always appreciated about Haiti is how dark it gets at night. Sadly, Haiti's not nearly as dark as it used to be. The electrical grid in Grand Goave, which ran only four to six hours a day during the year after the earthquake, now operates about twenty hours a day and sometimes provides power for a week or more without a blackout. Off-grid locales still depend on generators, but fuel is more plentiful than it was and much cleaner, so generators run longer and break down less often. A year ago the generator at Mirlitone ran a few hours each morning and evening, if it ran at all. We shut it down by eight, and by nine everyone was asleep. Now the generator bellows all night, lights burn, and air conditioners hum.

Toward the end of my trip, the generator at Mirlitone breaks down, and we return to darkness. I am the only person happy about this situation. I love the dark. I love how our other senses sharpen when sight is compromised. I love easing my way along the path from my room, across the veranda, down the steps, and through the chaconne to the beach, guided by nothing more than dinner's lingering scent, a starry night's faint glow, and the steady pounding of the surf. When there is light I speed down the stairs, but in the dark I engage each tread; I monitor the pressure in my hands and feet to make sure I always bear two points of weight. Darkness heightens my consciousness.

I sleep better when the generator is off. Absent the machine's rumble and the drone of Gama's air conditioner, night sounds fill my room: the waves, the barking dogs, the roosters that crow too early, and the church bells that peal moments before Gama's wake-up knock.

But for all that I love the dark, there are times when work presses down, and I need to extend light. On the last day of my trip, Gama and I have a long list of To Do's after the crews leave. By 5:30 p.m. the shack is dim, and the single overhead fluorescent burns out. Gama sends Francky to get another bulb on his *moto*. I prop a flashlight over my keyboard. Francky returns and inserts the new bulb, but nothing happens. Gama calls an electrician, who comes with a temporary light. We type away while the electrician climbs on our worktable and fiddles with the socket. Francky points the flashlight here and there. I could be upset, or at least annoyed, but instead I'm flush with giddiness, hunting and pecking in the shadows. A situation that would trigger anger in the United States just adds to the zany sense of adventure here. Gama begins to sing. Francky adds a different tune. I join in. Eventually we discover that we all know "La Bamba," though none of us speaks Spanish.

Ultimately the socket is fine. Apparently the replacement bulb broke as Francky's *moto* jostled up the hill. The electrician returns everything to its original condition, but he does not have a replacement bulb among his tools. He takes his work light and leaves us with a single flashlight. Without light we cannot work, and there is no light to be had. So we head back to Mirlitone. The best place to be in Haiti in the dark is in bed.

Aggregate

January–February 2012

It's 6:45 p.m., which in midwinter Haiti means it's black as midnight. I'm sitting at a picnic table under the lean-to roof at Mission of Hope. A bare light bulb illuminates the drawings in front of me. Beyond, the excavation for the new building is finished. Narrow trails wind up each side of the hole. The paths are little more than three feet wide; in some places the vertical drop is over ten feet. Storage buildings line the west path. These are the newest structures on campus and the only ones that survived the earthquake intact. Plywood sheds have been built on top of their roofs—temporary classrooms until our new building is complete. The east path leads to a string of outdoor toilets and shower stalls. Beyond these is the makeshift kitchen where short, stout women prepare three hundred plates of rice and beans every day for the students. During school hours children scamper along the treacherous routes and through the construction. Everywhere, I see boys in oxford shirts tucked into blue slacks cinched around their thin waists with homemade belts and girls in white blouses and pleated skirts whose lace anklets hover above the dust. They skip and jostle and chase each other along the precipices. If I worried about accidents the fear would paralyze me.

At this hour the schoolchildren are gone, but I have other safety worries. The site is crawling with workers who maneuver across exposed steel reinforcing beneath a string of dangling lights that create more shadow than illumination. We're pouring concrete in a section of the back retaining wall, which is three feet high by fifty-six feet long, including the seven pilasters that will hold the hill back when the rains come. We started at six this morning with a prayer circle. I spent most of my day working alongside two Haitians, cutting and bending several hundred pieces of rebar into different shapes. Agile climbers mounted the walls and installed the reinforcing, tying them with metal twists and extending them vertically to connect to future pours. Another crew removed the forms from the lower section of concrete then oiled, repaired, and reinstalled them at the higher level. Now we are pouring the concrete itself, dumping close to a thousand buckets from high ladders. The poured concrete is compacted with a vibrator, a hand-held machine with an oscillating hose that snakes between the formwork and the reinforcing to fill any voids and ensure a consistent mix. Finally, the top of the concrete is troweled to a smooth finish.

There are at least fifty people in the construction area. Most of them are young Haitian men. John Amour is on top of the forms giving direction and emptying buckets at the same time. There are a few other *blan*, Mission of Hope volunteers with chequered construction experience.

As darkness sweeps in, I pull rank and decide to sit out the remaining work; I'm not steady enough to dance over rebar in the dark. The concrete mixer churns, and the workers chant as they toss ingredients into the mix while in the shed beyond me the girls' choir practices its hymns for next Sunday's service. It's an odd duet.

The electricity goes out. The crew continues to dump concrete in complete darkness; we're not going to stop. This is John Armour's last day at MoHI and his third concrete pour in two weeks. John is an engaging guy, a Nebraska farm boy with tremendous common sense, a terrific rapport with the Haitians, and a fundamental distrust of designer-types like me. He's tossed all kinds of changes into the construction. So long as they do not compromise the structural integrity I don't care; the project is big enough for everyone to have ownership.

Power resumes, and a hoard of young boys buzz about me like bugs to an incandescent bulb. Actually, it's my computer that draws them in. They hang on me as I type their names; they gape at the letters that appear on the screen. Three- and four-year-olds in the States know how to use keyboards, iPads, all manner of technology, but here a laptop is exotic, and ten-year-olds have no idea how to use a mouse or click on a space bar. I guide them to type their own names, but they're wary of this strange machine. They prefer to watch me, studying my fingers as they glide over the keys and make magic symbols that glow in the dark.

The power goes out again. Work continues unabated. The lights return. By 10:00 p.m. the concrete pour is finished. The workers eat mounds of rice and beans and guzzle soft drinks, a bonus for their extra effort. Lex makes a speech of appreciation for the hard work and then sharpens his voice to make sure everyone cleans up before going home; the site will be full of children again to-morrow.

I sleep in the next morning and don't get to BLB until after 8:00 a.m. Immediately outside the gate a slight, weathered man has set up shop. He sits on a pile of rocks under a blue tarp—a remnant from our Samaritan's Purse houses—supported by four sapling trunks stuck in the ground. He sits with his back to the sea. To his left are small boulders, four to eight inches in diameter. On his lap is a flat white stone. In his right hand he holds a small mallet. He picks up a boulder, taps it with his hammer into dozens of smaller pieces, and slides the pieces down the pile to the right. He's been at his task every day since I arrived. He sits and hammers and breaks rocks all day long.

I was twelve years old when the Beatles came out with "The Fool on the Hill," the perfect age to be captivated by a song that denounces conventional motivation. I always wanted to be the guy whose "eyes in his head sees the world spinning round." Except that I was always too busy. Paul McCartney credits the song's inspiration to Maharishi Mahesh Yogi, but today, forty-four years after the song's debut, I discover a man who embodies the complementary mystery, serenity, and inanity of the lyric.

Apparently there's a market for this man's effort; people buy crushed rock to use as aggregate, one of the raw materials used to make concrete. When I ask Gama the value of the rock splitter's work he waves me off; the man cannot make much.

My fool on the hill is a deaf mute, which adds to his allure. When someone lacks ordinary powers we ascribe to him unknowable depth in other faculties. His posture is erect, his face benign; he appears at peace with his work, comfortable with his place in this world. When I approach he waves, when I lift my camera he smiles as if to say: *People like to photograph me just being who I am.*

Of course this is all projection; the man has no opportunity to voice his thoughts. Perhaps he is frustrated, a Stephen Hawking genius trapped in an eternity of rock tapping due to circumstances of birth and life beyond his control. But somehow I doubt that. To all the world he appears as a man who knows his purpose, neither humbled nor exalted by his station. He is the man who taps rocks all day under a tarp, the fool on the hill. The rest of us marvel at his tenacity, we thank god that we are not stuck with his lot. Yet, we wonder if perhaps his quiet persistence endows him with a deeper understanding of life than our constant scurrying.

The first week of work flies by. It's late Saturday afternoon, and I'm finishing a report documenting MoHI's status to the engineers. I have to sort through dozens of detail photos, create a site diagram that shows the location and orientation of each image, and email them all to SGH for their review. The report doesn't have to go out this afternoon, but it's been a day of constant interruptions, and I want to complete the task before we close out the week. Gama asks when I'll be ready to leave. By 5:30 p.m., I reply, glad to assign a time frame to my effort. Gama is writing his daily report to which I add a few lines. I need to post my pictures from his computer; the files are too big for my netbook. We hit snags. Gama's computer loses power, and he has to reboot; the photo transfer gets messy; I have to change my email settings to send the files from his laptop. The task presses against me, exacerbated by the random malfunctions that characterize Haiti. I could shrug the report off until Monday, but Monday morning will bring a new set of tasks, so I fight against Haiti's lethargy and push against the magic island's rhythms.

Frustrated, I curse, which sends a shudder through the missionary sensibilities of the construction shanty. Then I bark at Gama, blame it on his computer. He's a handy repository for my outburst, but there's no satisfaction in yelling at Gama, so endlessly calm and patient. He absorbs my rage with detachment; I get no more feedback than if I'd screamed into a black hole. Even as I lash out I know I'm making things worse, but frustration throttles me, and I cannot calm down. I need to take a break, contemplate the view, strike a few yoga poses, but instead I think, if I just finish this, and just finish that . . . so I bumble on, angry and irritated. It's well after six before we finish; my personal battery is kaput.

I crawl into the furthest recess of the pickup and stare out the window. After exploding, I always retreat. Gama gets behind the wheel, a load of Haitians jump in. We stop at MoHI and other places in town. People pile in; people peel away; all the while, I sit in silence. By the time we arrive at Mirlitone, dinner is already cleared, but I am past needing to eat. I curl on my bed and nurse myself back to being human with a complex Sudoku, something I can master. Later, Marieve delivers a plate of rice and beans for Gama and me to share. I apologize to him for my rude behavior. He brushes me off: *no problem*. But it is a problem, for me.

In the morning, a beautiful Sunday with a rippling sea, each wave offers a meditation on life's endless unfolding. Sometimes we find comfort in its consistency; other times we need the excitement of turbulence. The waves do not always break in accord with our personal rhythms.

I am a man who measures his worth in direct proportion to his work. When my productivity crashes, so does my equilibrium. Therapists have made a small fortune exploring my inability to simply be, though none has ever loosened the tyranny of busyness that throttles me. At this age I accept my fate, my need for constant activity, but it seems odd, even masochistic, for a man of my temperament to be drawn to Haiti, a place guaranteed to thwart my thirst for usefulness.

Haiti is a place that accepts things. Perhaps it's because the climate is benign, and people don't feel the seasonal tug we do up north. Perhaps it's because the world shunned independent Haiti, forcing its citizens to make do with what they could scratch from the land. Perhaps it's because Haiti's isolation led to a culture steeped in family and the supernatural rather than in science. Most likely it is all of these things and others I have yet to discover.

Strolling along the shore, I contemplate the pain I suffer and inflict on others when things don't go according to my arbitrary plans. Work here is satisfying, and my contribution is direct, unlike my complex, collaborative hospital projects back home. Every day in Haiti I experience flashes of being complete and present.

But those moments never occur between 4:00 p.m. and 6:00 p.m. That's when my self-imposed need to complete some arbitrary objective runs up against the setting sun, when Haiti's complacency to shrug off until another day gnaws at my core. That's my American Hour.

My Sunday walk along the beach leads me to the mouth of the Grand Goave River. The water is just a trickle this time of year. I stand in the middle of the riverbed and take in the panorama across town, up the foothills, past the orphanage construction, to the mountains beyond. As an architect trained in the 1970s, I cannot help but conceptualize Grand Goave according to Kevin Lynch's *The Image of the City*, a scholarly treatise of the obvious that illustrates how humans understand our world through a hierarchy of familiar patterns, accented by unique places that provide variety. *The Image of the City* established the terms *landmark*, *node*, *link*, and *edge* as the vocabulary we use to describe urban environments to this day.

Grand Goave has no zoning, no building regulations, and little government, yet the classic elements of urban planning prevail here as in any formally planned city. There are two edges—the Bay of Gonave on the north and the river on the east. Haiti National Route 2, which runs parallel to the coast, sits about half a mile back from the sea. It is the city's main link and only blacktop road. Between the highway and the bay is a grid of streets with arteries running north/south and tertiaries perpendicular to them. The market sits beside Route 2; a collection of wooden stalls that spill along the road's shoulder every Wednesday and Saturday. I often see Grand Goave's own pill man, cousin to the guy who mesmerized me on my first trip, wandering among the stalls. *Tap-taps* congregate here, near the bridge to Port-au-Prince.

Midway between the highway and the bay is the city square, a full block of open space surrounded by a sprinkling of two-story buildings with stately porches that survived the earthquake intact. This pleasant space was the center of Grand Goave life before the highway sucked commerce in its direction. Now, the city square is a cultural rather than a commercial center; music plays continuously and sometimes people dance.

South of Route 2 the land rises. The few roads in that direction are very steep, but there are many footpaths.

Since Haiti is not a country of robust institutions, Grand Goave is short on built landmarks, but the organization of the city is clear. Mountains to the south, bay to the north, urban grid on the flats, and meandering paths in the hills.

On Monday afternoon, for a diversion, I walk a different route from the orphanage to the school site. I follow the mountain foot-path instead of the road, taking photos of the city as it descends toward the sea. It's been two and a half years since I first came here, and the physical change is phenomenal. The bright blue Samaritan's Purse sheathing that wraps temporary shelters stands out against the tawny brown of older construction. Calling such shelters temporary is a misnomer; most are more solid than the houses they replaced, and many have become the nucleus for additional construction. I spot one house that Andy and I built a year and a half ago. In the ensuing months the owners have added a lean-to, a deck, and are now in the process of building a permanent concrete-block structure into the side of their hill.

The city existed; the earthquake pulled it apart, and now it is being knit back together. There may be no master plan, yet the rudimentary patterns of urban form are manifesting themselves just as they have done in human habitations for centuries.

Thursday, the last day of my visit, comes fast. "Mangoes for Breakfast!" Gama proclaims when I enter the shanty after my morning walk of the site. "Do you want to eat mangoes Haitian way or American way?" He slides a bucket of water across the floor of the construction shanty. Five mangoes float in it. "When in Rome," I reply. Gama gives me a quizzical look; idioms don't translate. "Haitian way," I say. He smiles, straddles the bucket, picks a fat mango from the water, gnashes it with his teeth, peels away the skin and chomps down.

I look at the water. I'm adventurous but not stupid. I cannot set my teeth into a mango washed with local water. "American way," I shrug, pull a mango out and use my thumb to break through the soft peel. "American way is with a knife," Gama points out. "You are doing Haitian way for Haitians with no teeth." It's a good joke, but then again, maybe not. People without teeth are common here.

At lunch we have goat head stew. The head is placed in a large kettle and boiled in a buttery sauce with chunks of yam, a papaya-like starch, and the obligatory onion. When the head is tender it's cut into pieces and mixed with the broth and starch. The skin turns deep gray and curls around the underlying muscle. It has a nice texture, but I don't find it as flavorful as the goat meat cubes in our evening stew or the charbroiled chunks that sometimes garnish our rice and beans. When it comes to goat, I'm developing a discriminating palate. Too bad I will have to wait two weeks before having some more.

Buckets and Wheelbarrows
February–March 2012

A five-gallon bucket measures 11.5 inches in diameter by 14 inches tall. When filled with concrete, it weighs over 120 pounds. We mix concrete by pouring the basic ingredients of gravel, sand, cement, and water into a rotating drum according to proportions that SGH developed for consistent strength. The drum deposits the mixture into a ten-foot-square shallow trough that we built on the west side of the BLB orphanage site. It reminds me of a large sandbox. Four guys in hip boots shovel fresh concrete, which is called 'green', into five-gallon buckets. They fill them about half full. Workers form a line and hand the buckets from one to another across the yard and up a ladder. Another guy hoists the bucket on his shoulder and balances sixty pounds of concrete along a grid of steel to the far end of the building where he dumps the bucket. Over the next two weeks we will repeat this process over nineteen thousand times as we pour BLB's second floor slab, working our way from east to west, back toward the ladder and the concrete mixer.

Throughout our first week of pouring concrete at BLB, our productivity increases every day. By the start of the second week our crew of sixty Haitians pours thirty-eight cubic yards of concrete in less than six hours. In the United States a handful of guys could pour the same amount of concrete with five ready-mix trucks and a pump, but that feat wouldn't be half so impressive. Here, spirited cooperation compensates for rudimentary tools.

We start at 6:30 a.m. Two laborers chip away at the key joint from yesterday's pour while another guy uses a hand broom and a Shop-Vac to clean out the formwork from the 1,100-square-foot area we plan to pour today. The finisher snaps lines that determine the top of the floor slab. Down on the ground five guys arrange plastic buckets against piles of sand; another five set up for gravel, two men stack bags of cement, another gets the concrete mixer rolling, while Felix hoses out the inside of the drum. When Boss Pepe gives the signal, workers converge on the mixer with their materials while Boss Pepe counts: twenty-one buckets of sand; twenty-one buckets of gravel; five and a half bags of cement. Felix keeps the mix moist by adding water in an amount that has more to do with Boss Pepe's intuition than SGH's calculations. Once combined, the mixer dumps a cubic yard of concrete into the trough where four monstrously strong men use long-handled spades to shovel it into waiting wheelbarrows.

Concrete by wheelbarrow is our new innovation. After two days of pouring concrete by bucket alone we realized that we could take advantage of the site's slope. We built a bridge from the back hill right onto the second floor slab. Now, twelve guys snake their barrows up the steep hill, roll them across the plank bridge, wheel over to the pour area, dump the concrete, and loop back down to get another load. The wheelbarrow guys love their gig. They sing and run up and down the hill all day. Meanwhile, we still have a bucket brigade that passes concrete up the stairs. Sometimes the two groups compete for speed.

After the material is dumped, a mason vibrates the fresh concrete to make sure it fills in around the reinforcing and into the corners of the formwork. Once the buckets and barrows fill the nine-inch-thick slab depth over an area fifty to sixty feet square, two finishers trowel the slab, making it smooth and level.

Watching the concrete pour from the top of the hill is a bit like observing Cirque du Soleil visit Richard Scarry's Busytown. Buckets of concrete move fast; the empties arc through the air like trapeze fliers, and wheelbarrows follow a convoluted route up and over and back. There is a blur of motion, yet closer inspection reveals that the "wheelbarrowers" are the only people who take more than one or two steps. Everyone else is arm's length from his mate in the sequence. When I lift my eyes just a few degrees all the activity falls away and I am staring out to sea. The shrouded hump of La Gonave seems a distant, surreal landscape beyond the mortal realm.

• • •

The first concrete falls from the chute a little after 7:00 a.m. By 1:00 p.m. the crew is done. They wash out their buckets and barrows while the finishers smooth around the last column. Everyone is exhilarated; the workers signal me to take their photos, dusty guys with huge smiles. Since the men are paid per diem they have great incentive to finish, and there is no logical stopping point for lunch. By 2:00 p.m. they're all sprawled in whatever shade they can find, eating heaping piles of rice and beans, content to have the rest of the day at ease.

The guys have poured a lot of concrete at MoHI as well; most of the foundation is in place. John Armour wants to supervise the remaining pours when he returns, so my time at the school is spent supervising erection of the first concrete-block walls. The heavy foundations needed in constrained concrete construction require us to build the block three feet high before we even reach the ground floor, but making walls feels like progress. After two days we have a low labyrinth; it's possible to identify rooms and corridors. I invite Renee to walk through the building and visit her future office. I point out the entry, the lab, the administrative suite, and finally her space in the far corner. Boss Pepe fathoms this is where she will work. He points upward and protests, *Madame Lex in the sky!* Since the earthquake Haitians seek as loose a connection to their structures as possible. If you cannot be outside, at least be at the top or on the edge, never buried in the basement where the rubble will be deepest. But Renee likes her place just fine; she trusts in our construction and craves this remote location as her best opportunity for privacy.

After more than ten years in Haiti, Renee's biggest challenge is the lack of privacy. Like many Americans, she had her own room growing up. When she and Lex decided to move here and start Mission of Hope they anticipated struggle and deprivation, but she never reckoned how public her life would be. "We take privacy for granted in the United States, but Haiti is a social country. People are everywhere, few people have their own room, and almost no one lives alone." In the United States, we are defined by our accomplishments. In Haiti, people are characterized by their interactions.

Renee and I share introverted temperaments; solitude recharges us. Yet one-on-one, Renee is an engaging conversationalist who's led a remarkable life. She was raised a Jew and emancipated by her adoptive parents at age seventeen. She worked odd jobs, managed a McDonald's, survived a failed marriage, became a Christian, married a Haitian, bore two children, and moved here. Renee is a keen judge of character, yet the breadth of her experience enhances her empathy toward every human condition.

The benevolent February sun relaxes our spirits and loosens our tongues. Talk of Renee's childhood leads us to trade tales of our own children—parenting challenges, education, instilling values—until eventually our talk turns to god, a subject that hovers close to the surface here.

"Do you think there's something more than this?" Renee gestures across the site, which in its current state does not make a compelling argument for humankind's ultimate destiny.

"There might be more, or there might not be. I don't really care either way." I'm ambivalent about the promise of eternity. "I believe there's something bigger than us out there, but I don't see the need to humanize it in the person of Jesus Christ." I hold my tongue at that. There's no reason to tell Renee that I consider conjuring god in human form to be a narcissistic failure of imagination or that as far as I'm concerned, she and I have the same claim to be the son and daughter of God as does Jesus Christ. Jesus' message resonates in me—that we should overturn the power paradigm, elevate the weak, and exalt the humble—but it doesn't draw me to religion. I've never found a church that pulls off compassion with the conviction the gospels demand.

"I can't see how that way of thinking can motivate you to come to Haiti," Renee says. Hundreds, maybe thousands, of missionaries have passed through Lex and Renee's locus of hope in the past decade. The vast majority engaged in what they consider good works in order to bolster their claim from this world into the next. But that mode of thinking means nothing to me. My motivations for being here may still be emerging, but the afterlife is an irrelevant factor in my calculation.

"You are here because you believe there is something more," I say. Renee gives me an encouraging nod. She's not pressing for conversion, but she would be mighty pleased if I leaned in that direction. "I am here because I believe this is all there is." Now it's my turn to gesture across the site; a compelling tableau of human struggle to improve our condition. Our eyes meet. We hold each other's gaze and reach an unspoken accord: she answers a higher calling; I respond to an inner voice. Such differences are not to be surmounted; they must simply be accepted.

Boss Pepe jostles my shoulder. He wants to know if we need to add another reinforcing bar at the doorjamb. In pidgin Creole and gesture I communicate that we always need two vertical reinforcing bars on each side of every doorjamb. I know that Pepe will install two rebar because I tell him to, but as I extend my tape measure to show how long the rebar needs to be, I want more than that. I want him to know *why* we need two rebar. I want him to understand the rebar's purpose and benefit. I want him to realize that he is not powerless against the forces of this world, that through knowledge and labor he can make his future better, safer, than his present. I don't want him to install two rebar just because the *blan* says so. I want him to understand that these rods of steel are our protection against the next time. Pepe smiles and nods, as he always does; I have no idea how much he understands.

The day after Renee and I tour her new office Lex greets me with a scowl. "Len is upset. He doesn't like that the concrete crews are finishing their work so early; he thinks they are abusing their per diem pay. He wants to cut the crew size."

I take a moment to absorb Lex's words. Miscommunication is integral to the daily rhythm of work in Haiti. Everything must be described many times. I build physical models to explain our intent, spray paint every electrical box location on the wall, and ask workers to repeat back their instructions, yet things still go wrong. I accept this as a natural part of interacting across cultures, but I'm caught off guard catching it from Len. I tell Lex not to worry; I will make things smooth. I walk up the hill to BLB trying to fathom Len's point of view. It's not an easy fit. We laid out ten concrete pours to finish the second floor, we negotiated that amount of work from the crews, and we are achieving excellent results. I know Len to be a man of lavish generosity, but I've witnessed his frugality and anger if he feels bested in a deal. Justified or not, Len feels taken advantage of, and it's my job to coax him to a comfortable place.

When I reach the shanty I discuss this problem with Gama. We agree that cutting the crew size will devastate morale. I analyze the data. We've completed six of ten proposed pours for the second-floor slab; each successive pour has been larger, and we've completed it faster. I attribute our 100-percent increase in efficiency to two factors. First, the crews have tightened their procedures; second, we did not initially anticipate using wheelbarrow transport. Productivity skyrocketed once we built the bridge and began wheelbarrowing directly to the second floor. I decide to highlight this fact and draft an email to Len.

I need to offer an alternative to cutting the crew size. I suggest we keep the crew intact but combine the last two pours into one 50 cubic year endeavor; an amount that would not be feasible without wheelbarrows. My suggestion offers Len a 10 percent savings in labor costs. I hit "send" and hope for the best.

As I wait for Len's response, I ponder our predicament and realize I am in the midst of a crisis worthy of a Harvard Business School case study: how to distribute the efficiencies achieved by accelerating productivity among labor and management. In an economy as rudimentary as Haiti's, the basic relationships of labor versus management and technology versus muscle reveal themselves with stark clarity.

During my last trip here, we outlined our options to pour the 280-cubic-yard second-floor slab. First we had to decide whether to pour the concrete using traditional hand methods or to rent a portable batch plant. The traditional approach would require approximately nineteen thousand buckets of concrete, employ sixty local laborers for many days, and cost about $150 per cubic yard installed. The batch plant alternative required renting equipment from Port-au-Prince for a fixed price of $16,000 and would enable us to pour the slab with rotating crews in one continuous overnight operation. Getting the equipment up the steep hill could be a problem, but once in place we would achieve better quality control without construction joints. The batch plant approach cost about 10 percent more, but we ultimately chose the traditional system because it employed more local labor.

Our next challenge was to determine how many different pours we would need for the by-hand method. The building shape suggested two scenarios; we could make seven pours of thirty-five to fifty cubic yards each, or ten pours at twenty-five to thirty-five cubic yards. Fanes, the local superintendent, was wary of pouring more than forty yards in a day, so we selected the ten-pour option and constructed our control joints accordingly. Since we were planning so many pours, the workers agreed to forfeit the customary premium for concrete work. They would work for their standard per diem. We got faster through standardization and adding wheelbarrows. Every day we pour more concrete, and every day the crew finishes earlier. But management (i.e., Len) wants its cut of our increased productivity.

Len agrees to our alternative plan. The following day the crew finishes by 1:30 p.m. again; spirits are high. Gama calls everyone to gather under the mango tree and explains that we plan to complete the remaining work in two days instead of three. The men listen in silence until the leaders erupt in passionate rebuttal: *We were promised ten days work . . . we work by the day, not the hour . . . if we finish early it is our reward.* Gama remains calm; the crowd does not. A few men jump up and gesticulate. The energy is raw. I have seen Haitians argue enough to know that what I'm witnessing is more show than substance. Faneus, head of the bucketeers, gives a fiery speech. Laborers nod in agreement. When there is a lull in complaints I intervene.

"Gama and I are very happy with the work you have done." I speak slowly to cool the temper of the meeting and to let Gama absorb and translate. "We are a good team, and you have become very fast at pouring good concrete." The men are remarkably quiet. Whether earned or not, respect is given to a *blan*. "But we have also become faster by using the wheelbarrows." I avoid using words like *productivity* which will not have a Creole equivalent. "We want to be fair to you but also to Boss Len." I will be the bad cop so Gama can come out the winner. "If you do not agree to do the remaining concrete in two pours, we will reduce the crew size." There is a collective hiss against the white oppressor. "I hope that you will agree to finish the remaining concrete in two days."

I stand back and let Gama take over. He doesn't get the undivided attention I receive, but I rely on him to close the deal. After a few minutes the protestations simmer; they reach *d'accord*. Faneus approaches Gama and grabs his shoulder; everyone shoots their arms to the sky and high-five each other. Whatever animosity existed evaporates. I smile and shake hands all around, happy to have agreement, although I have no idea what we agreed.

After the men are gone Gama explains the deal. "Two pours, and if the last pour takes longer we will pay overtime that day." I suspect a problem. "Len hasn't agreed to that." Gama shrugs. "If it comes to that, I will handle it."

Day eight hits a snag; the mixer breaks and is down for two hours; we finish around four, which everyone feels is fair. The last pour is a marathon: fifty-one yards. We start right at 6:00 a.m. The crew is cooking for a few hours then the mixer breaks, and doubt sets in. The conveyor is broken and cannot be repaired. The workers have to load the sand and gravel and cement by climbing up a small ladder. The rotating barrel gives out in the afternoon. The mood is glum. The mechanic gets it rolling again, but the flow is clogged. I grab a carton of energy crackers, courtesy of an aid organization, and pass a package to every worker. These guys can use the 450 calories and 15 grams of protein. Gama jumps into the line and passes buckets up the stairs with the rest of the crew. That makes all the difference. Management and labor melt into one; the men give their all, and we finish by 7:00 p.m., pouring concrete beneath a string of bare light bulbs and a full Haitian moon.

The workers leave tired and happy, with the understanding that they will get a bit of overtime on payday. Gama and I stay until 10:00 p.m., return to the mission house, and flop into bed. The concrete slab is poured; the workers were well respected and honestly paid. Intellectually, I understand that Len was entitled to save some bucks in the bargain, but the episode shrinks my heart toward him. The few hundred dollars he saved took extraordinary effort and jeopardized the workers' goodwill. I've seen Len drop more than that on dinner with the single flourish of a pen.

Saturday is a workday in Haiti, but the crew knocks off at 2:00 p.m. Good thing for them this week, because they're exhausted. Unfortunately for us, it's the busiest day of the week in the construction shanty—payday.

All morning Gama and Toto, the resident bookkeeper, go over lists of who worked when during the past week. This includes up to one hundred men on different days at different tasks at different rates of pay. It's a painstaking process of check marks on ledger sheets, a task that cries out for a computer spreadsheet, but Gama is the only computer-literate Haitian here. Around noon a well-scrubbed young man in a Lacoste shirt shows up and hands Gama bundles of bills. He's from the bank, though the only place I have seen the word *bank* in Haiti is on the brightly painted tin sheds that sell Lotto tickets along the side of the road. Grand Goave has no retail bank; there are no checkbooks, no credit cards, no direct deposit. I've heard a rumor that there's an ATM in Jacmel, forty miles away.

Haitian money (the gourde, forty-two to the US dollar) is nicely designed with pastel pictures of Haitian heroes and large font numerals designating 50, 100, 250, 500, and 1,000. It's the same shape as the dollar, but since wallets are not common, it does not maintain the rectilinear organization we give money. A gourde is just as likely to be crumpled into a ball as to lie flat.

At workday's end, Gama and Toto sit at the table in the shanty with their paper spreadsheet of names and days worked and their piles of gourdes several inches high. Since every business in Grand Goave is doing this same thing at this same time, I wonder if the Lacoste man has any cash left in his bank.

Workers queue outside. Rank has its privilege in Haiti, so the first man paid is the head carpenter. "Ah, Clebert, you get to go first." I shake his hand and smile. "Clebert lives in Port-au-Prince," Gama explains. "He has a long drive home." *"Moto?"* I ask if he has a motorcycle, I know no workers own cars. "No," he laughs at me, *"Tap-tap."* It will cost Clebert a couple of dollars and four hours to get home in one of those contraptions.

Toto explains to Clebert his pay for the week. Clebert agrees to the amount and signs next to his name. Gama hands him a fistful of bills. Next. The crew leaders come in first, sign, and leave. We work our way down the ranks. The signatures get shaky. By the time we get to the laborers they turn into symbols. Each worker has his unique way to make a mark, however foreign a pen feels in his hand.

And so it goes, one worker after another. Felix, the old man who tends the water for the concrete mixer, receives 1,000 gourdes for four concrete pours. One of the aftershocks of the earthquake has been inflation: basic laborers now make $6.25 per day while very strong workers, say, the fellows along the bucket brigade who haul concrete up the stairs, make a premium, and workers who endure the most backbreaking work, the men who wade in concrete and shovel it all day, make even more. Still, no laborer tops $10 a day. Manager pay is much higher; Clebert and Fanes make close to $20 a day, a lot by Haitian standards but still less than half what I make in one hour back home.

What does their pay buy them? No one owns a car; a few workers have motorcycles, but most have only their feet for transportation. They rise, dress, and travel in complete darkness to get here by 6:00 a.m. Many men own a piece of property with a house, even if it's only a shack. They don't have extensive wardrobes; most wear the exact same clothes every day. Gama's assertion that a man can eat well in Haiti for $1.50 a day covers rice and beans with onion gravy and a garnish of meat, but a barbeque chicken could run half a day's wages. A man with a wife and children will have to spend his gourdes judiciously to fill so many bellies.

The men wait patiently to receive their pay. The last leave at 6:00 p.m. as dusk turns to night, but Gama remains; he has hours of accounting to do. Toto and Francky, Gama's buddies since childhood, stay with him. Haitians are almost never alone. I finish my work for the day, walk down to MoHI where I can catch a ride to Mirlitone. On my way I pass Leon, the rebar crew boss. He must live nearby, for he's already clean and changed, wearing a pair of tan slacks and a snappy black linen shirt. A very attractive woman is by his side. He gives me a big smile and a firm handshake, obviously happy.

The pay workers receive in Haiti may seem like small change to us, but payday is the same everywhere in the world. The workweek is done. I have money burning a hole in my pocket; it's time to go out on the town.

With the second floor slab at BLB in place and curing, we can begin to install the vertical reinforcing for the second floor columns. Unfortunately, I have only two days to get this work started before I have to return to the United States. We have to fabricate eighty-eight column cages, similar to those we made at MoHI in January. Each cage will have eight heavy vertical rebar, bent ninety degrees at the top to engage the concrete roof, as well as a dozen or more horizontal stirrups to restrain the concrete column from bulging. Our challenge is that the orphanage roof slopes a quarter inch per foot toward the south to ensure drainage. That small dimension adds up to a height difference of almost two feet from front to back. Each row of column cages running along an east/west column line has its own unique height, but along each given column line they are all the same. In the north/south direction, each column line is made up of differing height cages with the tallest cage at the north wall and diminishing to the south. It is critical we get the column cages at the correct height so they engage the roof slab at the right elevation to maintain our slope.

We spend a full day building cages to different heights with no success. Leon and his rebar crew cannot fathom why each cage has to be different.

As so often happens, an idea comes to me overnight, and in the morning I introduce a new construction aid. The rebar crew is used to my inventions by now; they roll their eyes and laugh when I get excited. Back when we were installing rebar in the second-floor slab I created a plywood template shaped like a capital letter *E* to correctly space the upper and lower reinforcing within the two indents. When we needed to support the top bars at the right height within the slab, I showed them how to bend a piece of thin rebar like an extended paper clip to hold it in place. This morning, to overcome our challenge with multiple height column cages, I create a measuring pole, not unlike the doorjamb where parents mark their children's growth. I label in color the proper height to build each column cage and spray paint each east/west column line that corresponds to that color. The simple device works. Leon and his crew set the top of the cages perfectly, and we have one complete line in place before I leave.

My last day turns out to be a food bonanza. In the morning I enjoy my first *paté*, a Haitian empanada, steaming hot on the inside, crispy outside, with tangy spice in the meat. Lunch at MoHI is a huge pot of macaroni, platters of guanabana (*crosstlier* in Creole), a smoky brown fruit called *riossole*, and chunky sweet potatoes served with smothered onions. Everyone eats their fill, and no one bothers with the macaroni; a smashing victory for Haitian cuisine over the American classic.

Forty-five World Racers have invaded Mirlitone, too many to get to know well. They are a ravenous group, the only cohort I've ever seen who empty every pot of food Marieve sets out. They commandeer the chaconne, swaying and singing, "I am worthy because You love me," beating drums and acting more African than forty-four white kids and one black ought to, but I have no right to squelch their feeling native. After supper I escape to the beach.

The world darkens quickly; twilight is short this close to the equator, but tonight, the sky is a dome of wonder. The constellations are clear, though in different orientation than I am accustomed to seeing when I am in New England. I have strayed far. My Haiti trips are in cycle with the moon. It reaches peak fullness just before I leave, an orange disc so ripe I could pluck it from the sky. Mars and Venus are a pair of brilliant jewels above the cliffs of Petit Goave. Every one of these celestial bodies is pointing at me as I stand in my unique spot on this particular beach. For the first time since coming to Haiti, I do not feel like I am frittering away my time at the edge of the world. In this moment Haiti is the center of the universe, and I am centered within it.

Street in Grand Goave two years after the earthquak

View of hills south of the city

Samaritan's Purse house Andy and I built, with later additions

Beach near Grand Goave

Mission of Hope School
Rendering by David Huang

Erecting reinforcing for MoHI School columns

Concrete mixing at MoHI School

Bucket brigade at MoHI School

Topping off Phase 1 construction at MoHI School

Carissa with schoolchildren and hula-hoops

Dieunison and Dieurie

The author in Haiti (*photo by Dieunison*)

88

Gama addresses the crew at morning meeting

Be Like Brit under construction

Be Like Brit entrance

CMU
March–April 2012

The centeredness I felt last trip returns as soon as I land in PAP. I turn off my cell phone, settle into the passenger seat, and watch the world pass as Cherybin navigates us home. We arrive in Grand Goave where I'm pleased with the progress at both sites. I want to stretch my legs after the flight, so ask Lex and Renee if I can walk the two miles between MoHI and Mirlitone. Missionaries are not allowed to venture alone for safety reasons, but I'm so familiar with Grand Goave they grant me permission. Although I'm accustomed to walking the hill between BLB and MoHI, it's an adventure to turn right outside the school and head over the river on my own.

I pass along the market section of Route 2. A few vendors set up booths every day, but on Wednesdays and Saturdays, market days, merchandise runs deep into the flats and spills onto the pavement itself. Retail geography governs here just as it does in America; the charcoal sellers squat next to one another, ditto the mango sellers and the chicken sellers. Although *blan* are less of a curiosity since the earthquake, everyone looks at me stone-faced until I say *bonswa*; then their mouths relax, and they respond in kind.

I am not naïve to Haiti's dangers; I put my wallet in my front pocket and keep my shoulder bag slung across my chest. If I sense someone shadowing me I cross the street. Still, nothing the least bit frightening occurs. I am now accustomed to the market crowds that overwhelmed me on my first trip; I give a passing nod to Grand Goave's pill man when he approaches in his pharmaceutical headdress. Still I am startled to hear someone call out *"Bonswa, Paul!"* and not see anyone I recognize. It's unnerving.

I begin walking home every afternoon, and it soon becomes a cherished habit of my Haitian life. If it hasn't rained I take the shortcut across the riverbed, past the women sweeping dirt from in front of their houses and the young guys washing their motorcycles in an empty lot. I pass the above-ground tombs in the cemetery, and the names spray-painted on buildings, remembering those who never made it to that final resting place. *A dieu* Edith. *A dieu* Dion. *A dieu* Phillipe. Names fixed to the walls that killed them.

Locals dump garbage where the street ends at the riverbank, which attracts goats and pigs. Spring births have swollen the animal population; one mama pig has eight piglets scurrying after her, each a different color. When the rains come, the rising river will wash this garbage to the sea, turning the bay murky. But on dry days the distant bay is a crystalline blue. On the opposite bank the pace is slower, people are poorer, and few people know me. Still, friendly adults stop to chat, and brazen children try for a dollar.

When the river is running I have to stay on Route 2 and cross over the bridge where young guys with *motos* seek customers to drive to Leogone. They heckle me, but they're not dangerous, simply disgusted by the *blan* who doesn't want a ride.

At the first bend in the road, a footpath descends to a drainage channel—remnant of some long-abandoned aid project—and leads into the jungle. I leave the city and enter a shady realm thick with banana plants and palm trees. Bony cattle gaze at me with hungry eyes. Lattice huts are stitched together with palm fronds. The cooking fires are small, the children are naked, their bellies distended, yet I am never out of earshot of laughter. I pass by a clearing where a gaggle of skinny boys kicks around a soccer ball. Sometimes they're so engrossed in their game they forget their ritual begging.

Regardless of which route I take, I pass hundreds of people on my way home. When I make eye contact with someone I exchange a pleasantry; sometimes I even listen to a tale of woe, but mostly I am alone with my thoughts in the crowd. I've finished a worthy day of work and have no expectations for the evening. I roam the twilight paths and let the setting sun determine my pace to arrive at Mirlitone just before dark. When I reach the chaconne, I can join in dinner conversation if I choose, but I'm equally at liberty to retreat to my room. I never feel like I'm missing anything because there is nothing much to miss. Rather than being a deficit, this lack of activity is a psychic gift. With no diversions, my mind soars. Time is generous here and expectations different. Obstacles to progress are myriad; any forward movement is considered success. Such reduced pressures afford greater opportunity for peace.

The Creole word for happy is *kontonn*, whose primary English translation is "content." I appreciate that as a language of few words, Creole uses this deeper, more satisfying term to express well-being. It might be a stretch to say I am happy on my walks home; "happy" implies a level of energy that I've exhausted this late in the day. But I am certainly content. And though I am not sure how they manage it, the people around me seem content as well. They confirm my hypothesis that contentment is nourished by mental calm rather than physical comfort. As I approach Mirlitone I come upon a hedge covered in pale purple flowers. Beyond, a mango tree stands heavy with fruit, and in the distance shadows creep over the mountains. The details of this island are more vivid when I have the leisure to absorb them. I am here by myself but I am not the least bit lonely. I am content with my own company, and a sweeter life is beyond my imagination.

The peace I enjoy during my walks home helps counter the frustrations that boil up during construction. On my third day back we have to set the northeast corner of MoHI's new school—a relatively simple task, I think, but I am wrong.

Here's how we set the corner of a building in Haiti: Take a big group of guys, at least six; eight is preferred. Run a nylon string along the length of one wall, about a foot off the ground to correspond to the top of the footing. Extend the string beyond the end of the wall and tie it to a stake made from a length of number 5 rebar. Repeat the process along the adjacent wall, eyeballing the location of another stake. This creates an approximate right angle between two lengths of string.

Next, take a framing square and place it against the string. A framing square is an *L*-shaped ruler with two legs, one eighteen inches and one twenty-four inches long, while the corner we are setting defines the outline of a building that is fifty-four feet by ninety-four feet. In other words, a framing square error as little as 1/32 could translate to the building being out of square by more than an inch. Three men balance the framing square, one at each end and one at the fulcrum. They suspend it in midair along the two lengths of string and shout at each other whether it is *bon* or *pas bon*. Two guys twist and turn the rebar stakes this way and that, depending on who appears to be winning the argument over the accuracy of the floating framing square. The boss men stick their hands in the mix, point, and shout loud opinions. If this seems confusing, it is. If it seems inaccurate, it most certainly is.

Finally after much deliberation and, to my eyes, no real change, everyone agrees *bon*, and the trio removes the framing square. The guys holding the stakes push them into the dirt to make a mark. Then, they set the stakes aside on the ground, and go get hammers; a Haitian with a ready tool is a rare sight. They come back with mallets and pound the stakes into the ground more or less where they made the depressions, rendering all of the deliberation over the floating framing square irrelevant. When both stakes are in place, the crew checks the framing square again. If it is off they wiggle the stakes. If they wiggle one so much that it comes loose, they jam pebbles into the widening hole to stop the stake from wobbling. There are no limits to how many times one can adjust a stake, but removing and resetting is forbidden. That would be akin to admitting a mistake. Finally, everyone says *bon* once more, and general satisfaction reigns.

This process takes from ten to fifteen minutes, time I use to advantage by doing meditative breathing and anticipating my peaceful walk home. I have no confidence in their approach, but I'm patient while they go through their steps. Then, after all Haitians are satisfied, I announce that we will check the diagonals, a method of determining squareness that actually measures the entire building rather than relying on a floating framing square. They look at me in tragic disbelief, as if to say, why does this *blan* doubt us? But just as I humored them through their shenanigans, they humor me in mine.

We make a diagonal measurement from opposing corners of the building. When we find the measure off by six inches the crew gasps, distrustful of mathematics. We move the stakes; they go through their deliberations again; I check diagonals again. We repeat until group consensus by both floating square and Pythagorean theory is achieved.

It's 8:00 a.m. when we begin laying out the final foundation corner of the MoHI School. We finish just after noon. We have lunch and then take another two hours to slide the strings up and down their stakes to get them at an agreeable vertical elevation. By then it's too late to begin excavating. In one full day we set about a hundred feet of string. Instead of fretting over the gross inefficiency, the crew seems pretty pleased with itself. I decide it's not my place to argue with progress, however painfully achieved.

I am learning that any work that involves unfamiliar practices proceeds at a snail's pace while we achieve speedy and high-quality results when tasks are familiar and repetitive. After we set all of our lines and corners, the MoHI crew makes quick work of installing formwork for footings, bending hundreds of lengths of rebar, and within a week we pour the remaining footings for the new school.

Three visiting missionaries stop by and observe the pour. I don't pay them much attention since I'm occupied with the concrete crew. However, the next morning, while I'm sitting under the chaconne waiting for Gama to take us to work, John, a visiting pastor who witnessed the construction, sits down opposite me. Apparently, his group is leaving this morning, and he's all ready to go. We exchange a few pleasantries. He tells me he's been to Haiti several times and that he enjoyed watching the concrete pour. I think it a bit odd when he says the crew worked like slaves but take it as a compliment to their stamina. Then he elaborates.

"You can't do anything for these people; all they want is money for today. We come down here, we set the vision, we start to implement it, and then we return in a year and what has happened? Nothing."

I am taken aback by his words and wonder if I've heard correctly. John continues, oblivious of my reaction.

"These black people are tribal, just like Africans. There are no leaders, only followers. We must lead them, yet they resist being led."

He describes a side trip his group took to the beaches near Port Salut, places beautiful enough to be resorts. I do nothing to prompt the man, but he will not be quiet. "The people out there, they swim naked on the beaches. Of course we would have to stop that, tourists don't want to see naked people."

He sighs; his belly heaves against his belt buckle. "In America we have everything. We come down here, we preach and we give them money. But they just use it for today; they never plan for their future."

Thankfully, Gama flicks the truck's lights, our signal that he's ready to go to work. It's too early and I am caught too off guard to respond to John with any coherence. Besides, what could I say that would matter? I mutter a goodbye. He chortles platitudes about the good work I'm doing. I hate that crap. I especially don't want to hear it from him. I avoid shaking his hand.

I slide into the truck. Gama looks tired. I'm glad he's not talkative. I need to dissect my disgust.

My mind is a jumble of rage. How can someone who has been here so often see Haiti so different than I do? Why can he only see a future that mimics America, or worse, creates an Americanized precinct? What entitles him to create the long-term vision?

Then I realize that what angers me most is that John comes to Haiti, ostensibly to witness and to help, and yet is so dismissive of its people. If John's firsthand experience shapes his opinions, what chance is there that the billions of other humans on this planet will ever consider Haiti as anything other than the world's most treacherous backwater, a cesspool of Voodoo, cholera, and AIDS?

I remind myself that not all missionaries are like John. Many come here to live among Haitians, to view the world through their eyes, and apply whatever skills we bring to enhance their perspective. Renee best embodies that approach. She doesn't bank on big changes, conversion statistics, or posh resorts to save Haiti. She moves humbly among the people, guiding them to opportunity.

Still, I abhor the missionaries who declare themselves saved and fly down here to save others. So smug and sure of themselves: a week in Haiti is like a trip to a shooting gallery where they can score a few converts by preaching the virtues of eternal life to easy targets. Offer up a few loaves of bread, and the locals will literally eat out of your hands. I've heard missionaries exclaim how they love to come to Haiti because it's such a pure expression of Jesus' teaching to help the poor, as if Haiti's misery exists simply to bolster their own virtue. Such reasoning makes me so angry I grit my teeth and turn away.

Gama pulls through BLB's gate. I need to get to work—get my hands dirty, my back sore, and my shirt sweaty. I need to labor alongside these men I've come to respect. I need to get John out of my mind.

There are enough challenges on site to make his complaints disappear. The site is overrun with concrete block. The correct construction term is *concrete masonry unit,* or CMU, but whatever we call it, we need more than 2,000 to construct the orphanage's second-floor walls. CMU is the most common building material in Haiti. Every construction site has a pile of sand, a pile of gravel, some sacks of cement, and a collection of molds that are 16" long by 8" high by 6" wide with three cylindrical inserts that, when the mold is filled, create three voids in each block. Workers fill the molds with the raw ingredients plus water, tamp the mixture down, let it set up an hour—sometimes less—then remove the mold and let the block dry in the sun. The typical Haitian CMU breaks under a force of approximately 300 pounds per square inch (psi). Standard American block, which are 16" long by 8" high by 8" wide and have two holes in the center, are ten times stronger.

Our buildings require stronger block and continuous vertical reinforcing tying the building together. Since Haitian block is too weak and the hollows do not align when each course of block is vertically offset, we've built a CMU plant on a bit of land that Lex owns near MoHI. We make CMU by the hundreds rather than the dozens, we make the size we need, and we employ more Haitians producing better quality products. We have not achieved the strength that we do in the States, but our block break at about 1,200 psi, which is four times better than most Haitian block. We sell our block to other aid organizations, but unfortunately most Haitians still opt for the inferior block when rebuilding their own homes. It's a tragic choice from my perspective, but our CMU cost twice the Haitian standard, and most families simply cannot afford that premium to guard against future disaster when all of their money goes for today's needs.

· · ·

CMU have been accumulating because we haven't been laying them as fast as we planned. Each mason is expected to lay at least ninety block a day. Considering that we're building the second floor, virtually identical to the one below, and that every mason has a laborer who brings him materials and fresh grout, ninety block a day is not unreasonable. Considering that they are laying block in brutal sun with no shade, ninety block is a long row. The masons have failed to meet their quota for several days. Yesterday, Fanes told them they would be docked pay, so they walked off the site. Today we are rich in CMU, but we have no masons.

By and large, Fanes is representative of what I've witnessed among Haitian managers—he's extremely polite, avoids unpleasantness wherever possible, and has a sixth sense for finding shade. I have never seen Fanes anticipate a problem, and he often ignores them until they mushroom. I figure the lack of masons might simply ease his load, but happily, Fanes proves me wrong, and in the process helps revise my opinion of Haitian managers.

Fanes arrives at 7:00 a.m., selects a laborer to assist him, climbs up to the second floor, and lays block. He works consistently and carefully, skips lunch, lays 140 CMU, and knocks off at two.

The word is out to the masons, and they will return tomorrow. They will each be expected to lay at least 90 block, or they will receive short pay. My esteem for Fanes has risen greatly. Our stacks of CMU are about to diminish.

In midafternoon, clouds come over the mountains from the south, the sky turns black, the construction crew scrambles for cover, and we have a fifteen-minute deluge. Rain in Haiti is fierce and sometimes long, but this storm ends as quickly as it began; the sun returns, and everyone goes back to work.

The air is so fresh that when the crew knocks off I log out and commence my leisurely walk home. The storm has disrupted life's daily rhythm among the cluster of houses at the base of BLB's hill. The woman who sits in front of a woven platter of packaged snacks for sale is still there, though I've never seen her sell a thing; her neighbors still squat on their stoops and chat, the children—I have no idea which belong to whom—still chase after me shouting *Photo! Photo!*, but the narrow gallery with its covered roof between two houses, where a hugely pregnant woman has sat for months, absorbing whatever breeze comes her way, is empty. Instead, the woman is gripping a tree beside the road. Her hands are clasped high on the trunk. Her hips shoot out behind her, and her belly hangs free. She sways imperceptibly in the breeze. Her eyes are wide. She stares past her actual surroundings. She doesn't make a sound, but her silent screams pierce me. I don't say a word or offer any aid; her body language announces a private agony. I fear she cannot bear the burden of her belly another moment.

When I reach the bridge, the river runs strong. The Grand Goave River is almost a quarter mile wide, and it gets wider every year. According to Renee, its width has doubled in the twelve years she's lived here. When I arrived three years ago, three houses stood between Mirlitone and the river; now there is only one. The river has grown not because it rains more but because when it rains, the runoff is so much faster. Water eats away at the banks; high ground yields to its power. With every rain the mountains give up more of themselves, more bare earth is exposed, and more topsoil is washed away. After this afternoon's shower, the bridge spans a turbulent swirl of mud. The epidemic of erosion feeds on itself. The mountains are just a little bit shorter, the river is just a little bit wider, and Haiti has given up just a little bit more of itself to the sea.

Beyond the bridge the *moto* gang greets me with the usual harangue. Though they are more annoying than dangerous, they remind me to be cautious; a *blan* with a backpack can be a target. Since I began walking through town people who disapprove of a *blan* on the streets alone tell me tales of treachery. A few weeks ago a young woman, the sister of a MoHI staffer, was abducted in Port-au-Prince, robbed, and murdered. She was on a buying trip and had a good amount of cash. Her murder was not random, but it may not have been premeditated either. Someone might have seen her, realized she had money, and followed her. Two towns away a Haitian killed a missionary. The police, who are notoriously ineffective, did little, but local vigilantes, who are notoriously effective, skunked out the murderer, dragged him to the side of Route 2, and burned him alive for all to see. In many towns missionaries are the primary source of economic activity; the vast majority of locals want us here and value our contribution. I rationalize that I am in the country, not in Port-au-Prince, and that I carry only a few dollars in my wallet. But I cannot deny I am a target. I will stop walking the minute Lex or Renee tells me it's unsafe, but I enjoy it so much, I want to continue the habit as long as possible.

When I turn off the paved road and onto the dirt path, people are more inclined to talk, so I get to practice Creole. I begin each conversation with a stranger by saying I work for Pastor Lex and am on my way to Mirlitone. A big guy with a machete asks if I can help him feed his ten children. I tell him to ask Fanes for a job; he looks strong enough to do construction. Children clamor after me for one dollar, but I give them bread instead. A dozen or more young men play marbles in a clearing with the enthusiasm of soccer players in a World Cup match; their elegant torsos and long arms arch over the tiny spheres of glass. The tales of danger I've heard simply do not correlate with my benign experience. The *blan* passing through their game is no more than a curiosity.

Where the footpath merges with the dirt road that leads to Mirlitone, a spry old man in a pair of jean shorts but no shirt or shoes comes out of the driveway of what I consider to be a prosperous Haitian farm; he has a horse, a pig, and four goats. We exchange greetings. He walks beside me. I offer my name. His is Palido. We walk farther. I tell him I'm going to Mirlitone. He nods. We keep on. We come over the rise to the gate of the Mission House. He stays in step with me. He walks up to the gate, slides it open, and gestures for me to pass through. Theo, Mirlitone's caretaker, comes to the gate and nods to Palido, acknowledging the handoff.

I'm sure that it's wise for me to be cautious on my walks, but it seems most unnecessary. The eyes and feet of this countryside are always looking out for me.

There is a similar specter watching over me during my workdays in BLB's shanty. Len's "To Do" list hangs over my chair, a white board full of numbered tasks scribed in alternating red and blue markers with his trademark three exclamation points after each one. Work Gama and I must complete before Len returns. On the first day of my two-week stint the two of us review the list. Within a few days I complete my tasks and then take up my own design issues.

At the start of week two Gama and I review the list. Then on the last day, we repeat. He scrutinizes me with what little annoyance he can muster, tells me he will get to his tasks, and goes about his business. It's not that Gama isn't busy; it's just that he works in a Haitian way, which is non-linear and infused with socializing. He is even-tempered to a fault; nothing lights a fire under the man. His day is open—he's content to work until nine or ten at night rather than focus his efforts on getting home by sunset. His attitude doesn't really bother me until my last day, when Haitian habits crash against inflexible airplane schedules.

On my last day of this trip we have four tasks from Len's list still to complete: mark all the second-floor partitions and electrical devices in spray paint, meet with the metal door fabricator to review the proposed door design that I drew up last week, organize the drawings and throw away the ones that are out of date, and, most important, review the roof cornice details with Fanes and Clebert, the head carpenter. Since today is payday, which entails so much work for Gama, I tell him I can handle the spray painting myself; he assures me we will complete the other items before lunch.

I return to the shanty after marking. The metal door guy comes by, and we review the sketches. I complete a stair layout for MoHI while Gama does I don't know what. I only know it's not what I asked. I have to go to MoHI for lunch and meet with Renee to review the school's next round of work. I barely mask my aggressive tone when I ask Gama what time he prefers me to go to MoHI. He tells me to go now; we will finish everything upon my return.

I head back up the hill shortly after two, passing Fanes, who is on the way down, heading home for the weekend. I greet him pleasantly but seethe inside. Fanes needs to review the details to be built next week; I do not want the inevitable misinterpretation of his getting sketches secondhand.

I reach the site. Construction is finished; the workers sit outside the shanty waiting for their pay. When I walk in Gama smiles and says, "How are you?" "Not good," "Tell me what is wrong." He remains patient. "Not in front of other people." I glance at the laborer standing silent, waiting for his pay as I plunk down my computer. Gama shoos everyone out of the office. "Tell me now." He asks for it. I deliver.

I think of myself as a willow tree. I like to believe that I'm flexible, that I can absorb a lot of movement, but when bent too far I snap, and once broken, I am difficult to splice whole again. I also know that my temper is torrential, that when my anger unleash-es, its fury is so great it eclipses whatever triggered it in the first place. All of this self-knowledge evaporates as I spew at Gama.

"I saw Fanes leaving. I told you I wanted to meet with all of us to review those details. I don't ask much from you, but you must do what I ask. I am not Len, but I am Len's stead. You jump to every request he makes but you don't pay me half that respect. I do not like to harp, I really do not like to yell." At this point my voice shakes the jalousie windows, the workers beyond gape at the *blan* in his primal state. "If you do what I ask, when I ask, then I won't have to yell."

"You are right, I did not act correctly, and I will make good."

It would be convenient to hate Gama, or at least dislike him, but I can hardly fault someone just because he commands greater composure than me. Gama gets on his phone and jabbers in Cre-ole. "Fanes is coming back, and we will do it now." I look at the workers outside, dozens of men now have to wait due to Gama's casualness, or my determination, depending how you view the situation. Fanes returns; Clebert comes in. I feel two inches tall. I am exhausted and suddenly ravenous. I want a hamburger, with bacon, something greasy to assuage the anxiety in my stomach. I tap aimlessly at an email while Gama rambles around for the drawings I gave him yesterday.

I am rich in faults except when it comes to my work. By the time all is in order I am an exemplary mentor. I explain how the draw-ings are organized; we go to the second floor and stand exactly as each detail is oriented so they can correlate the drawing to the reality. I relate each graphic to the construction in place. I ask for questions, and they have some, which is a good sign that they are paying attention. After we walk the entire building I tell Fanes and Clebert how much I appreciate their work and wish them a good weekend.

It's almost four by the time we finish. I don't pester Gama about the drawings Len wanted organized; that will go undone. Gama resumes distributing the payroll. I want to pack up and leave, but it is the hottest, stillest time of day, so I sit in the air-conditioned shanty and twiddle on the Internet while the men trundle in, one by one, to receive their hard-earned pay.

Formwork
April–May 2012

The pilot of American Airlines Flight 1291 into Port-au-Prince makes the craziest descent today. He remains high in the air until the city comes into view, then circles through two complete arcs, 720 degrees of centrifugal pull, to reach the ground. Outside my window the view rotates from sky to water to coast to city to coast, and then the sequence repeats. The pollution is worse than usual. We descend from clear blue to sooty green. By the time the pilot levels over the runway, the sky and the water are the same disorienting shade of lima bean.

On the ground this disequilibrium continues. The airport gauntlet is quiet; the red shirts barely heckle me. Lex picks me up, which is unusual, and describes the situation as we drive through the city. A member of Haiti's Congress was stopped last week at a police checkpoint. The officer found a concealed weapon on the congressman's chauffeur, arrested him, and put him in jail. The congressman, irate, went to the jail and demanded his chauffeur's freedom. Three hours later the arresting officer was shot and killed. Lex is unclear whether the congressman, the chauffeur, or a hired gunman shot the policeman. In any event the congressman enjoys immunity from prosecution. The police, in solidarity, went on strike today.

The dominoes fall fast. Stores close, as shop owners feel unprotected from thieves. Schools close, as parents fear for their children. Gangs gather. They throw rocks and build barricades and set bonfires at busy intersections. The rationale for their protests is as murky as the thick smoke enveloping the city. They riot because they can. The streets are empty; there are few pedestrians, no street vendors, and scant traffic. The massive open-air market is deserted. UN tanks manned by Brazilian soldiers barrel down the thoroughfares, more menacing peacekeepers than police in sedans. After the tanks pass, the city is silent. The quiet feels explosive.

The US State Department issues warnings advising Americans against traveling in Port-au-Prince, though American Airlines fails to announce this to the hundreds of people they deposit into the melee.

As we drive, Lex maintains regular cell phone contact with a striking police officer who updates trouble spots. We navigate by our personalized, riot-centric traffic report. Evidence of agitation abounds—intersections are crowded with boulders from barricades, and rings of black soot mark extinguished fires. We weasel through the gaps in Port-au-Prince's terror. With so little traffic, we reach Grand Goave in less than two hours—a personal best.

Lex explains that he tried to contact me to remain in Miami, but I was already in flight. Since my regular trips began, we've had a contingency plan in case no one meets me at the airport; I am to seek out the head of airport security, Mr. Big, and put my fate in his hands. But Lex's commitment to his volunteers is supreme. He monitored the situation, decided better to pick me up before things got worse, and took meticulous care to ferry me safely. It is hard to imagine how my love and respect for this man could grow, but now I can add personal protector to his list of strengths.

Grand Goave has none of Port-au-Prince's chaos, and my two projects are each proceeding according to their own particular style. On the surface, MoHI School and BLB are similar; they share a design team, construction crews, tools, and materials. One might assume daily life on the sites would be similar. Yet the culture of each endeavor is as different as their respective owners.

Be Like Brit would be considered an efficient job site by American standards; in Haiti it is unparalleled. The construction shanty is headquarters for Len, Gama, and me, as well as Toto the accountant and Francky the gofer. It has an air conditioner, though when Len is gone I prefer the breeze through open windows, which is pleasant all day long. Fanes, the job superintendent, is the only person who enters the shanty without knocking, yet even he never uses it as a place of work. He enters only for morning greetings and scheduled meetings. When crewmembers have questions, they knock and wait for us to come outside. Laborers cross the threshold only on payday.

The trades at BLB are well organized. Every crew has a boss, and there is a clear hierarchy of communication, from Len to me to Gama to Fanes to the boss to the crew. If I pick up a broom to sweep the floor before marking locations for plumbing fixtures, a laborer takes the broom, and sweeps for me. No one allows me to do any manual labor. At BLB, pay is tied to performance. Each trade has its expected quota, and workers who don't achieve their target receive short pay.

The three women who set up makeshift breakfast and lunch establishments on site, the Haitian equivalent of lunch trucks, serve competing versions of *diri et pwa* (rice and beans), embellished with chicken or goat or fish to suit any wallet and any palate. Workers cluster at their kitchen of choice.

MoHI is less hierarchical, both by circumstance and by design. There is no construction shanty. I set up my drawings and computer on a picnic table under the lean-to, a mere arm's length away from the concrete mixer. Schoolchildren run through the site. When Lex is present he wanders among the workers his primary tools being his voice and his cell phone. Since the site is so compact, the trades cannot segregate; everyone works everywhere.

Crew designations are less clear at MoHI. If I am marking something up, no one volunteers to assist me; yet if I need someone to hold the end of the tape while I measure, the nearest guy is happy to help regardless of his title. MoHI workers are paid by the day. If daily productivity is low, Lex gives a pep talk the next morning to inspire the men, but output expectations are less stringent than at BLB. MoHI is a more complicated building with more challenging conditions; if masons lay fifty block a day, they are doing well. No one grouses when asked to do something outside his customary role. The laborers work hard, but the output is less remarkable.

MoHI provides lunch for the workers at midday or, if we're pouring concrete, whenever the pour is finished. Sometimes they even provide soda. The food is standard Haitian fare, usually *diri et sos pwa*, a variation on rice and beans in which the beans are pureed and then ladled over white rice. Simple but delicious. It's cooked in giant pots and served out of five-gallon paint buckets.

The delicacies available up the hill are not on the menu here. Lex and Boss Pepe serve the food; everyone jams under the lean-to to escape the sun. We talk and joke. The guys have so much fun with half an hour of free time and a plate of rice that my spirits lift even though I understand only a fraction of what they say.

One afternoon I ask Renee if MoHI pays workers less since they feed them. She tells me that MoHI pays the standard wages, but she feels that feeding the workers has the benefit of making sure they eat and making them more receptive to working late when needed.

As I walk home I consider these two variations on a theme—the proto-capitalist BLB site versus the social-democratic MoHI site.

As a member of management, whose incentives are independent of either system, I should be able to make an objective assessment. But I cannot. At BLB I feel more productive; at MoHI I feel more connected to my fellow man, which pretty much sums up Len's and Lex's essential differences.

Probably the biggest difference in the two projects from my perspective is that I see Lex all the time when I'm in Haiti while I rarely see Len. Communications with Len are formal; most everything with Lex is spontaneous. One evening, Lex tells me to hop in the Mitsubishi with Renee and the three of us drive up to Saint Etienne, their satellite mission in a small mountain village along the road to Jacmel. Lex is building a restaurant there to provide local jobs and cash in on travelers moving between Port-au-Prince and Haiti's largest tourist destination.

We are deep into the rainy season. We have sudden afternoon downpours every day and torrential rain all night. Humidity cloaks everything like a shroud; mechanical objects have gummy works. The water pump at Mirlitone is on the fritz; the main generator is kaput. I actually prefer the lights out because when they glow, hordes of rain bugs, ugly winged creatures, buzz around illuminated bulbs and cast eerie shadows across my ceiling.

As we climb into the mountains I witness for the first time the rainy season's benefits. Corn, so scrawny just three weeks ago, is reaching Kansas proportions. The banana plants are huge, and the mango trees' branches droop with ripe fruit. When we reach the restaurant I'm surprised to discover Lex is building a wood-frame structure, very light and flexible. The site is a narrow strip along the road that falls off dramatically on either side. The first floor will be a kitchen with takeout. Upstairs they're cantilevering a long porch. The tables will literally hang over the valley. The concept is good, but we have a few challenges. I help Lex determine the best location for the main staircase and describe why the cantilever joists need to be deeper. The roof must be tin and the railings filigreed ironwork. This building is the antithesis of the school; everything must remain light, flexible enough to sway when a quake hits.

We finish our work as the evening mist floats over the terraced hillsides. I scan the valley, a patchwork of cultivated plots, precariously rooted trees, and narrow, steep paths that defy physics. Their vertical rise before me is so exaggerated I envision the cartoonish swales of a David Hockney painting. In the silvery atmosphere, this Haitian valley becomes a fantasy landscape of slope and sky, dense foliage and exotic flora suspended in an otherworldly haze—Tolkien's Middle Earth made real.

The tranquil reverie of St. Etienne is annihilated the next day. The sky is unusually clear, and I have a faint headache. It could be due to too much sun, but more likely it's from the constant din at the construction site. The Haitian approach to labor follows the dictum *Work requires banging*, and today it is particularly loud.

Haitian builders are remarkably strong, and much of the site camaraderie is based on shared displays of physical prowess. There is nothing praiseworthy in the carpenter who cuts concrete formwork with such precision that it slides into place. Ah, but if the plywood is too long, and the carpenter can draw a mallet over his head, pose with clenched muscles, then swing the mallet through a giant arc to force the plywood into submission, that is work. Better yet, the wood does not comply at once, and so the worker has the opportunity to pound repeatedly, the sound reverberating over the entire site. Fortunately, plywood cut too short offers the carpenter a similar opportunity: force-fitting shims to fill the gap.

A concrete building is essentially built twice. First we build it in wood, creating formwork that takes the inverse shape of our design; then we fill our mold with fresh concrete and remove the plywood after the concrete hardens, which takes twenty-eight days. Concrete is terrific at withstanding forces that push (compression), but lousy when pulled apart (tension), so we suspend steel reinforcing inside the concrete to carry tension. The steel must be fully covered by the finished concrete, as exposed steel will rust and deteriorate. Sometimes, as in columns and walls, we install the reinforcing first and build the formwork around it. Other times, for beams and floors, we install the formwork first and then place the reinforcing. Both approaches offer multiple opportunities for banging.

Reinforcing must be installed straight and plumb, the steel cut, bent, and tied off with thin wire called *fille alegature*, alegature being perhaps the longest word in all of Creole. Even the strongest Haitian cannot do much damage banging on a 5/8-inch-diameter steel rod, yet gratuitous banging goes on all day.

The key to installing formwork around steel is to make it generous enough for the plywood to stand clear of the reinforcing, thus avoiding exposed metals in the finished product. We require at least one and a half inches of concrete cover. Two inches is preferable. We never get it. The concrete walls are supposed to be twelve inches wide. If they are thirteen or fourteen inches wide, no matter, so long as they're consistent. But there is no fun in erecting a piece of formwork and just letting it stand there. The carpenters routinely install the formwork ten or eleven inches wide. The result, of course, is that the reinforcing is too close to the walls, which then affords the wonderful opportunity to insert cleats and stone shims and hammer the forms wider apart.

The conflict also affords the carpenters and ironworkers the equally enjoyable opportunity to stop work and negotiate who is at fault for the problem, a pastime they love and I loathe with equal passion. I identify location after location with insufficient clearance, and the workers argue. They are in a no-lose situation: if I prevail they get to bang some more; if I capitulate, they have triumphed over the *blan*.

We have yet to complete one concrete pour with a cover of one and a half inches everywhere. The engineers at SGH would be disgusted with my track record, but then again, they're back in the States while I am here, surrounded by fifty really strong guys with big mallets. I console myself that Haiti is not New England. We have no freeze/thaw cycles that will spall the concrete and expose reinforcing, and the finished concrete will be covered with stucco to provide another level of protection.

CMU walls provide their own banging opportunities. In theory, our 16-inch long CMU are offset by 8 inches on each course. This allows the vertical reinforcing to run up the middle of hollows that align.

But the masons like to work in pairs and prefer to start both ends of a wall and work toward the middle. Inevitably, the middle block is either too short or too long. An opportunity for banging! This means the ideal 8-inch offset gets fudged on both the second course and the third. The vertical joints shift so much that the rebar no longer align with the holes, so the masons bang a crimp in a rebar to shift it to a new void. The virtues of beginning the wall in the middle and working toward each end (where we frame into a column to be poured later, and therefore have some slack) seem clear to me, but no matter how I try to enumerate and explain this to them, the workers give me a weary nod and start a new row from opposing sides.

Haiti is a tradition-bound country, and the methods of concrete construction have evolved over hundreds of years. The earthquake proved their techniques inadequate if you think like an engineer, but Haitians put more faith in tradition than in calculation; trying to explain why a particular piece of steel is necessary to protect them in the future is a daunting challenge. I comfort myself that we have come so far; that the walls are being reinforced, imperfectly; that they are tied to the columns, fairly well; that the concrete covers the reinforcing, good enough; and that the quality of the work is increasing, ever so slowly. We make progress every day, we tear out and rebuild less and less all the time. And when we hit an impasse, the workers find a way to bang it out, which always makes everyone feel better.

"Do you believe in God?" Gama gets my full attention when he starts, apropos of nothing, a theological discussion midmorning in the shanty. His question is accompanied by a hopeful smile that broadens when I say that I do. Since our exchange is not in writing I am spared having to clarify that I do not believe in his capital *G* God but find comfort in a force greater than man in this world, a force that I am content to call small *g* god. I don't explain that I see no need to put a face to my god or worship it and that I deplore the notion that it guides my actions, which would be an abdication of my personal responsibility.

"So, then you believe in sin?" Gama continues. I don't make a straight-line connection between god and sin, but understand that logic according to his faith. The problem with theological conversations between evangelicals and me is how quickly we hit an impasse.

"Not really," I reply.

He squints, dissatisfied. "Do you believe in good and bad?"

"I believe in good."

"If you believe in good, you have to believe in bad; they are the opposite. Just like God and Satan. If you believe in God you have to believe in Satan."

"No, I don't. I can believe in god but not believe in satan."

"But when Satan possesses people and makes them bad . . . "

"I don't believe in bad people."

"You don't believe people are good or bad?"

"No, I believe all people are good. Sometimes we do bad things, but we are all good."

We iterate a few more times, but our morsel of mutual ground is exhausted. Gama's belief in good is dependent upon the existence of evil; they need each other for balance. As far as I can discern, this conflicts directly with the evangelical objective of spreading the Word so that all can see the Light and embrace goodness. If evangelicals ever achieve their long-term aim to convert everyone, then everyone will be good, and evil will be eliminated. Yet they are bent on defining one in relationship to the other, eternally locked into embracing both.

That evening, in the generous time I have between lights out and sleep, I consider our conversation. Contemplating good and evil means I lie awake a bit longer than usual; reflecting on evil is not conducive to rest.

Defining people as good or bad is just another way of creating division in the world, like identifying communists and capitalists, Americans and Haitians, black and white, us and them. If I believe in good, must I believe in its opposite? Such balance appeals to a mind tuned to science, but labeling some sector of humanity as bad violates my deeper sense of human potential. My mind sifts through scenarios until I finally acknowledge the obvious. The opposite of good may be bad, but the alternative to good is simply "not good," and the difference is more substantial than it might appear.

I was once the recipient of affirmative action: accepted to MIT as the geographic diversity student from Oklahoma. They did not actually print those words on my acceptance letter, but I figured it out. I spent seven years there and received three degrees, yet in all that time I never met another student with weaker admission credentials. I was personable, studious, and reasonably intelligent, but mere intelligence hardly registers in an environment where brilliance is the norm. I was hundreds of points shy of perfect SAT scores. Most of my classmates entered freshman year with calculus under their belts and drooled over differential equations. I had never even heard the term *derivative* before my orientation picnic in front of the Great Dome.

Had there been an opportunity to fail my first year at MIT, I would not have survived. But failure was not an option. All freshmen took a core curriculum, and we were evaluated by a simple system of pass/no pass. If we mastered the work, we passed. If not, the course did not show up on our records, and we could repeat it with impunity. The beauty of the system was not only its simplicity, but also the tone it set. The goal was to take each of us, from whatever starting point, and instill a common body of knowledge from which to pursue deeper study. For some students freshman year was a brisk walk. For me, it was a marathon of lectures, textbooks, and tutorials. Yet I never considered that I wouldn't make it, because when MIT accepts someone it commits to ensuring that student succeeds.

Mine is a privileged example: an institution of boundless resources ought to be able to nurture eager students even when they start with deficits. Now, thirty-nine years after being that MIT freshman, I'm in Haiti on a hot Saturday night trying to fathom the evangelical mind and how to communicate my design to laborers I cannot understand. My conundrum leads me to examine the beauty of Creole, which, like the culture it describes, is simple and direct. The Creole word for good is *bon*. The word for bad is *mal*. When I walk the site each day to check dimensions, measure reinforcing, and verify plumb, I do not describe the work as *bon* or *mal*. The convention here is *bon* or *pas bon*; good or not good. When I say *bon* the crew smiles; when I say *pas bon* they shrug and make adjustments. *Pas bon* is not pejorative; it is simply something that can be made *bon* with a bit more effort.

I drift off to sleep as the raucous Saturday night music pounds across the river, content in my reasoning. The world need not be a zero-sum game of good versus bad. Some people commit bad actions—murder, rape, abuse—that deserve retribution; we should all strive to minimize such deeds. Many people do good in the world, which we should acknowledge and applaud. And then there is a whole lot of not good—prejudice, envy, greed, injustice—attitudes and actions that demean perpetrator and victim alike. If we acknowledge them as impediments to our better selves rather than as immutable wrongs, we can lift ourselves up and tilt the balance between good and evil so far that we liberate ourselves from measuring one in terms of the other.

Truth is, though I appreciate Creole as a reflection of Haitian culture, I am making very little progress in learning how to speak it. Part of the problem is that Haitians are more interested in practicing their English on me, and I realize they have more to gain by polishing my language than I do by mastering theirs. But I also admit that my fifty-seven-year-old mind has grown dense as cured concrete when it comes to languages: Creole just isn't sticking. So I decide to be proactive and ask a group of my favorite laborers to share English/Creole classes at lunch; sometimes we meet after work as well. We use my phrasebook as a starting point; pick a page, and begin reading. They read the English words, and I help their pronunciation; then we flip roles, and I attempt Creole.

Some pages are worthless; being able to ask if your flight is delayed means nothing to someone who's never been on an airplane. The most relevant phrases cover the basics of time, weather, work, and family. I learn that Emmanuel has a wife and four children—two boys and two girls. Drivle is single, not even a girlfriend; we all laugh that he is *lib* though I applaud his honesty since every other Haitian man boasts of a girlfriend, even as I suspect many are fabricated. Webert is single as well, but parrots the conventional description of a girlfriend back home. Quiet Fanil allows that he has seven children by several women, none his wife. I flip through my phrasebook seeking the Creole word for *stud* but cannot find it. It figures that a dictionary that defines single as *silibate* omits sexually charged slang.

I ask where they live, and all four say La Gonave, the island visible in the bay. I ask how they get there, and they tell me *tap-tap bato-a*, a water taxi. I picture the hydroplane that ferries commuters from Hingham to Boston, though the reality is sure to be more rudimentary. I ask how long it takes to get home, and after some discussion they settle on forty-five minutes, which proves to be an awkward period of time to translate. I ask if they go home every night; in the United States a forty-five-minute water commute would be reasonable. They laugh and say no, only weekends. Later I learn how inaccurate our conversation is; the ferry is a four-hour ride in a paddle-powered dugout.

I ask where they stay, and again they reply La Gonave. I finally ask where they sleep, and they point to one of the shacks at MoHI, where, apparently, they bunk every night, four of them, maybe more, in a space no more than ten feet square. Suddenly our workdays take on new perspective. The workers get here so early and don't object to working late because they never leave. Work is the most stimulating part of their day; once everyone else departs, the émigrés from La Gonave have only themselves for amusement until the sun rises again.

On Saturday I ask if they're going to La Gonave this weekend. They look at me oddly and say no. "Then, when are you going?" I inquire. July, they reply, which is two months hence. The more I know about them, the less I understand.

Among the four, I know Emmanuel the best. He's worn the same gray T-shirt and loose, checkered pants since I first met him in December. In a past life I'm sure they were pajamas. He has a light heart and a ready smile, and the thought crosses my mind that he may have no other possessions. When the weather is fine, and our construction projects need labor, he works. If neither site wants him, he's at liberty. I often encounter him chatting with people along the path between our two sites. He loiters with the same buoyancy with which he works. Emmanuel can read; his English is quite good. By all measures he's an adult, yet he carries buckets of concrete for a living. That meager opportunity takes him far from his family, for a ferry ride, whether it be forty-five minutes or four hours, is dear to a man of such limited means. Still Emmanuel seems completely at ease with his lot in life.

Emmanuel causes me to reflect on my own habits. I never go anywhere without carrying a book, a magazine, or my computer. I always have something on hand to occupy my time if I hit a lull. I'm conscious of time and don't waste it. Although I don't consider myself particularly anxious, the idea of roaming about all day in my only clothes without so much as a pencil terrifies me.

These guys are not dullards. They're literate and funny; their minds are quick. Yet they spend large periods of time in a sort of physical and mental limbo. I wonder if they're frustrated, if they crave something more, or if acquiescing to hours of quietude is integral to the Haitian psyche. By all appearances they are content; untroubled by grievances and disappointments, appreciative of what comes their way. One could make the argument that such placidity sets Haiti back in her struggle to compete in the wider world. Conversely, when I consider the time and money I've spent on yoga, meditation, and therapy, I could benefit from some of that serenity myself. I wonder if they can translate it for me.

Another thing I would like them to translate is the Haitian custom of men holding hands. They do it everywhere. One late afternoon I'm checking the work on BLB's second floor when I look up and see Faneus, our lead mason, and Nicolai, a laborer, hand in hand walking and laughing while the sun sets over their shoulders. I know that Haitians touch each other all the time, on purpose and by accident, that holding hands is common across genders and signifies deep friendship between men. But this image of two beefy guys sauntering together with the glistening sea in the background could be an ad for a gay cruise. My eyes linger longer than professional conduct allows.

When I first came to Haiti I waved to people when I greeted them. Then I started shaking hands. Now when I greet a worker I take his right hand in mine, clasp my left hand over it, and look him right in the eye. As a politically correct American who never touches anyone in public beyond right palm to right palm, this

degree of contact is outside my comfort zone, but I can tell they
appreciate it. A few of the guys, as I take their hand, throw their
left arm around my shoulder, and I've learned not to flinch where
it lands.

Walking home, fresh from my romantic musings about Faneus
and Nicolai, I run into Drivle, my Creole language class buddy. He
grabs my hand and swings an arm over my shoulder. A few steps
later I run into Clebert, a mason's assistant. Clebert is a small,
spry guy with a gregarious nature and constant smile. *Mister Paul*,
he calls out, thrilled to discover me off the construction site. He
too grabs my hand and clasps my shoulder. I continue on, over
the river, and turn off where my path dips into the jungle. As I
descend into the cool evening I hear footsteps behind me. I slow
and step aside to let the approaching person pass. It's Clebert once
again, hurrying at a good clip. *Ah, Mister Paul*, he exclaims as if it
were years, rather than minutes, since we last saw each other. He
reaches out and takes my right forearm in his left. His hand slides
down into mine. He grasps my fingers.

I am surprised. My initial reaction is to pull away, but I don't.
I suck in a breath and acknowledge that his warm palm is rather
nice. We walk hand in hand. I run through the small repertoire
of questions I have at my disposal with someone who speaks no
English. I learn that Clebert was born in Grand Goave, has lived
here his whole life, and has a wife and four children; a resume
indistinguishable from that of most other workers. After a decent
interval I point out a flowering tree, which allows me to free my
hand from his grasp. I do not return it. I've reached my limit for
holding hands with a Haitian today. We continue along with a more
comfortable distance between us, at least for me, until he shouts a
hearty *m'ale* and turns off toward his home. I reach Mirlitone and
get to bed early. Tomorrow will be a very early day.

Something's coming. Gama and I can feel the pulse as we drive
along Route 2 before dawn. The anticipation is as strong and insistent as the pounding bass of the street bands that permeates
Grand Goave on a Saturday night. We pick Renee up in the 5 a.m.
blackness and get to MoHI early. Renold, the fastidious keeper
of tools and supplies, arrives on his bicycle before six. How he
can maneuver along the rutted roads in the dark is a mystery to

me. Dawn breaks on the twenty tons of rebar delivered yesterday. Workers stayed until nine last night organizing the forty-foot lengths into neat stacks, labeled by diameter size. As workers arrive they're not allowed to sip coffee and nosh on stiff white bread as they usually do. Instead the moment a man enters the gate Renold puts him to work: pick up trash, stack plywood, shift sand piles, make wider paths, sweep the tops of the footings. By the time the schoolchildren arrive in their green-checked uniforms, MoHI is spotless.

Boss Pepe and I put select crews to work doing stuff that will make good video footage: erecting block walls and reinforcing cages, removing formwork. Renee gets the call. They are less than an hour away.

I march up the hill to lend a hand at BLB, where parallel preparations have rendered the site ghost town clean. The west courtyard is naked. The sun casts such severe shadows on the concrete columns that I'm afraid I've stumbled into a de Chirico painting. Here, too, the crews are engaged in high-profile activities: laying the broad stone wall up the road, building the top edge of the cornice formwork, pouring concrete into tall columns, finishing a floor in bright colors. I take my position, supervising the floor pattern, but my mind is distracted, my ears poised for the vehicle gunning up the hill.

Nightline is preparing to air a twelve-minute segment on Len Gengel for Father's Day. A reporter and two producers are in Haiti for three days gathering material. Lex joined them in Port-au-Prince on Monday evening. On Tuesday they filmed an orphanage there and visited the Hotel Montana, where Britney died. They're coming to Grand Goave today to film BLB, MoHI, and the block factory and take a boat ride to capture the sweeping view of the orphanage from the bay.

Projects like BLB and MoHI need media attention in order to raise consciousness and money. Yet when the media arrives, real work comes to a halt. It is the semblance of work we strive for, the visual metaphor for effort rather than any meaningful progress.

Since late last week, when Len informed us of ABC's upcoming visit, my mind has been racing through possible, and improbable, video scenarios. I see myself crouched before the model of the cornice, in front of the real thing, describing the intricacies of construction on national television. I practice explaining the boat analogy: *the deep foundation is like a boat's ballast, to withstand the earthquake's waves.* I try out phrases that will make me sound spontaneous and succinct. I polish my answer to the inevitable question, why am I devoting all my time to this endeavor. *Len is doing this because his daughter died. I have a daughter Brit's age who's still with us.* Never mind that national news would never air such details. Never mind that the sentiment is irrelevant to anyone except me. Never mind that the segment is about Len Gengel and not Paul Fallon. Such are the fantasies we all harbor about media, the vehicle by which each of us will become a star.

The white Land Rover arrives; I knew they would be in a Land Rover. Len climbs out along with reporter Matt Gutman; Julia, executive producer for Diane Sawyer; Elizabeth, executive producer for *Nightline*, and a Haitian driver. Matt is brutally handsome, skin smooth as plastic, just one waxing away from a figure at Madame Tussauds. I feel so course in his reflection it actually hurts to look at him. He and Len stroll around the orphanage. Julia and Elizabeth shoulder cameras and walk backward in front of them. Gama and I straggle behind, invited into the conversation at their bidding.

Given our alternating schedules, Len and I can go weeks, even months, without actually seeing each other. In person, the force of his physical presence can overwhelm me. I need time to brace myself against his energy. But there's no such time today. The interview starts immediately, on the wrong foot in my opinion, as Len tosses off an erroneous vignette about the two of us having a fight under the mango tree regarding the *B* shape of the building. It was not a fight; it was a discussion; and it took place under the chaconne. Irrelevant drivel, warm-up material, yet I take offense. Len, master of the media, heightens our drama. No one wants to hear about collaboration or engineering details; they want conflict, and if we have to bend the truth to hook them, that's a minor compromise in the service of good television.

Before we even walk through the first floor I realize why I've never heard of Matt Gutman, or watched *ABC World News* or *Nightline* or any TV for that matter, beyond sports. TV has always felt fabricated to me, and today I am a guilty conspirator in feeding the fabrication mill. Worse than guilty, I was foolish enough to foster expectations that ABC might want the content I had to offer, when I really just wanted my face on the screen.

It takes about an hour to walk the orphanage, much of that time spent staging the lighting and angles just right. I envision how the building looks through a camera lens, and I'm satisfied by what I see. But Len's answers to Matt's questions are so dumbed-down they make me wince. His words flow like soupy concrete, stuff we would discard. Matt asks why the columns are so fat, an opportunity to describe how each of the structural components are tied together, perhaps even make the boat analogy, but Len simply raps his fist on a column, grins and says, "Built to last."

After the tour we climb the hill at the back of the orphanage to set up the money shot of the building with Grand Goave and the Bay of Gonave in the background. When they get Len and Matt poised in the frame, Matt squeezes the emotional juice, "What would Britney think of this?" Len misses a beat. The gut-punch transition from construction details jams a stake through his heart. The man quivers a bit, his eyes tear up, and then Len finds his flow. He meshes true feelings and showmanship with such panache that I ache for the guy, exactly as I did when we first met almost two years ago.

The crew packs up and leaves for other locations around town. Gama and I are not invited, which is fine by me. I am ravenous, my usual poststress response. I eat a huge plate of rice with beans and roasted goat, though it's only 10:30 a.m. I try to focus on my tasks, but the morning's charade leaves me angry. Around noon Len calls. He tells Gama and me to come to Mirlitone. I pump myself up for another media round, but when we arrive the crew has gone; they cut the shoot short and headed back to Port-au-Prince. In their absence all we have left are the recriminations over what we did not say, what the camera never captured. Len is despondent, unhappy somehow with his performance. He decides to go out on the boat anyway, to savor the view of his orphanage from the sea. Gama and I return to work.

Back on site I redirect attention to moving the project forward. Len, Lex, BLB, MoHI, me; we have all been willing fools in the dream machine. We need the media, so we think, for money and notoriety, and so we play the game. But everyone comes away unsatisfied. It would never suffice to air twelve minutes of *here are people doing good work, and here is how they do it*. Instead we reduce the complexity, foment drama, and gouge a grieving parent's heart.

Parental devotion is not the sole province of Americans; I witness touching displays of love among many of our crew and their children every day. Tatay, our best mason, has become one of my favorite lunch companions at MoHI, He's an engaging man with a friendly demeanor and a great attitude. A few days after ABC leaves town, a young boy—ten, maybe twelve years old—sits with Tatay at lunch. The resemblance is striking. Workers' children often visit at lunch and share their fathers' portion of rice and beans. Although there is no balance in scale between what Len is doing and giving up part of your lunch, the fact that these hardworking, hungry men share their meals with their youngsters always moves me.

I take a photo of Tatay and his boy; they smile at their image in the viewfinder. After lunch I go to Renee's office and make a 5x7 color copy, cut a piece of cardboard to keep the image flat, and slide it into a manila envelope. Before Tatay leaves work I hand it to him. He looks at the photo of father and son and smiles, but then a shadow of doubt flashes beneath his joy. He tries to understand why I did this and decipher whether he owes me anything in return. *"Tatay et Paul zami,"* I say, to diffuse his concern by affirming our friendship. I wonder if he's ever seen a photo of himself or his child. He nods, understanding that our ledger is balanced. His mouth relaxes; his grin turns wide; he shakes my hand vigorously and tucks the photo back into its envelope.

The warmth I feel toward Tatay and his son must be contagious. Perhaps it's the Haitian spring. That same evening, driving home across the river with the setting sun illuminating his gentle face, Gama reveals the romantic tale of how he met his wife. Angela came to Haiti on a mission trip; they worked together in a clinic where she provided nursing services and he worked as a translator. When time came for her to return to Massachusetts, he made his move. "I realized that Angela was the woman God sent for me; so I translated my heart to her." I'm pretty sure no woman on earth could resist that line.

Angela and Gama married and lived in the United States for five years. They have a son, Nathan, who's now three. They dreamed of returning to Haiti, like Gama's cousin Lex and his wife, Renee, before them. When Len Gengel met Gama he intuited immediately that this smart, patient man could bridge the American and Haitian attributes of Be Like Brit. Lucky for us all, Gama signed on for the duration. Angela and Nathan joined Gama here in February; the room next to mine at Mirlitone has evolved from a bachelor pad to a family suite.

Angela is beautiful, a large woman with jet-black hair, clear complexion, and piercing eyes. Features that no doubt sweetened Gama's urge to translate his heart. In earlier eras Renoir would have relished Angela's generous proportions, and Rubens would have made her a goddess, but in an epoch that equates beautiful with thin, Angela is tormented by her stature and dismissive of her assets. She also has a powerful set of lungs, which give her both a powerful singing voice and a sharp yell. Judging from how casually she calls across the compound, I figure she comes from a family accustomed to using their voices rather than their feet to seek someone out.

Angela possesses many attributes common among Americans. She likes to shop, enjoys being pampered, and finds solace in material goods. These are difficult cravings to satisfy in Grand Goave. Her disposition is sweet and her countenance helpful, most of the time, yet Angela possesses a brittle, demanding side that she struggles to control. As a devout Christian, Angela longs to be eternally caring and generous, but her nature is more complicated than simple perfection allows. When her human inclination toward complaint and anger swell, she shellacs herself in a veneer of good cheer until, inevitably, the rage beneath her forced smile erupts and the full spectrum of her bottled emotions uncork—loudly.

As the resident heathen unhindered by any expectations of perfection, I accept frustration and rage. I always regret when I vent on someone, but I don't beat myself up about it. I acknowledge my dark side; I release my steam valve rather than implode, and when I'm finished I collect myself, assess the harm done, pay reparations with apologies, and strive to be more composed next time. Angela battles against such release. When her too-loud voice teeters between anger and remorse I want to reach out and comfort her; I want to tell her that expressing life's underbelly is not a failure. Unfortunately, Angela and I are not that kind of close.

Sunday is my upside-down day in Haiti. Construction crews have the day off so I spend my time at Mirlitone. In the morning everyone goes to church. I attend occasionally, but more often I stay behind, practice yoga, read a book, and savor the quiet chaconne. By late afternoon I need to move, so I walk into town and attend MoHI's Sunday evening youth service—heavy on singing, light on preaching. Sunday is the only night I ever go out in Haiti.

Angela is the best thing about the Sunday evening service. She leads the singing, and when she stands on the platform, strumming her guitar, fronting the backup band and girls' chorus, Angela is the person she wants to be. Her voice is clear and strong. She would have been a bang-up country singer if she'd headed to Nashville instead of Haiti. All the conflict she struggles with gets channeled into the sweat and energy of performance. Her love of the Lord oozes from every pore. Such conviction makes for good music.

Toward the end of service Angela performs her signature number. The verses are about the cross and Jesus' wounds; the lyrics are gory and graphic. The bridge is mostly instrumental. Angela beats hard on the strings; the other instruments fade in comparison, and she wails a counter line: *He conquered the grave. He conquered the grave. He conquered the grave.* The first few times I heard the song I was transfixed. It's a great number. Then, once I digested its raw power, I began to consider that refrain: *He conquered the grave.*

In the States, I spend less time thinking about eternal life than I do about tying my shoes, but if the thought whistles through my brain at all it gives me the willies. I cannot imagine why anyone would want to live forever, regardless of what future fantasy they can envision. Most popular notions portray heaven as a place of peace and light, but I don't believe humans really seek peace and light, or we would make more of it here on earth. We like drama and conflict; we like to proclaim our higher instincts while indulging our baser ones. Every description of heaven I've ever heard is totally boring.

The real problem with eternal life, as I see it, is not that we aspire to something antithetical to our true nature so much as it pollutes how we act in the here and now. Eternity is not a strong motivator.

If I'm going to be around forever, the present lacks urgency.

I have no wish to conquer the grave. When my time comes, whether in a week or a year or fifty years, I want my remains tossed back into the soil to become a few more grains on this rotating ball of gravity. Maybe I will be reformulated into some other creature that lives and dies in some other time. What becomes of me seems immaterial compared to what I do today. Regardless of what faith we proclaim, none of us know the future, while each of us knows our present all too well.

Angela soars when she sings "He Conquered the Grave," but I wonder whether her faith is a blessing or a crutch. For all that Angela's music rejuvenates me, I come away convinced that fixating on the afterlife shortchanges the difficult work we must all undertake to make this life satisfying.

Rework

May–June 2012

With seven billion people in the world I might have guessed that one would be a Hula fairy, but I could never have imagined that I'd fall under her spell beneath the thatched chaconne at Mirlitone. Any adjective short of a superlative fails to describe Carissa. She is tall, blonde, gregarious, charming, effervescent, frivolous, fabulous, utterly useless, and utterly lovely. Every moment in her presence is electrified by the alternating current that she adds no measurable value to the world, and yet she makes the world an immeasurably better place.

Carissa runs a nonprofit, Hoola for Happiness, a group that makes Hula Hoops and distributes them to Third World outposts like Haiti, Nicaragua, and India to spread joy and a bit of gospel. The hoops are shipped as five attachable pieces, each one an Olympic color, that snap together. Carissa's website hawks them for thirty dollars a pop, and she travels the world distributing them to poor children. When Carissa fixes her gaze on me and describes Hula Hoops as the communication bridge between cultures, I laugh at her ludicrous suggestion. When she gets me to try one, I am all bones and no swagger. But when she steps into a hoop and gently sways, when she sends an Olympic ring around her waist and hips, adds another around her neck and arms and a third along an outstretched leg, I convert to her enlightened form of communication. The hoops shimmy up and down her body, unhinged from gravity, innocent as Sesame Street, enticing as Salome.

Carissa arrives at the MoHI construction site midmorning with dozens of Hula Hoops over her arm. She alone knows that what a tight construction site burdened with fifty laborers, piles of aggregate, rebar cutters, a concrete mixer, and three hundred schoolchildren needs is to have all those children gyrating in Hula Hoops. Within moments of her arrival the site is a jumble of lithe black bodies in tan uniforms stirring up Hula Hoop frenzy. The girls are good; the boys are amazing. I discover a new force field in the world about twenty inches off the ground, where Hula Hoops attain equilibrium and children can spin them forever.

Carissa departs as quickly as she arrived and the hoops vanish. Carissa brings nothing as rudimentary as food or clothing or buildings to Haiti. She brings rings of colorful plastic and she brings joy. The only physical remnants of her visit are a few broken segments of green and red that get kicked into a corner. But the exhilaration she brings lingers. The children return to their studies and the crew to our construction, each of us better for the fairy that anointed us with her circles and her spirit.

The next day, Carissa's bubble of joy bursts. It is my worst day in Haiti. The trigger for this emotional spiral is benign enough— revising the service gate design to accommodate the metal fabricator's limited capabilities. The service gate is a recent addition to the BLB project. The road that used to terminate at the corner of the orphanage site has been extended along our front wall, up the steep grade on our west side, and over the hilltop to access the many new houses being built beyond. If we knew the road would bypass BLB I would have flipped the entire building to separate the main entrance from the service entrance, but it's too late for that now. Len wants a second access, but it relates to nothing. I walk past the far side of the building to verify the gate's opening dimensions when I notice a first-floor bathroom window half covered with plaster. I stop, I stare, I curse. The guys milling around the concrete trough worry what they've done wrong. I wave my hand to indicate this isn't about them, and go about my dimensioning. By the time I return to the shanty I've descended into a deep depression.

Depression is my oldest and sometimes dearest friend. I've suffered bouts since childhood and undergone years of therapy. When I was in my twenties psychiatrists promised relief if I learned how to conceal my inappropriate feelings about men. So I married and had children. Then psychiatry changed its mind and counseled that until I embraced my attraction to men, I would never escape my demons. Not a simple thing for a grown man with family responsibilities to do. Neither of these opposing theories, nor any medications, ever alleviated the gnawing stomach, the plaintive stare, and the blank affect so familiar to me.

Over time I've learned how to manage my moods pretty well: excessive exercise, little caffeine, and minimal alcohol. Still, depression grips me from time to time. It hatches sudden as mosquitoes after a summer shower, paralyzes me for a few days, and then lifts so abruptly I can actually visualize the curtain of despair rising from my brow. When depression visits I lay low until it passes. I am not cured, nor will ever be, but I am finished with shrinks and drugs. The damage they wrought exceeded their benefit. This is the body and the mind that god gave me, so I work with it, chinks and all.

When I am depressed, my primary coping mechanism is to get away from people. During those bouts, I am irrational and ugly, and once I subject others to my dark side the memory of it clouds the atmosphere when I turn bright again. I've also learned not to do anything rash. My depressions are triggered by real problems, but if I try to address them while feeling low, I inevitably make everything worse. I've never been depressed in Haiti, but as soon as it hits I realize how difficult it will be to deal with here. There is no getting away from people in Haiti; people are everywhere.

All day I itch to lash out at my depression's trigger. I'm furious at Len for compromising the lines of the orphanage by blocking up a window. The more I think about it, the madder I get. This is not the first time he has corrupted the architecture with his slap-dash decisions: the clinic layout he rearranged without any consultation is an enduring testament to his narrow design sense. What galls me is that we've discussed the challenge of having large windows in a few of the bathrooms and decided to use curtains on the interior for privacy rather than compromise the rhythm of the building's openings. Len obviously forgot, and during his last trip, told some guys to slap plaster on the window.

The dagger that bleeds my depression is not the sand and cement. It's Len's attitude. I'm just another hired hand, a very cheap one at that, whose efforts he can take or leave as he chooses. His arbitrary design decisions are usually bad and always costly, but his disrespect for me, and the value I bring to the project, sends me spiraling down.

I have a full docket of work today; I cannot simply leave the site. So I go on autopilot, motor through my tasks, and rub against others as gingerly as possible. I meet nary an eye, return nary a greeting. I am not exactly rude, but people figure out pretty quick to steer clear of me.

At lunchtime I go down to MoHI, where I feel loved. I eat my *diri et sus pwa* and recall how just yesterday Renee explained: *When we signed on to build an engineered building, we undertook the responsibility to follow through. There is a lot we don't understand, but we know we can't pick and choose what to do right and what not to do right.* It's ironic that Len, a builder, doesn't get it. He trots out his architect and engineer when it's good for media but conveniently forgets about us when he violates our work. I don't believe Len harbors ill intent, but considering all the petty decisions he includes me in, he certainly knows I would care about blocking up a window.

Revenge fantasies are ambrosia to a depressed man. I decide to quit, to just stop working. But conscience trumps faulty brain waves. Instead, I fill my deranged mind with delicious threats. I will tell Len that if he ever does this again, I will quit. That scenario has more satisfaction than simply walking away; it encourages more twisted conversations to play out in my head and foments more mind games. Walking home, still not meeting one person's eye along Route 2, I compose nasty phrases that cleverly reveal my wounds. The only saving grace is the self-knowledge that I am depressed, that I will not act on these damaging illusions, and that when the curtain finally lifts, there will be a way to work this out.

Emerging from depression is tricky business, like bearing weight on a sprained ankle. Instead of atrophied muscles I have to revitalize the sinew of human connection: to greet people once again, to meet their eyes, to engage in conversation, to care about them.

By Saturday my spirits are hardly recovered but at least they're balanced. I'd like to complete all the masonry on MoHI's ground floor today; it would be a satisfying way to end the week. But I realize we're short of rebar and cement, so half the crew gets sent home. I send an email to Len about blocking the window. Unfortunately waiting twenty-four hours hardly softens my tone. I receive a rambling commentary of apologies and excuses and counter accusations in return. I read it once and file it away, as if getting it out of my inbox will purge it from my mind. No need to keep that discussion raging. I am frustrated in every direction. I take a cleansing breath as my yoga teachers advise. I try to let go of everything beyond my control, which is pretty much everything, but when stuck in depression's grip, letting go is particularly hard.

Since nothing's happening at MoHI I head up the hill to address rebar fabrication at BLB. Michelle, my female carpenter friend, descends. She looks beautiful, her hair a ball of exciting curls, her skin radiant. She is poured into hip-hugging jeans and a tight yellow T-shirt with a sequins front; Michelle has just the right mixture of curves and sass to remind me how sometimes I miss a woman. She runs toward me with news of Jenison, whom I haven't seen in months. I cannot understand everything she says. I take out my dictionary and ask specific questions to make sure I have the story straight.

Jenison is in Port-au-Prince. Michelle could not afford to keep him after his mother died. The boy lives with his grandmother and his sister. Michelle explains that this is permanent. She gives me her hand and says good-bye. Hearing that Jenison is gone, still shrouded in depression's veil, I need more than a handshake. I reach over and hug her shoulder. Instead of bringing me comfort, our embrace leaves me hollow and brittle. I realize I've been in Haiti too long; I have accumulated connections and I suffer regrets. I miss the simple days of constructing temporary shelters with Michelle and Andy and Jenison handing up nails. Building three houses a day was good work with immediate satisfaction. Now thoughtless bosses and material shortages bog me down in a complicated, frustrating attempt to create these concrete behemoths.

Michelle continues on to the market. If she can turn my head, I imagine what havoc she will wreak there. I start up to BLB, but my feet can barely move. I want my buddy Jenison at my side. Port-au-Prince will either chew him into submission or sharpen him into a thug. Perhaps I should try to find him when I pass through the city. I dismiss that fantasy as soon as I formulate it.

He is one in five million, lucky if he's living in a side-street flat, unfortunate if trapped in the maze of a tent city. A few pointless tears well in my eyes, insufficient to streak my face. I feel sorry for Jenison and just as sorry for myself.

Dlo, dlo. A small voice comes up behind me. A young boy points to my water bottle; he looks five, he's probably eight. I want to brush him away; I resent the constant barrage of people here, but I catch myself, open my bottle, and offer him a drink. He walks with me awhile. Ephron, or something like that, is his name. He speaks too quietly for me to understand. He wears a dirty Spider-man T-shirt and carries a bag of scabby lettuce from the market— just another one of Haiti's roaming children, constantly on the move with no place to go.

I recall Jenison walking up the hill with me, telling me that his mother died, then laughing and skipping away. Life bears a frightening dichotomy here. Every day is utterly predictable—the same hot sun, the same still afternoons, the same somnolent boredom of nothing to do with little seasonal variation and no future plan. Until life changes, abruptly. People die or move; their fate is wrenched in a moment. Then they settle into a different yet equally predictable pattern.

Four more children catch up to us. They dance around me and show off their market goods. Fate tossed Jenison away and gave me all these others. Perhaps I am supposed to nurture them now. But my heart feels nothing for them. It is heavy as a rock, tethered to my little friend.

Tears, even weak ones, are a call to action. The morning after I learn of Jenison's fate I wake up resolved to do something about it. I understand that Port-au-Prince is a teaming mass of five million people, that all I have to go on is Michelle knowing Jenison's grandmother's phone number, but great sleuths find truth with thinner threads. Before I start inquiries I ask myself the obvious question: *How far am I willing to go for Jenison?* I don't wish to adopt him—he's so thoroughly Haitian—but I am willing to foot the cost of a stable living environment and schooling.

I do an Internet search of Port-au-Prince schools; only the exclusive private ones show up. I know four Americans with connections there; I email each of them asking for advice, and they respond with names and contacts at several schools. Gama agrees to broker communication with Michelle, call the grandmother, and help me assess the situation. My despair dissipates. My depression lifts. At least I'm doing something.

Having purged my toxic depression I am filled with purpose. I may not be clinically manic, but I'm in an awfully good mood. Lunch with the MoHI work crew is raucous, and toward the end of the meal I unroll a present I brought, pin it on a wall of the shed, and show the men a map of the world.

The idea for the map came during my last trip when workers asked if I had lunch with John Armour when I was in the United States. John lives in Jacksonville, Florida, closer to Haiti than to my home in Cambridge. Their question made me wonder what the world looks like to men who've never traveled more than forty miles and always lived among their own until the earth rattled and *blan* sprinkled out of the sky like salt from a shaker, strangers bearing tents with flags of Italy, protein crackers with flags of Great Britain, rice with flags of Brazil, backhoes with flags of China, and pop-up shelters with flags of the United States. I thought the world might baffle such men and that they might benefit from a map.

I bought a brightly colored rendition of the earth at the Harvard Coop. Renee sent me pictures of the American volunteers working on the school. I printed their photos, stuck them to the map and drew circles around their hometowns. I also drew a big red circle around Haiti. I show the men Haiti and the United States, and where John and Len and Daniel and Kim and Travis and I all live when we're not building their school. I don't even touch upon the two-thirds of the earth that is Africa and Eurasia. The guys pay rapt attention. Some have never seen a map; some have never seen a colored print hanging on a wall. A few get up close and point to their red circle; incredulous that Haiti is so tiny. Still, they like the photos of the people they know, and perhaps they understand that we all come from very far away.

The map does not dispel their notion that John and I should have lunch together when I'm home; the Haitian penchant for socializing with friends eclipses their map reading skills. But the map stays up for the rest of my trip, and I take every opportunity to describe geography and scale and distance. I point out the people they know who are scattered across the globe in the hope that every time I do it, the world gets a little bit smaller and a little bit more familiar, and they become a little bit bigger part of it.

After lunch, on my way back up the hill to the orphanage site, I discover a crew hauling rebar up the hill. They remind me of the brute strength it takes to make things happen in this backward land. I'm also reminded of the ancient Greek myth of Sisyphus, a deceitful ruler who gets his comeuppance through the gruesome torture of pushing a huge boulder up a hill, only to have it slip away and roll back to the bottom so that he must start all over again. Some days, when progress eludes our construction effort, I feel we are acting out our own Greek drama on Be Like Brit's hill. Surely, hauling heavy rebar a quarter mile uphill is a Sisyphean effort.

The orphanage will have more than 2,500 lengths of reinforcing in its slabs, columns, and walls. Most of it is number 5 rebar (5/8 inch in diameter) which comes in forty-foot lengths. Each bar weighs over forty pounds. Loaded delivery trucks cannot climb the steep hill, so they dump piles of rebar at the base and laborers carry it up. One man can drag a single bar up the hill, or a group of three to five guys can hoist a bundle on their shoulders, the bundle size being one bar per man. The round trip takes about half an hour, which means we have 1,250 man-hours devoted to hauling steel uphill. It will not take an eternity to move it all, but it will take eight man-months of labor, which could seem like eternity with all that weight on their shoulder.

Wanting to be helpful, I slip my shoulder under a section and take up my share of the load. I do fine for twenty or thirty paces. Then I start breathing hard. Soon I cannot keep step. After a few minutes I drop away. The laborers do not mind; they smile at my effort and revel in their superior muscle.

I wonder how much this is costing Len, a construction expense never reckoned in any estimate. The answer appears to be very little, on a dollar-per-ounce-of-sweat basis. Hauling over 100,000 pounds of steel up the hill will cost less than $1,000, and we have no shortage of men willing to do it. They are not being punished, as Sisyphus was. They're paid the going wage and their trial will end, but not before they carry a lot of heavy loads up that hill.

The cheap cost of Haitian labor amazes me. Yet, beyond a general sense that Haitian wages fall short of providing a comfortable life, I don't actually know what a day's pay buys. I know the cost of construction materials from all my estimates, but I have little idea what everyday items cost. I live in Haiti without money. Perhaps that is why, if money is the root of all evil, I experience so much good here.

I have some money; I just don't spend it. I carry a hundred dollars or so in my wallet in case I get stopped at customs and need to pay a levy on a hockey bag. I also have 350 gourdes I picked up months ago, less than ten dollars in local currency. I bought a few painted tin pieces on my first trip in 2009, and sometimes I buy coffee, vanilla, or rum for friends at the airport. Otherwise I spend no money here. None.

At first it seemed coincidence, but once I started coming down on a regular basis, I made a conscious decision to ignore my wallet. Opportunities to spend money are limited, but they exist. I could purchase creature comforts like a two-dollar straw hat or twenty-five-gourde soda. Six fried paté cost a dollar; they would make a satisfying meal. But I forgo those momentary indulgences for the Zen satisfaction of living beyond currency.

Although there are all-inclusive aspects to my life at Mirlitone, it is not a resort with a constant buffet and open bar. Meals are served at specific times, and if work demands prevent me from sharing them, I go without. Gama and I always leave before breakfast, and I compensate by carrying leftover bread from last night's supper. At one of the two construction sites I always manage to snag a lunch. Occasionally circumstances leave me hungry; and when that happens I choose to be content with the feeling of hunger because another meal will come my way sooner or later.

The decision not to buy casual items leads me to a deeper level of living consciously. Partly out of respect for Haiti's limited resources, partly as a game, I decide never to ask for any special consideration. If the generator is running I turn on lights and use my computer, but if it's not, I use my headlamp, run the laptop on battery power or, more likely, go to bed early. If the water pump is out, I am content with a bucket bath. If there is no vehicle going in my direction, I walk. Whatever minor inconveniences these events present are trivial compared to the centeredness I receive from being so conscious of my surroundings.

I derive many benefits from my position here. The crew always gives me my lunch plate first with extra *sus* on my rice. Sometimes I accept it as a sign of their respect; sometimes I pass it along to the next guy and take a later plate. Per Len's orders Gama keeps Diet Coke on hand, a real luxury in Haiti that I enjoy sparingly; and I can always raid the Gengel snack-food shelf in the construction shanty, though stress drives me there more often than real hunger. I have so many advantages here my commitment to a basic life is not hard. Still, I find it a worthy mind-set to remain cognizant of the huge gap between perceived and actual needs.

When I return to the United States I find it difficult to maintain this frame of mind. Our country oozes power, water, roads, and food. Our culture is dedicated to gobbling them up. We talk about conservation, but it's a tough swallow in a country that became great by magnificently spinning resources into stuff. Conservation is a niggardly diminution of the American character, counter to our fundamental being; it challenges who we are.

Perhaps someday I will walk through the United States with the same light impact I leave on Haiti. For now I focus on making sure I do nothing to cause any more damage to this fragile island.

Since the days are growing longer, I often have time to stop and chat with Renee before my walk to Mirlitone. Renee is my touchstone for understanding Haitian/American differences, though we both acknowledge the cultural gap between our countries can never be fully understood, let alone bridged.

"Haiti is a country of teenagers," she says during this evening's ruminations. Instantly I realize it's the most succinct description of this country I've heard. Teenagers are unformed yet egotistical, lack competence yet are overconfident, wound others recklessly yet are so thin-skinned they bruise easily. Teenagers are fiercely defensive of their clan, prideful beyond reason, focused on narrow desires, and clueless to others' interests. Their passions run hot and quick, but unfortunately their consciousness ends about two inches beyond the surface of their skin. They are self-absorbed, self-centered, and oozing with potential. Just like Haiti. I am one of those rare parents whose favorite period of child rearing were the teenage years. Perhaps that is why I love Haiti so much; teenage Never Never Land.

The superintendents at our two projects provide good insight into the Haitian inclination to be perpetual teenagers. A superintendent is the person who works across all trades and makes sure that people, materials, and tools are in the right place at the right time to keep construction moving. He is responsible for building the project according to the drawings and ensuring quality. A good superintendent needs to be able to manage people and time, be skilled in construction, accept criticism, and give direction. It is a job for an adult.

Fanes, our superintendent at Be Like Brit, is close to me in age, but our worldviews are decades apart. My biggest run-in with Fanes began last month. As crews formed and installed the reinforcing for the second-floor slab, I asked Fanes to fully complete one section so we could review it, understand problem areas, make necessary adjustments, and develop realistic expectations for progress. Fanes nodded at my request but didn't do anything about it. I asked again; I got the same nod and zero action. Every time I found an error in construction he told me they weren't finished, yet he wouldn't actually finish anything. Eventually, as unresolved errors piled up, he told me all I did was complain and that my demands were unrealistic. By this time he was right, because the list of unsatisfactory work had grown so long I was a complete nag.

I changed my approach. I applied enlightened management techniques to work our way out of this quagmire. I wrapped Fanes in the cloak of senior management, spent extra time reviewing the drawings with him to make sure he understood the intent and the details. I insisted that Fanes join Gama and me whenever we walked the site. Fanes responded like a trapped rat frantic for escape; he found any excuse to be absent.

On this trip conditions are worse. In a confrontation all too reminiscent of Hal and me at Forward in Health, Fanes yells at me to stop chastising him for the bad work because he didn't do it. With logic that exactly mirrors that of my thirteen-year-old, Fanes tells me he is responsible to get the work done, but he is not responsible if the work is bad. I realize, too late, that Fanes takes every criticism personally. I have wounded his honor. He pleads, *Why don't you ever tell me what's good?*

American muscle may be no match for Haitians', but our hides are a whole lot tougher. We focus on the work; we give a passing nod to the overall product and then dive right into the meat of the issues. In Haiti, where the meat is so close to the bone, I am learning this approach is a disaster. Perhaps Fanes and I can rebuild some trust, but we will never be simpatico; he is simply too high-maintenance for the results he delivers. Like most teenagers, he puts off whatever can be put off, winds up creating more work down the road, pouts about the fallout, and stores grudges in his personal arsenal.

I've learned a few tricks to improve our relationship. I start every conversation with Fanes by asking about his family then move on to praising all aspects of the work that are good, and though it seems a waste of time to me, I have learned that when I sugarcoat the criticisms he digests them better, which is not to say he actually acts on them.

Huguener, the superintendent at MoHI, arrived in Grand Goave almost twenty years ago, a shrimp of a kid who looked four when he was eight. He is another of Lex's cousins, emigrated from La Gonave. Despite Huguener's small stature, his mind is quick, and he soon became top of his class. He grew tall and swift and became a talented soccer player. Then he picked up a guitar and laid down a good lick. He became a hit in the Sunday morning church band, pushing the limits of loud twangs and sliding across the stage on his knees before screaming, quivering girls. His studies slipped, but genius is not a prerequisite for the ultimate teenage fantasy of being a rock star.

Unfortunately, Huguener's fame did not extend beyond Grand Goave, and his music brought him no fortune. Six days a week he worked for Lex, doing construction or driving errands or whatever chores appeared. Reality is no match for a rock-and-roll fantasy, and Huguener barely applied himself to work. A clever, lazy guy is the worst possible employee, much more creative in his evasions than a lazy guy who is just plain stupid. Lex and Renee bristled at so much potential frittering away in a country that needs every bit of talent it can muster. Huguener was none too happy either.

When construction at MoHI began to move with the same intensity as Be Like Brit, Huguener became a natural interface for me. He is a serviceable carpenter, but his excellent English and obvious intelligence made him better suited to be my translator and keep the project running in my absence. But he was magnificently lazy, disappearing at all times of day, shirking any accountability. I have no patience with bad attitudes and was not about to play the ridiculous Fanes-and-Paul game with a guy twice as smart as Fanes and half my age. Last month I told Huguener straight out he was the sharpest guy on the site but also the laziest and most disappointing. I told him he should be running things, but his attitude was holding him back. I don't think he much liked me, and I didn't blame him. I am not here to be liked; I am here to nudge Haiti forward every way I can, and sometimes the most effective nudge carries a bite.

This month I return to find MoHI has met our most ambitious construction targets; the site is clean and tidy, the workers focused. Lex says, "I don't know what you told Huguener, but he is a new man." The change is Huguener's doing, not mine, though I am happy to capitalize on the momentum and stoke his engine. I tell Huguener everything he has done right as well as what needs to get better. He listens to both with equal care. We review the MoHI drawings, construction details, and spreadsheets. I add him to our email distribution list. He organizes meetings every day before we start work, has an agenda planned, even wears nice shirts to address the crew and then changes into construction clothes. He describes the pushback he is getting from the guys who used to be his peers and now have to take his direction. We become confidants. The project, Huguener, and I all benefit from the change.

Between Huguener at MoHI and Gama at BLB we establish some aggressive targets for work to be completed while I'm away. Late Thursday afternoon, the day before I return to the States, Gama and I evaluate what's left undone. We haven't been able to find Michelle to contact Jenison's grandmother, so I'm resigned to postponing action on Jenison's plight until my next visit. While I review our To Do list Gama glances through the glass shanty door. "There's Jenison." "What?" My back is to the opening. Gama repeats, "There's Jenison, outside." I turn and see my boy, taller, thinner, the same profile, standing still as a statue staring across the site. The butterflies in my stomach flutter up my esophagus. "Jenison!" I shout as I leap for the door. "Come in, come in."

Jenison steps toward me. He hesitates to enter. *Vini*, I repeat. That simple pause tells me how much has changed. Last year's Jenison never hesitated at anything.

Jenison sits at the end of our table. I'm so glad to see him yet after we exchange pleasantries I have nothing to say. It's pointless to ask someone how he has been when "fine" would be a lie and the truth is too hard to either tell or hear. I want to know if his calm demeanor is a mark of increased maturity or the result of some gruesome trauma. Gama fills in our gap. He asks more appropriate questions. Jenison's story unfolds.

Apparently, Jenison's grandmother farmed him out to a man from Martinique who abused him. Jenison fled back to Grand Goave. The boy's outward appearance is good; he has grown, he has no bruises. He tells us the Martinique spanked him even when he did nothing wrong. Jenison knows right from wrong and he does plenty of wrong, which adds up to a heavy dose of spanking. I want the details of every step of his saga, but I hold back. Jenison tells us he has missed a year of school, but he was never good at it anyway. He tells us he is back in Grand Goave permanently, but he ducks the question of where he's staying.

Happenstance caused both Gama and me to be off site at lunch. Our pan of rice and bowl of sauce are sitting on the back counter. I ask Gama if we can offer Jenison some food. I settle the boy on a chair next to the cooler and give him a plate. As he eats, Gama solicits my intentions in English. I tell him I plan to support Jenison; he offers to make it happen. He will find out where Jenison is staying; he will get him a tutor to help him catch up; we can find a school for the fall. Jenison's plate is clean. Gama jokes in Creole about the tiny portion the *blan* dished out. He asks Jenison if he wants more. Gama fills the plate with rice and sauce and adds a small piece of chicken, no more than a garnish, on top. Jenison's eyes stare at the meat coming his way. I lower my own eyes, embarrassed to witness such gratitude over a shred of chicken. I am simultaneously astonished at my joy at seeing this little boy again and reeling from the responsibility I've just undertaken.

Concrete
June–July 2012

A week or so before I return, I send a "Mule to Haiti" email to my stateside connections asking what they want me to bring down. I usually fill two hockey bags with requested supplies. After this trip, I may reconsider that offer.

I'm flying to Haiti with two electricians, John Picard and Greg Smith; they came to Be Like Brit last winter to oversee wiring the first floor and are returning to wire the second before we pour the concrete roof. Len got us an upgrade to first class, which means wider seats and fresh juice, but more important, we are allowed three seventy-pound checked bags each.

The Thursday before our flight, we all meet at Granite City Electric in Quincy; Greg's company is donating all the fixtures and fittings for the orphanage. I bring a collection of hockey bags and the items I've acquired thus far for the trip. Everything packs into seven bags; the heaviest one weighs sixty-six pounds. We are good to go.

The next day Greg emails me that he has another bag of goods, and Renee tells me to expect a keyboard MoHI needs for an upcoming conference. That brings us to nine pieces, still good. On Sunday the keyboard is delivered to my house, along with piles of work gloves, C-clamps, medical supplies, and two cartons of cleft-palate nipples. The keyboard, swaddled in bubble wrap, is too large to meet the airlines unified dimension requirements, so I repackage it in corrugated cardboard, custom cut for a snug fit and tuck the rest of the items elsewhere.

We convene at Boston's Logan Airport at 4 a.m. for our 5:30 a.m. flight. John arrives first and checks his three bags. Somehow Greg and I have seven bags between us; we do a quick shuffle to reduce the number to six and take them to the skycap. Someone's scale is off; our bags now weigh over eighty pounds each. We open the duffels along the curb and start to sort when the skycap informs us that American Airlines does not accept cardboard packages to Haiti; the keyboard cannot go. We shoehorn it into the largest bag, which leaves all sorts of paraphernalia on the pavement. Thankfully it's four in the morning; at any other hour state troopers would rain down on our pandemonium.

The skycap is no longer an innocent bystander; he asks us where we're going and why; he suggests improved packing techniques. We play our Haiti card and tell him we are building an orphanage. He believes us, as we're far too disorganized to terrorize anyone. He tells us to toss everything in a bag, checks a huge coil of wire that won't fit anywhere, doesn't bother to weigh anything, and hands us a sheaf of baggage claims. John palms the guy a twenty, money well spent.

These are the things we carried:

48 Granite City T-shirts
30 pairs of Granite City sandals
8 pairs of safety glasses
6 rolls of blue wiring tubing
6 bags of construction gloves
4 cartons of light switches and receptacles
4 heavy C-clamps
3 rolls of undersurface drainage filter fabric
2 cartons of masonry anchors
2 cartons of cleft-palate nipples
2 cartons of blue tube fittings
2 rolls of insulated tubing for solar panel connections
1 new computer for Gama
1 carton of personal items for Angela
1 keyboard

Until this trip I've breezed past customs in PAP, but as we load our nine duffels plus wire coil on three carts at baggage claim, I know my luck is over. Officials rifle through every bag. The Oreos in Angela's personal box receive the most attention. I consider handing them over in exchange for safe passage, but in the end we strike a deal—$110 for the whole lot. If there is any science to determining that sum, it gets lost in translation.

When I get to Grand Goave, the first thing I seek is a status report on Jenison. Quite a bit has changed since the last afternoon of my previous trip, when Gama and I plotted Jenison's future while the boy gorged. The day I left, Gama took Jenison to the market, outfitted him with new clothes and shoes, found him a place to live with Toto, the BLB accountant, bought him a bed, sheets, and a toothbrush, and gave him pocket change. He sent a photo of a smiling Jenison in garish shorts and T-shirt that only an eleven-year-old could coordinate. Gama reported that Jenison loitered on site that entire day, eating continuously.

The next day, Sunday, Gama brought Jenison to church. When Gama went to the pulpit to translate, Jenison slipped out and was AWOL until ten that night. When Toto returned to work on Monday, Jenison in tow, Gama told the boy he could no longer wander off as he pleased. He reminded Jenison that he had a benefactor now, a person to care for him in exchange for Jenison going to school, a gift most Haitian children only dream of having. Jenison listened politely, nodded in comprehension, ate a good breakfast, slipped out of the shanty, and hasn't been heard from since. Gama hasn't seen him; Michelle hasn't seen him. He's gone.

Unfortunately, Gama has no new information. I could be angry at Jenison; I could worry that this jewel of my heart is wandering a challenging land alone; I could be desperate knowing less about his whereabouts than ever. But I'm not. I remember telling my own children that a parent's job is to give kids plenty of rope but not let them hang themselves. I can accept Jenison's independent streak; actually, I'm rather proud of my headstrong Haitian. My affection for him doesn't spring from Jenison being easy; it flows from his being unique. I'll never know what induced him to compass back to the BLB shanty in Grand Goave; he may have only been looking for some food or a pair of free shoes. Our vision of Jenison as a productive, well-educated Haitian suited us well, but it obviously didn't suit him.

Still, I believe what Gama and I did was worthwhile; for whatever confusion may be swirling through Jenison's immature head, I'm confident he knows that someone in Grand Goave cares for him. When life proves daunting for a too-young man on his own, Jenison knows that Grand Goave is his port in life's storm. I'll be here to rudder him whenever he's willing to steady on.

Meanwhile, I have little time to worry about Jenison—we have concrete to pour!

It's 10 p.m. on Friday night, and we're pouring MoHI's first-floor slab, 160 cubic yards of continuous concrete. More than a hundred men are on site as we change crews. Exhausted laborers with hardened concrete clinging to their pants are replaced by men with fresh faces and clean shovels ready to work through the night. Fanes appears with a young kid in front of him, fourteen years old at most. The boy has baby clear skin and wears a purple T-shirt, blue stretch pants, and heavy rubber boots. "He wants to work, should I let him work?" I grin. "Yes, why not." He gives the boy a pat on his rump, and the kid follows the throng. Twenty minutes later the boy clips past me with a wheelbarrow. He shoots me a high five and a smile wide as Kansas. He rekindles the excitement I felt at his age when I got my first job.

By midnight, the fresh crew is moving along well so I unroll a mat on Renee's office floor to get some shut-eye. I wake at 4:30 a.m. to unsettling quiet. No concrete mixer churns; no shovels scrape against gravel; no wheelbarrows squeak; no Haitians chant. I pull my stiff limbs to sit, slip on my shoes, and venture out. Nothing moves. Darkness clings to every shape just before it dissolves into dawn. We are eighteen hours into our concrete pour, and our game plan to run alternating crews straight through the night has obviously hit a snag.

A few souls drift across MoHI's site, but construction is still. The specter of last night's frenzy, the careening wheelbarrows, the flying buckets, echoes against the present silence. I drift up the stairs and take a photo; the splotchy image of my harsh flash bounces off the concrete already in place; the full length of the building but only about a third of its width: less than half of what we need to do. The concrete is already setting up; the exposed edge will create a cold joint, a point of structural weakness. The engineers will be disappointed. But they aren't here, and I can't stop the concrete from turning hard any more than I can stop the sun from rising and turning this crisp night into scorching day.

I sense people all about me, Haiti style; invisible forms snoozing on benches or curled in darkness. No one speaks. We are all too tired, and the night is too magic to puncture it with words. *Why do I love it here?* I am surprised that oft-asked question percolates against my weary skull; I'm too fatigued for analysis. Yet the answer reveals itself with the clarity of the emerging dawn. The answer has nothing to do with adventure or curiosity. I realize, for the first time, that this hulking school in this Podunk town is likely the most gratifying piece of architecture I will ever lay my hand upon. I understand, with amusement, that Lex and Renee are the best clients I've ever had, maybe the best I'll ever get. How could I have anticipated how well they respect me and what I bring to the project, how seriously they adhere to design requirements both onerous and foreign, and how their faith instills a different form of budgeting than I have ever encountered? They are building the design that stirs their soul, and they let their higher power guide them to the money they need to complete the task.

This pile of masonry woven together to defy shaking will not be a masterpiece by any standard definition of the word; it will never win an award or grace a magazine. I have designed larger buildings, more complex ones, and more elegant ones. Yet this school possesses qualities that elevate it above mere function; it will be a sturdy guardian for this community, providing a safe and dignified place to meet and to learn. Its ponderous, elementary construction is the antithesis of the architecture of transparency so much in vogue today, yet that very solidity will be a critical comfort to this shattered community. The building's nobility speaks to me in the dark, in the flesh, with the same directness it does on paper. I am so committed to preserving its honesty that I remain on site through endless buckets of concrete just to make sure that every formed wall is as straight as our rudimentary tools can shape, every rod of steel is well placed, and every beam compacted to maximum strength. This is no longer just another building for me; it is the marriage of form and purpose I have always sought, it is everything I value set in three dimensions for generations to come. By every measure that I hold dear, it will be my masterpiece. That is why I am here, to safeguard its passage from lines on a page into the light.

The sun comes up, we resume work, and continue nonstop through the long, scorching day. We are closing in on thirty-six hours of pouring concrete, and in our second concrete night, the collective mood is high. The workers have just finished eating in shifts. The mix is flowing fast; the end is in sight. Summer evenings in Haiti are clear and almost cool. MoHI feels like a carnival; everyone smiles; everyone high-fives.

Renold, the MoHI dispatcher and accountant, steps out of his office and into the path of construction. He takes my hand. We saunter down the path toward the mixer. I deal with Renold every day, yet have never thought about him beyond his function. But when a guy decides to hold my hand, some consideration is in order. Renold is tall and thin, very careful, and a bit officious. He's respected rather than liked and responds to new situations by becoming hyper alert until he settles into a solution. In short he is remarkably like me. The gentle pulse of our palms helps me understand these similarities. Holding hands makes us twins.

We finish MoHI's floor slab late Saturday night. On Sunday morning I organize the curing tarps and listen to Lex's sermon, then turn full attention to Be Like Brit, which is planning an even larger pour: the orphanage's roof. Gama and I work all afternoon on preparations. I leave around 5:30 p.m. to walk home. The breeze feels fresh; the air invigorates, and in that moment I realize that ninety degrees on a late summer afternoon no longer feels oppressive.

Which reminds me how my housemate back home noticed that I put on a sweater when the thermostat drops below 70; I never used to get cold. How I've taken to eating rice and beans in the States more than beef; I never order a filet of anything anymore. How the occasional Creole phrase slips into my dreams. How I no longer say I visit Haiti; I say I live here half time.

Today marks the midpoint in my yearlong commitment to Haiti, and I am well along in my conversion. To what I'm not exactly sure, but I'm on board for the rest of the ride.

Len and Bernie arrive on Monday to participate in pouring Be Like Brit's immense concrete roof, scheduled for the night of July 3, to be finished on the Fourth of July. I'm anxious before Len arrives.

Except for the 24-hour media circus in early May, we haven't been in Haiti together since January. Len's always been demanding, but lately our Skype and email exchanges have become more volatile. The pressures on him to raise money and build this monument are tremendous. Cyberspace provides enough distance for me to exercise patience, but I've become accustomed to my own rhythm here, and I fear friction between us when we occupy the same space.

The moment Len arrives I realize how wrong I am to wish he remain distant. Everything that's best about Len Gengel shines through in person: his earnestness and humor, his contagious smile and friendly handshake, his genuine affection for other people. Within minutes I realize that although our alternating schedules may be efficient, they shortchange our connection.

By Wednesday night we're ready to pour, which means a celebration is required. In Haiti, every milestone demands ceremony. Last week, before MoHI's concrete pour, dozens gathered on plywood stretched across the rebar to join in prayer and to photograph the ceremonial dumping of the first bucket, as well as the second and third and fourth . . .

A little pomp goes a long way for me. Guiding wobbly benefactresses across bouncy rebar and watching them tentatively overturn a bucket of aggregate tries my patience when I am itching to do real work. But I acknowledge the importance of a ritual beginning, of dedicating energy to the task before us, and in keeping the progress of needy organizations in the public eye.

Tonight Be Like Brit will pour 440 cubic yards of concrete, the largest concrete pour ever in Grand Goave. We are utilizing a technology foreign to this part of the world—ready-mix concrete. Eleven cylinder trucks are scheduled to drive between Port-au-Prince and Grand Goave, delivering green concrete to a pump truck that will lift the mix thirty feet over the top of the building and deposit it on the roof through a giant hose.

Capping off the orphanage with this new technology warrants not one but two occasions. In the afternoon Gama gathered all the workers. Len made a speech. He outlined the history of the project, Brit's journey to Haiti, her death at the Hotel Montana, and our eighteen months of active construction. I had the misfortune to follow Len, never a good slot on the speaker's roster. I explained the logistics of ready-mix. Guys who'd never seen a concrete truck, let alone a pumper, could not fathom pouring seven yards of concrete in ten minutes. I told them this was an opportunity to learn how concrete is placed in many other parts of the world, how we hoped to increase their construction skills with this experience. Then Gama delivered the details of schedule and logistics, which might have been dry except that he announced premium pay for night work. That got everyone's attention.

The real occasion is now, 9:00 p.m. The pump is here and in place; the dispatcher tells us the first truck is less than an hour away. This is our moment for ceremony. Len, his son, Bernie, Lex, Renee, and I stand on the roof surrounded by the crew, the scene illuminated by a magnificent full moon. I expect a reiteration of this afternoon's words but am pleased when Len turns the focus to the workers arrayed before us in their rubber boots and secondhand T-shirts, holding their trusty shovels and trowels like David's slingshot against the towering pump truck. Between our two projects, most of them have worked seven days straight; this will be their third all-nighter, yet good cheer abounds.

Lex's invocation also takes a different turn. He describes the project in the larger context of Grand Goave, moving beyond the usual recitation of creating jobs and housing children in a safe building. Instead, like all great politicians and preachers, Lex stakes out a broader view. The project sets a new standard for Grand Goave, for all of Haiti. After a resonant pause, he ends, "Future generations will remember what we do here tonight."

I doubt that pouring a concrete roof deserves rhetoric with the same gravity Normandy deserves on D-Day, but it makes for one heck of a memorable event. The moon lifts full and bright over the mountains; the first truck arrives, and instead of being lugged up in buckets, concrete falls from the sky.

Concrete is the most widely used construction material in the world. Over two thousand years ago the Romans mastered it for their aqueducts and coliseum, yet variations of binding stone and water date to before the Egyptians. Labor-intensive, durable, and impermeable, concrete is the premier preindustrial building material. As societies became more mobile, the difficulty of transporting concrete became a problem until the 1930s, when we began mixing the ingredients together in a rotating drum on the back of a truck. So-called ready-mix concrete is prepared in a central plant and hauled to a construction site, where it can be discharged down a chute to build foundations or pumped up to create elevated floors. Ready-mix concrete is more liquid than its hand-mixed sister so that it stays loose during transport and flows through the pump. The advantages of ready-mix are improved quality control in the mix design and speed of placement. The disadvantages are limitations on the travel time between plant and site before concrete begins to set.

In most developed nations, a network of plants ensures that virtually every city has access to concrete by truck. No such network exists in Haiti; the only plants are in Port-au-Prince, two hours from Grand Goave under optimal circumstances. Cemex, an international construction materials company, is expanding their presence in Haiti and offering services beyond Port-au-Prince. When a trio of representatives showed up a few months ago promoting their product, both Len and Lex were intrigued. Pouring the orphanage roof's 440 cubic yards by hand would mean dozens of pours and multiple control joints. The opportunity for a monolithic roof seemed the perfect test project.

Jose, our sales rep from the Dominican Republic, and Michel, our technician from Petionville, introduce a Latin slant to doing business here that proves high on promise yet short on delivery. John Thomsen, the structural engineer from SGH, and I have serious reservations about transporting ready-mix from Port-au-Prince. In the US, two hours is the maximum allowable time for concrete to sit from truck to placement; three hours is an upper limit if the mix is doctored with additives. Since we cannot control what happens along Route 2, we will need optimal efficiency at the plant and on site. Everyone agrees on a night pour, 7:00 p.m. to 7:00 a.m., to minimize traffic impact and avoid quick setting during daytime heat. In a long trilingual conference call we explain why we need at least fifteen trucks, not the eleven Cemex proposes, to make the necessary forty-four round trips within a twelve-hour period; we advocate for a stronger mix to minimize cracking; and we want Be Like Brit to have some authority over quality control. Cemex trumpets its 100 percent replacement warranty, but ripping out in-place concrete after it's deemed defective is a losing situation for everybody. We want to place good concrete from the start.

Despite assurances on each of our requests, Cemex doesn't present the final contract until the afternoon before the pour. They will provide only eleven trucks, and they maintain complete control over determining acceptable concrete to place. With so few trucks, we won't be able to pour the roof in one night, and no matter how many hours the concrete sits, Cemex can still choose to pour it. We are unhappy, but we proceed.

On the day of the pour we arrive on site at 6:00 a.m.; plenty of time for final adjustments to rebar and formwork. The masons arrive at three in the afternoon. The first truck is scheduled for 7:00 p.m.; it does not arrive until ten, and five more come directly behind it. Then we wait ninety minutes for the next one. Concrete requires a continuous flow to maintain a "wet edge" for structural integrity. Trucks arriving as a gang with gaps in between compromise this requirement. Around 4:00 a.m., with less than a third of the roof poured, Michel approaches me about suspending operations until the next night, which means building a construction joint and introducing a seam. I simply refer him to Len, who, as I expect, growls that if he had wanted seams he would have used wheelbarrows. Dawn arrives after an hour's sleep; things slow down even more. Michel confides that they are running only a ten-truck rotation, not eleven, that they have never transported ready-mix this far, and that the trucks are only 80 percent full, because Cemex fears losing concrete out of the drum coming up our steep hill. Forty-four trucks now become sixty, the headway between them, promised as twenty minutes, is over half an hour. We are in for a long pour.

The sun comes up fast and strong. By 9:00 a.m. I have an unanticipated problem—the concrete poured overnight is setting up and its surface is cracking. We are prepared to cover all the concrete and keep it wet for seven days, standard curing procedure, but we did not reckon on having to cure some sections while pouring others. By now the crew is facile at maneuvering the pump and placing a truck of concrete in ten or fifteen minutes, then dozing until the next truck arrives. Suddenly I need the time between trucks to unfold tarps, spread burlap, and wet concrete. Haitians are allergic to multitasking. Len and Gama have gone to Mirlitone to sleep; I have no translator, and no one is interested in what I have to say anyway. A water hose is not going to counter the quickly drying concrete. We need to flood the roof with water straight from the well; we need a bucket brigade. It takes me over an hour to organize the effort, by which time the roof has significant plastic cracks.

Cemex pumps every truck of concrete that arrives, no matter how long out of the plant. It is pea soup, so full of admixtures to retard set-up you could drink it with a straw. Boss Fanes and Boss Pepe are disgusted. *Concrete no good! Concrete no good!* They keep shouting at me, incredulous at the muck I allow to be poured. I try to explain that this concrete is different from hand-mixed, that Cemex added drugs to it, but even without a translator they understand that my hands are tied. We spread whatever Cemex pumps up there.

The day passes, another night, and another day. The fifty-ninth truck finally leaves at 1:00 p.m. on Friday, July 5. BLB's roof pour takes thirty-nine hours, exactly the same time as the MoHI pour the previous week. To Cemex's credit they steer the calamity to its conclusion—Michel is just as wretched as the rest of us. In two locations concrete sets so long between pours that cold joints develop. I send SGH pictures of the plastic cracks, but once our curing crew is in motion the roof stays wet.

Despite all of our problems, I cannot say we made a wrong decision; pouring 440 cubic yards of continuous concrete is well beyond what any wheelbarrow operation could achieve. The lesson to be gained from our arduous experience is not that the technology of ready-mix doesn't exist in Haiti but that the peripheral supports are missing. Cemex was never responsible about what it promised; the company did not do the simple math to determine the number of trucks needed and how often they would have to cycle to provide a continuous flow of concrete. When SGH and I presented our proposal, the company's representatives nodded and ignored us. They refused to establish any parameters of acceptability or share with the owner any say in quality during the process. The result was a business transaction rooted in bottom-line gamesmanship rather than professional conduct. Cemex is a huge multinational company with a stellar reputation throughout the world. It's unfortunate that it does not bring those same standards of care with them to Haiti. Haiti cannot become a forthright, transparent place to do business until the players stop treating it like a crippled stepchild and employ the same analysis, production, and delivery used elsewhere in the world.

After the last truck leaves and we cure the final section, everyone is so exhausted our minds turn muddy. I try to make sense of the perplexing web of connections that ensnarl me in Haiti. Len and Lex and Renee and I work together; our interactions bump up against the same boundaries one finds in the workplace. We don't talk politics or sexuality, and even though religion weighs on this place like the afternoon thunderheads, we observe bounds on that discourse as well. Our main purpose is the work, and we all understand that enflaming our differences can only undermine that objective.

Still, we are more than workmates. We live together; we share the unique challenges of navigating Haiti. We are not really friends; I don't envision myself spending weekends at the beach with them. Yet that is exactly how we spend Sunday afternoons under the chaconne. We are not a family by blood or choice, yet I think naming us a family is apt. We need each other, we love each other, we take care of each other, and if we sometimes don't like each other, well, that's all part of being family.

The Venn diagram of our Haitian family is simple. There are two alpha males, one has a loyal beta female on hand, and there is one beta mediator. Any anthropologist will tell us that this is an unstable diagram; alpha males do not share. Therein lies the essential imbalance of our family: too may top dogs for harmony. But therein, too, lies our strength: it takes a lot of testosterone to get anything done in Haiti.

Haiti is awash with alpha males. Guys strut, pose, rev their *motos*, taunt, compete, and seek domination rather than cooperation every time. This is one reason Haiti appeals to Lex and many evangelicals. The Bible's gender hierarchy is everywhere evident here; men rule and women submit. Lex's cleverness, cunning, and bravado make him a big man here, just as Len's confidence, brass, and sheer size render him formidable. I imagine that some social scientists and a couple of million dollars could show an inverse correlation between a nation's development and its prevalence of alpha-male behavior. Emerging nations need charismatic leaders to create a simple vision and harness manpower to build basic infrastructure. But as countries evolve and their challenges become

more complex, they require more collaboration. Intellectual capabilities become more important than physical power; society
needs fewer mavericks and more people who subsume their individual interests to the greater good. Lex and Len possess strengths
that would make them successful anywhere in the world, but they
thrive in Haiti.

In less than two years we've raised money, built roads, dug
foundations, poured concrete, and established the predictable
patterns of bickering that define most families. Almost all of our
quarrels fall into the category *this will seem funny tomorrow*, but
some wounds have cut deep and left ugly scars.

Len suffers that odd duality common to many Americans—he
wants everything his own way, yet he wants (needs? demands?)
to be loved. Lex savors his role as the guy with his fingers on the
pulse of Grand Goave, but he is happy only so long as everything
flows through him. When Lex wants to sell Len CMU for $2 apiece
and Len looks elsewhere for a better deal, things get prickly. When
Len decides to use ready-mix concrete but Lex sticks with wheelbarrows and bucket carriers, things get prickly. When Len directs
Lex to negotiate the land deal and Lex cannot close it on Len's
exact terms, things get prickly. When Len expands his road without prior agreement of the abutters and Lex fears reprisal, things
get prickly. In all of these interactions, and dozens more like them,
I strive to maintain an air of objectivity; everyone knows I don't
have any interest save the ultimate outcome for both projects.

But none of us act as pure as those descriptors imply. Len flips
from sharp businessman to grieved parent in an instant; he cannot
understand why Brit's story does not move everyone to simply
allow him to do what he wants. Of all of his foibles, I am most
dumbfounded when he rants: *I don't want them to think I'm the rich
American up on the hill.* How else, I wonder, are the citizens of
Grand Goave supposed to see him? He breezes into town, buys
whatever he wants, builds a palace in memory of his daughter,
and gets upset when he doesn't receive special treatment from
people whose family members may be memorialized by nothing
more than spray paint on crumbling walls.

For Lex's part I'm sometimes embarrassed by how he intercedes where he isn't needed. Len's decision to use ready-mix concrete brought new players to Grand Goave, outsiders who weren't

Lex's people. Lex interjected himself into the negotiations more than necessary, and the team squirmed uncomfortably while he bragged irrelevantly about his concrete prowess.

Although I try to take a balanced view on all of our family squabbles, in the end I align myself more often with Lex. I kid myself it's because Lex is the guy with a long track record and broader vision for Grand Goave. But my objectivity is compromised. I respect and admire Len; I work hard for him, but I register his faults. Lex has captured my heart, and like all believers blinded by love, I overlook his shortcomings.

It's after 6:00 p.m. on my last day here by the time we clean up from BLB's concrete pour, outline the work with Len for my next trip, and have a similar meeting with Lex and Renee at MoHI. I catch a ride to Mirlitone and try to calculate my total hours of sleep over the past ten days. It's a tiny number, but I'm too tired to do the math. My legs ache, my head woozes, my breath is too quick, my eyes burn. I haven't been so tired since graduate school. Which is not a good omen, since graduate school fatigue always led to getting sick. I pack, go to the bathroom, and hit the sack by 7:00 p.m. I lie like a mummy, the daylight receding along with my consciousness. I close my eyes and embrace dizziness as precursor to a dream.

But the dizziness is real, as is the pressure in my groin. I rise and go to the bathroom again. Back in bed, I welcome sleep, but it teases me. The moment I embrace slumber the need to eliminate returns. After three or four toilet visits every solid within me is gone. I spray brown water and figure I've hit the end, but lying prone creates distress. I develop a fever. My innards *boing* like a glockenspiel. There is no sleeping now. There is only time on the toilet followed by lying flat until more toilet time is required. By midnight I have been up more than a dozen times. Finally, exhaustion eclipses intestinal distress. This creates a new problem. At 2:00 a.m. I wake to the foul smell of nursing home incontinence in my own bed. I'm too debilitated to be properly ashamed.

Somehow I rise at 4:30 a.m. and withstand Route 2's bumps all the way to PAP. I figure it's a twenty-four-hour bug, and I'm on the downside. I orchestrate my bathroom needs in the terminal and on each leg of the flight. I sleep en route to Miami, I sleep on the floor in the Miami terminal, I sleep on the flight to Boston. My housemate, god bless him, picks me up, and I'm in my own bed by 7:00 p.m. My toilet treks are less frequent, maybe every two hours, and I get some sustained sleep. I rise around 10:00 a.m. the next morning. A tentative awakening. I lay low all day, nibble on bread, eat cereal dry from the box. I am very sick.

By Sunday I can move again, but nothing tastes good. I go to yoga and do some poses. I envision myself as a reed, a tall and hollow life form billowing in the half-moon. Being sick makes me keenly aware of my body. My breath races into voids I never felt. My torso aches from the intestinal tugs, my cavities are so empty they echo. I am hungry. I must eat, but nothing appeals. I nibble a few more crusts of bread. The closest I come to satisfaction is a saucer of egg noodles.

Another ten-hour sleep. I wake Monday convinced I've turned the corner. My step is purposeful and unaccountably light. I bounce onto the scale to discover I've lost ten pounds in three days. It's not a weight loss plan I would wish on anyone.

Carpentry
July–August 2012

The main design feature of the Mission of Hope School is a pair of staircases that begin at the ground floor near the central front entry, ascend away from each other to access the perimeter galleries along the first floor, and then turn back to rise to the second floor where they come together on a generous landing at the main entrance to the church. Stairs that begin at the same place, diverge, and then come back together are called sweetheart stairs. Ours are wide and grand to accommodate hundreds of people climbing to church services. They will also make a great circuit for children playing tag.

We're starting to build the stairs. First we need to establish key dimensions and erect very specific wooden formwork. It's as close to finish carpentry as this project will require. Later we'll install the rebar and pour the stairs in concrete.

Like all first days of new work, progress is slow and miscommunication rampant. It takes us three hours to determine the stairs' beginning and end points. We mark the top of the future ground floor (the ground-floor slab will be poured after we install underground electric and plumbing connections). We dangle a two-by-four from the first floor to measure the vertical distance between floors. I would prefer to measure from the ground up, but I learned that Haitians have a predisposition for suspending building elements in space when they determined the initial square of the building by floating a framing square. Perhaps they don't trust the solidity of the ground; perhaps they like the challenge of establishing equilibrium in open air; or perhaps they just don't like to crouch down. In this case our method, however haphazard yields a result exact enough; the total height is 10 feet, 3-3/4 inches, only a quarter inch off our 10 feet, 4 inch design dimension.

Two factors determine the comfort level of climbing stairs. The first is the relationship between the vertical face of each step, the riser, and the horizontal plane where we place our foot, the tread. The dimension of these two planes must be within a proportional range; the steeper the rise, the shallower the tread. Monumental stairs have long treads, as much as fourteen inches, with risers as little as five inches. Service stairs can have risers as tall as eight or nine inches, but the treads must be correspondingly narrow for comfort. The rule of thumb architects use is that rise times tread equals 75+/-. Seven in eleven is the most common stair ratio in the United States, and exterior stairs should never be steeper. Our vertical dimensions divide evenly into eighteen risers, each 6-7/8 inches high. Therefore we will need seventeen treads, each 11 inches wide.

The second factor in stair comfort is that all risers must be exactly the same dimension. The human gait can differentiate changes in riser height as little as 1/8 inch. Uneven stairs force us to look down and concentrate on our feet, rather than allowing us to ascend with grace and certainty. Riser heights in Haiti are notoriously erratic, and if Renee has made one firm demand on this project, it is that she wants perfect stairs.

I explain to the carpenters that I want to create a reverse form-work to outline where the stairs meet the wall. This goes over easier than I expect, and within a few minutes, bits of 11 inch by 6-7/8 inch plywood cascade diagonally along the block wall. Now I have a problem. There is nothing inherently wrong with what they are doing, but the opportunity for small mistakes accumulates with so many small pieces of wood. If each plywood rectangle is only 1/16 inch off, we will generate a one-inch discrepancy over the entire staircase. I fetch Renee, whom I rely on for subtle negotiation. I tell the workers their plywood rectangles are not wrong, but they might lead to cumulative error; whereas, if we cut multiple stair teeth out of single piece of plywood, we can be more accurate. Words like *cumulative* do not exist in Creole, but Renee is a master at converting my vocabulary to local vernacular. She tells them what they have done is good, but if we use larger pieces we will be *plus exactement*. That phrase goes over well.

We get a full sheet of plywood. We score it with riser increments along one line and tread dimensions along the other. We do not measure 6-7/8 inch increments over and over, rather we measure from a datum line to 6-7/8" followed by 1'1-3/4", 1'8-5/8" (and so forth) in one direction and 11", 22", 33" (and so forth) in the perpendicular. Datum dimensions are more accurate than sequential ones. I'm not sure if the workers understand the benefit of what I explain, but we lay out the stair with only three separate sections of saw-toothed plywood. When the outline of each opposing stair is tacked against the wall we verify that the future landing between them is level. Everything is square. These two lengths of formwork constitute the major accomplishment of six men over two days. We may not be getting any faster, but we are getting *plus exactement*.

Meanwhile, I am getting ever thinner. The runs that took ten pounds off me after my last trip never really went away. I improved, cautiously, until an ill-fated indulgence of BLT with French fries and salad purged my intestines anew. I went to the doctor. He put me on the BRAT diet (bananas, rice, applesauce, and toast) and ordered a three-day regimen of stool sampling. Lab analysis discovered I'm the proud host to Blastocystis hominis and Entamoeba hartmanni trophs, spooky sounding bacteria that are not usually pathogenic but for some reason are wreaking havoc swimming around inside of me. There is no surefire remedy, but the doctor suggested Flagyl might help. Being disinclined toward drugs, and having already left Boston to visit family in Colorado by the time my lab results were in, my doctor and I agreed to see if diet alone would do the trick.

The BRAT diet works like a charm, clogs me so tight I rarely seek a toilet. Problem is, so little protein leaves me lethargic. Over time I extend my repertoire. Beans with rice, good. Plain hamburger on toast, good. Grilled fajita beef on a tortilla, bad. Poached egg, good. French fry, bad. Bland food, good. Tasty food, bad. I can't even look at the really yummy stuff like ice cream and salad and chocolate without feeling queasy.

Back in Haiti the BRAT diet's a cinch. There's no applesauce, but bananas, rice, and beans abound. I expand my repertoire to include plantains. No toast, but good bread, plain. As long as I don't eat anything else I'm fine, but ladle sauce over my rice and my innards flow like the Grand Goave River after a deluge.

Midway through my trip, and three weeks into this tedious diet, I haven't made any improvement. I email my doctor, report my condition, and he promises a prescription for Flagyl will be waiting for me when I arrive home.

Before I can savor my Flagyl I have some very different work to do. Cherylann Gengel is back in Haiti with her longtime friend Moe Finley and my fellow architect Kim Cochrane. They are here to select the finishes and furnishings for the orphanage. We all visit MSC Plus in Port-au-Prince (Haiti's Home Depot) to choose tile, paint, and bathroom accessories. We bless the exterior pilaster details, oversee the first installation of the integral colored concrete floors, approve a luminous fresco mock-up of the finish plaster/paint mixture, lay out the built-ins for each orphan room, and guide the carpenters in making the first bunk beds out of used formwork.

One late afternoon we take a break in the shanty and compile a wish list for World Vision, a nonprofit interested in supplying big-ticket items for the orphanage. "No toys and no linen, they're easy to get from individuals. Kitchenware would be nice; we're going to need commercial quality." Cherylann rattles through our agenda, alternating between making decisions and making jokes, I can't help but recall the woman I traveled to Haiti with two years ago and the tentative hug we exchanged at the end of that trip. Now we are chums, and though I am at least a decade older than Cherylann, I always feel nurtured in her presence.

Our ambitious list grows, ranging from generators to spoons. As I scribe our wishes I discern the philanthropic balance between what we need and what people like to give. Cherylann has already turned away twice as many teddy bears as the orphans could possibly need, as if a child in the tropics wants to snuggle into a soft, warm replica of some animal she will never see. Haitians have no teddy bear reference; what we Americans wish to impart by donating them is not the actual felt and stuffing, but our own deep and positive associations with the stuffed creatures.

In Haiti, I am immersed in a world of giving. The Gengels give unlimited time and serious money to build this monument to their daughter. Family, friends, and strangers give thousands of dollars to make it a reality; businesses donate lights and toilets and solar panels to outfit it; and people say, all too often, how much I give by coming to Haiti. I laugh them off by proclaiming that living in the Caribbean two weeks a month with someone making all my meals is hardly a hardship, but their words actually make me cringe. I'm appalled when someone calls himself a "giver" and dislike having the term applied to me. Does anyone ever refer to himself as a "taker"? We all think better of ourselves than that. Yet just as every gift requires a recipient; every giver is also a taker.

My problem with the whole idea of taking and giving is that it becomes another way for us to categorize people, and categories divide more often than they unite. If I give something to you, I am, however subtly, deemed more capable, more affluent, or more enlightened. The act of giving creates a hierarchy, with the giver residing on an exalted plane. Once the hierarchy of the donor and the beneficiary is established, those designations foster relationships based on pity or sympathy rather than mutual empathy.

In a world where money is the universally acknowledged measure, the terms *buy* and *sell* describe pure economic transactions; they carry no moral value, whereas the terms *give* and *receive* describe exchanges that are economically unbalanced. People give money to Be Like Brit without expecting to receive a product of like value in return; businesses donate goods without expecting compensation, and volunteers actually pay to participate in construction.

We volunteers do receive things in return for our time. We feel useful and connected to our fellow humans. We feel that if misfortune strikes us someday we might receive help from others. When we reach beyond the concerns and confines of our private world, we experience an invaluable sense of meaning. These non-economic motivators may not be quantifiable, but they're real. Anyone who gives also gets, and for many of us, the more we give, the more we get.

The best human interactions optimize each party's needs, and the most satisfying solutions tap into motivators that transcend money. I do not come to Haiti to *give*, I come to Haiti to *do*, and what I do here is the most interesting and satisfying thing I've ever done. Receiving accolades for my good fortune obscures the reality that Haiti gives me at least as much as I give to Haiti.

For people who donate at a less intense level, the same analysis holds true. When Be Like Brit ran a fund-raising promotion asking people to "purchase" a concrete block, hundreds of people coughed up ten bucks. I'm sure every one of those donors had an adrenaline rush of altruism as they wrote the check. Helping to realize Britney's memorial and increase opportunities for Haitian children for the cost of a movie ticket is a good value.

The peculiar inclinations that prompt people to give teddy bears rather than toilet paper apply to larger gifts as well. Philanthropists have specific focuses; some organizations provide water-filtration systems, others provide computers. Some donor preferences align well with our project, others do not. Some donors give to Mission of Hope because MoHI is a religious organization; others give to Be Like Brit because BLB is not. We seek donors who will provide what we want, but sometimes, as with our solar energy system, we bend to accommodate what's offered. Every charitable donation is a marriage between a donor's particular interest and the needs of the recipient: the closer the fit, the better.

At a project scale, the same synthesis between a donor's wish and a recipient's real needs come into play. Haiti is overrun with philanthropy. The impoverished country takes pretty much whatever it can get, but that doesn't mean that Haiti always receives aid that addresses its greatest needs. The Gengels did not come to Grand Goave and say, *How can we most help this community?* They said, *We want to build an orphanage to honor our daughter's last wish.* Grand Goave is happy to have Be Like Brit, not only because it will support sixty-six orphans but also because it provides an economic boost through construction and long-term employment. Whether a $1.5 million orphanage represents Grand Goave's highest and best need is irrelevant. The Gengels' personal motivations, like my own and those of every other donor, drive our giving.

One challenge in my role at BLB is balancing the project's memorial aspects with its social purpose. It's an orphanage, but it's also a monument, and occasionally I do not navigate the competing objectives well. When we were selecting light fixtures I sent photos to the interior design group of what I typically see in Haiti—exposed sockets with screw-in fluorescents. The response was strong and swift; the orphanage would not have such rudimentary fixtures. A flurry of emails followed, including photos of possible options, some pretty fancy. I should have let the conversation fly loose for a while, but I sent an email suggesting we consider that the people who donate to Be Like Brit might not want their money spent on such elaborate fixtures. Len shot me a response that twisted my conception of giving in a whole new direction: *Cherylann and I have given the most anyone could to Haiti, and that's our only daughter.*

I was perplexed. How could Len say that he gave his daughter to Haiti when by any reasoned perspective Haiti took Britney away? I didn't respond, of course, I knew better than to get into an email argument with Len about the semantics of taking and giving. Still, his painful, distorted words rooted in my mind. I worried that Len's psyche convoluted the truth to make sense of Britney's death, revising the reality of January 12, 2010.

Len's words exposed his core need for control, because someone who gives is always in control, while having something taken away renders him feeble. As he shapes his hill in Grand Goave, as he builds a wide road and tall walls and terraces the landscape to his own contours, Len is claiming control over Britney's next scheduled itinerary stop; taking command of the very ground that swallowed her up. This realization deepened my sorrow for Len. I've always mourned his loss; now his inability to accept it wrenched my heart. Peace will never come to a person who must control everything.

Thinking about Brit always forces me to consider my own daughter, Abby, and how tortured I would be if anything happened to her. For all our differences, Len and I are alike in believing that we fathers are our daughters' ultimate protectors. We coach life and light into the world, we marvel at their beauty, we are awed by their grace. We give them every advantage we can imagine, experiences that transcend our own humbler origins. We send them away to college and to visit foreign lands so they will have a wider, more benevolent view of humankind. We give them enough slack to test their wings, but we reel in the rope before anything untoward can happen. That is our responsibility as parents, as fathers. But horror strikes, and the rope unravels, and even though the tragedy is random as an earthquake—nature's reminder that mere humans cannot control everything—we cannot accept that a daughter is lost to the rubble. Even though no one blames us, we have failed. For our main purpose, our whole purpose on this earth is to nurture and protect our daughters, and we cannot allow anything to take them away from us.

Only Len would use the term *give* to describe Britney's death, but if Len needs to say he gave Britney to Haiti in order to find a drop of peace in his soul, I must grant him that comfort. No one could ever accuse Len of failing his daughter, no one but Len himself. If tragedy ever strikes Abby, I will also suffer the same lifetime of questions, of doubt. It is irrational, but it is human, and I must respect it.

Our World Vision wish list is three pages long and growing, itemizing all kinds of useful stuff the orphanage will need. We continue our extraordinary dance of giving and receiving; we assuage some of Haiti's suffering while Haiti nourishes our own peculiar wounds. We appreciate all the people who assist in our effort as we live out our own grief through exhaustive activity. Britney Gengel is more widely known in death than she ever was in life. She will never be a living, breathing human again, but her spirit touches thousands of souls thanks to Len's Herculean, fatherly, effort.

I wish we could have what's on our World Vision list right now. We are out of everything, everywhere. There is no cement to be found in Haiti; as a result we cannot pour the septic system at BLB or finish the stairs at MoHI. There is no gasoline at BLB so we have no generators and no power. We cannot renew our wireless Internet because the local storefront is out of Natcom cards. There is no rebar at MoHI, so we cannot ready the stairs in case any cement arrives. And both jobs are short of the most important construction commodity of all—money.

The shortfall at BLB is just the natural ebb and flow of life with Len. Three months ago he sold his vacation house in New Hampshire to keep the project afloat, and for a while the cash faucet was gushing. Len loves building the road, the site terracing, and the retaining walls more than messing with finicky plaster and tile. Three huge earth-moving machines have lived here for a month now. They do useful site work, but they cannot make this mammoth concrete shell habitable. This week Len realizes we may come up short on some very essential items, like doors and windows and screens, so he shuts the faucet off. I am accustomed to the shifting currents of life with Len. His newfound prudence welcomes analysis, so I make careful price comparisons on materials and techniques. I do not mind because in my experience projects with tight budgets often distill greater architectural honesty. It doesn't mean we won't do things well; it simply means we'll be more judicious.

MoHI's shortfall is more elemental—they are flat broke. Renee made an embarrassing mistake last week when she requisitioned A Heart for Children for an additional payment. We all refer to the grant as $350,000, which it is, more or less. The grant is actually 255,000 euros. Renee had already requisitioned, and received, 255,000 euros, but she was thinking dollars and thought she had 95,000 of some sort of currency left. We knew the grant was tight for the scope of the project, but we thought it would see us through the superstructure. Post-earthquake prices are so inflated that the cost of construction is an endless upward spiral. We need $50,000 to finish the main structure and $110,000 more to complete this first phase of work. MoHI needs a big donor, and we need him now.

I offset the challenges of so many shortages by considering all the things we have too many of. BLB has too many rocks, they are everywhere and the septic excavation just keeps popping out more. MoHI has too many piles of sand and gravel awaiting cement; we can barely navigate the site. And both sites have too many laborers clamoring for work that is disappearing fast. When Gama and I drive up the hill in the morning, over a hundred eager faces meet us at the gate. But the days of hiring all comers are history. Gama chooses forty, maybe fifty, of the best laborers. The rest go home empty-handed and hope the local economy improves very soon.

The estimates and economizing necessitated by the shortfalls actually make more work for Gama and me. On my last night in Grand Goave we're at the shanty very late; it's midnight by the time we return to Mirlitone. We come upon a group of eight people draped in white, standing in a circle around an altar of flowers, mementoes, and candles at a street intersection. It's like the altars people erect in the United States to honor roadside accident victims, though more elaborate and more ephemeral. Voodoo is not a regular part of my Haiti experience—the evangelical crowd doesn't tinker with it—but the scene whets my interest in Haiti's pagan face, which I discovered reading W. B. Seabrook's *The Magic Island*.

Eighty years ago a little-known member of the Lost Generation arrived in Haiti intending to document his impressions unbiased by the polarizing attitudes of his day. While Hemingway was making his literary mark in Paris, the epicenter of Western civilization, W. B. Seabrook explored colonialism's collateral damage—Arabia, Haiti, and Africa—with a passion for the occult that led him well beyond the pale of acceptable taste. One could craft a respectable resume for this gifted writer, a war hero gassed at Verdun and recipient of the *Croix de Guerre*, a *New York Times* reporter, contributing writer to *Cosmopolitan* and *Vanity Fair* as well as author of eleven books. Yet a full reporting reveals a man immersed in life's extremes, however measured. He indulged in cannibalism and sexual adventurism, and his books address witchcraft, Satanism, sorcery, and Voodoo as well as a harrowing personal account of his extended stay in a mental institution.

Seabrook immerses himself in Haiti in the 1920s, when this free republic was under military occupation by the United States. He travels easily between the American power elite who live like princes in this impoverished country, the black and mulatto aristocracy under the thumb of Washington, DC, and the country peasants whom he embraces and befriends. He infiltrates each sector to explore how Voodoo and black sorcery resonate from thatched huts to the presidential palace and recounts his experiences eloquently in *The Magic Island*.

I am hesitant to draw too many parallels between Mr. Seabrook and myself. I have no intention of eating human flesh, seeking a psychiatric commitment, or committing a drug-induced suicide, which Mr. Seabrook did in 1945. Nor do I presume to turn a phrase with his insight and grace. Still I find a consonance of perspective in our adventures here. Both Seabrook and I came to

Haiti to witness rather than to judge, to accept the country rather than attempt to change it, to value what Haiti has to offer rather than condemn it for what it lacks.

Although the names and details change, Haiti versus United States circa 1920 and Haiti versus United States circa 2012 recount the same story. Fiercely proud of its independence, Haiti is reduced to the pitiful embodiment of that well-worn lyric, *freedom's just another word for nothing left to lose*. Set apart from a world run by white men, Haiti is so racked by poverty and corruption that it becomes their ward. At the beginning of the last century the marines played governess here; in this century it is the more than ten thousand NGOs and missionary organizations who keep the dependent nation afloat. Like medieval fiefdoms of goodwill they each lend a hand but lack the encompassing ability to teach Haiti to row, let alone discover the wind that could fill its sails. Seabrook's succinct summation of the American occupation ends by acknowledging, "Our attitude now in Haiti is superior, but kindly." Unfortunately that same sentiment is widespread today.

The Magic Island includes fantastic descriptions of Voodoo rites and customs which Seabrook, simultaneously reporter and ready participant, presents with the same legitimacy of any world religion. The climax of his night-long blood baptism centers around a young virgin and a goat channeling each other's spirits, chanting in each other's tongue, merging their identities before the sacrificial knife slashes the goat's throat, sparing the girl, to release the baptismal fluid. Anyone who knows the Old Testament tale of Abraham and Isaac must recognize the parallels. The point for Seabrook is not whether Christianity or Voodoo is correct but in acknowledging that each satisfies a fundamental craving that eclipses mere survival. Humans are driven to link our past, present, and future selves; to bond with our ancestors; to shape the context to our existence and envision continuity for those to follow. The Haitians he describes, expending their meager resources in spiritual pursuits, remind me of medieval serfs living in squalor while erecting Gothic cathedrals. Those with the least in this life invest most heavily in what might come next.

Gama is disinclined to discuss the midnight ceremony we witness. "Have you ever been involved in Voodoo?" "No, I am a churchgoer." "Do you have any interest in it?" "No." When you are Gama, when you believe the direct channel to God runs through the prophecies you accept and the tongues you speak, there is no need for other paths to the supernatural. But when you are me, a heathen voyager on this magic island, all forms of mysticism are equally fascinating.

This voyager gets little sleep because Pastor Akine, one of MoHI's regular drivers, insists we leave at 5:00 a.m. for my 10:00 a.m. flight from PAP. I drag myself out of bed when I hear his car horn blast in the pitch dark. I pay tribute to my intestinal distress with the toilet time it demands. I toss everything in my purple bag, including a heavy concrete sample from the BLB roof pour that SGH wants to test in their lab. The massive cylinder weighs thirty pounds and looks like a bomb to an X-ray detector; I will get a physical inspection at every security point.

When we pull out of Mirlitone in the clear dark night; that breathtaking Voodoo moon lingers in the west. I'm really hungry. Last I ate was yesterday lunch, when our hope of pouring concrete for MoHI's main stairs seemed impossible. But Lex found some cement, and the crews found their flow, and by nine o'clock last night we had created a pair of impressive stairs that will last for decades. I trudged up the hill to work with Gama and forgot to eat. I have a sack with some bread; I offer some to Pastor Akine and gnaw on a few pieces myself. When we hit paved Route 2, I recline my passenger seat and shut my eyes.

Sleep and Haitian driving are not compatible. My eyes flutter open at every bump, and I cannot help but witness the arcane delights of nighttime travel: the nearly empty *tap-tap* with its sole passenger sitting astride the center bench, staring down the road like a king surveying his kingdom as it slips away; the empty dump truck hugging the center of the road whose back wheels are so wobbly they might come off any minute; the bicyclist pedaling along the left shoulder with a huge bundle of sugar cane staked on his handlebars, no light, no helmet, no way to see where he's going in the dark against our headlights' glare.

I must sleep some because in an instant the sky's no longer dark. As we drive east, a pink band highlights the horizon's silhouette; the flat line of the sea on my left rises gently across the highway, extends through the settlements on my right and into the distant mountains like a graph of positive trending indicators. I pull my seat upright to watch the city grow before my eyes. Traffic is light, though steady. The *tap-taps* are full; workers wait on the side of the road in clean khakis. The new divided boulevard in Carrefour is impressive; the light standards with their integral solar panels extend graceful double arms, welcoming a new day.

We reach Port-au-Prince proper before dust rises to coat the world in gray grit. A *tap-tap* boasting a painting of Jesus with thorns on his head and blood glistening on his side is too graphic for my queasy stomach. City driving is chaotic; Pastor Akine passes on the right, the left, the right again. MoHI drivers are as aggressive as any of their urban cousins. The sun finally appears, a blistering white ball hovering above the metal roofs of the main market. It's going to be a hot one. The market is already crowded with rows upon rows of women crouching before bundles of greens. These mountain people must rise early in order to come and squat all day in this squalor. The pill man will move among them later, when the trials of a scorching Port-au-Prince day stimulate the desire for pharmaceuticals.

Billboards sprout like dandelions, thick steel tubular bases telescoping above shacks and tents, capped by rectangles five times the size of the dwellings they shadow. Some of the ads are peculiarly Haitian; two cartoon children with schoolbooks in their hands and a new Tuff Tank water container perched on top of their concrete house; a beautiful woman smiling in front of piles of rice sacks. In the United States we do not advertise running water or subsistence crops. But closer to the airport, and the money, the billboards are more sophisticated—insurance companies, Air France, brokerage firms. All this aid is making someone rich.

Curing
August–September 2012

My flight to PAP is uneventful. Neither MoHI nor BLB wants anything hauled in, so instead of picking up checked bags I collect the airport's newest attractions, flyers. One young woman distributes advertisements extolling a local restaurant; another hands out sheets for modular homes complete with air conditioning, though a similar ad in the United States might not promote a prefabricated orphanage for forty children. A third lady shoves *Magic Haiti* magazine in my hand, a glossy number with four-color photos of art, resorts, and food that resemble nothing I've ever seen in this country. I gather these offerings like an anthropologist collecting data on his subject culture and appreciate this new form of hucksterism, a step up from panhandling.

I don't see anyone from Mission of Hope when I reach the end of the secure walkway, so for the first time I step across security's threshold alone and join the crowd on the far side. I'm the only *blan*, but I don't feel anxious. Port-au-Prince Haitians look different than people from Grand Goave, they have rounder bellies but deeper scars. Eventually Ricardo arrives along with Alexis, who is dressed in hip-hugging jeans and a bodice-gripping top that test the outer limits of what her mother, Renee, allows. Alexis is sixteen now, and remarkably beautiful. Lex's older brother Raymond and his son, Tanyo, are with them, along with Fabi, Alexis's friend.

We exit the airport, turn left instead of the customary right, and motor to the National Convenience Store for a snack, which turns into a full lunch. Ricardo and Fabi flirt. He's drawn no doubt to the alluring blue extensions woven through her tiny braids. Lex calls. When he learns that we're still at the airport he gets me on the line and tells me to hustle. I tell him I have no control. I don't mention that I'm in no particular rush; this is the first time Port-au-Prince has seemed anything other than an ordeal to be endured.

Ricardo drives a circuitous route through the city, higher into the hills than I've ever been. The streets might be considered middle class. We pass houses with small courtyards. There are even a few trees. It's dense but ordered. We descend back into the center of things. The azure sea fills the voids in the cathedral's shattered rose window; what's left standing appears more sculpture than ruin. We scoot around the palace, still toppled. The tent city has disappeared; the trees are leafy and the ground is raked. Within two months rows of port-a-potties have been replaced by an open-air bookstore, Bibliotec Universal, which is Parisian in ambiance as well as name.

Port-au-Prince is improving, or perhaps it's simply that our summery mood soars above the corrugated shacks, piles of garbage, and sewer pigs. We're on a joy ride, and we only absorb the joy. We stop at a roadside stand to pick up sodas and sugar cane from a sidewalk vendor. Everyone in the car chatters in Creole, which sounds like bird warble to me. The Bay of Gonave shimmers, its color that sparkling aqua tint I associate with Bermuda, gorgeous and refreshing to behold.

We deposit Raymond and Tanyo in Leogone, wave to all of Alexis's cousins, and finally pull into Mission of Hope about 4:30 p.m. Lex bristles because we're so late, but nothing's so pressing it cannot wait until tomorrow. Marieve greets me at Mirlitone with a large bowl of bananas; I'm supposed to feed my still-sketchy intestines two a day. Her thoughtfulness triggers a rush of blood; my cheeks glow with the warmth of beach sun. I am in summer's thrall, relaxed and loved.

We make good progress on both projects until, on Thursday morning, Tropical Storm Isaac enters our consciousness. Internet pop-ups, US National Weather Service bulletins, and radar tracking maps show a swirl of clouds coalescing along the line of ocean between Africa's horn and the Caribbean arc. Yet the day is calm and fair. We finish laying out the detailed rise/run template for MoHI's second staircase. At noon all the bosses convene to assess what we'll complete before the storm. "Everything, concrete on both stairs and the guardrails; we pour tonight," Lex announces. Clebert, the lead carpenter, is skeptical, as am I. He and Lex argue in Creole. I have nothing to add, but I can tell their *d'accord* is slim. When Lex says *do it*, it will be done; Clebert's arguments hardly matter.

We all walk the site. I describe the order of work: underside formwork, sloped rebar, riser formwork, nosing rebar. Lex wanders off, disinterested in details, but Clebert, Leon, Fanes, and Huguener follow. I go up to BLB; a truckload of plumbing and electrical fixtures arrived from the States that has to be inventoried. Len sends a blitz to Boston media that Be Like Brit will open its doors as a refuge from the storm. He gives my contact information for interviews. *When the reporters call, tell them we will save the mountain people!* None call; Isaac isn't news in Boston—yet. I return to MoHI at five, the weather unchanged. The only indication of the storm's movement is on Renee's computer monitor. Little progress has been made on the stairs. Lex is gone, as are many workers. I spur some activity and cajole the carpenters to stay late, but we aren't going to pour tonight.

Friday morning brings overcast skies and heavy, still air. Isaac has leapt off the abstract screen and into our atmosphere. The carpenters completed a good amount, but nothing is fully done. Huguener and I target the pour for after lunch. At noon the first drop of rain hits my shoulder.

Isaac is an unlikely name for a storm, a biblical character best known for lying passive under his father Abraham's sword until the Angel of the Lord intercedes and proclaims the father's faith. We never know what the boy thinks as his dad prepares to murder him. When Isaac grows he fathers Jacob, who famously wrestles with angels and sires twelve sons who become the Tribes of Israel. Isaac is little more than a conduit between two more dynamic guys. He lacks weight in his own right.

Everything that was almost done on Friday morning is still almost done on Friday afternoon. That last 5 percent is always a struggle. Haiti's idiosyncrasies—the lengthy discussions to meet *d'accord*, the challenge to sequence construction in an efficient flow, the rudimentary tools, the intermittent power, the hierarchy of bosses and laborers—frustrate me more under storm pressure. But Haitians are proud of being slaves to no one, including *blan* architects and biblical-named storms. Time is fluid in this land of few appointments and no trains to catch. Tomorrow will be much like today, and if a storm comes along, we'll just sit it out until the next tomorrow.

But I have an American-style schedule in my head. I know that Lex and Renee leave for their annual fund-raising trip to the States in ten days; we will shut the project down for six weeks while they're gone. We need to finish the steps and pour the second-floor slab on this trip or else the rebar will rust and the plywood warp. I count the available days; we have no slack. Isaac is an inopportune visitor, but he's coming nonetheless, and we have to accommodate him.

The rising barometer suffocates my patience. I yell at Clebert when he sits about guzzling soda while his crew loiters. I rant about the section of too-long rebar that I asked be cut back days ago. Apparently the rebar saw is broken so the carpenters just formed around it. I roust the mechanic myself, get the saw fixed, direct carpenters to remove the forms and ironworkers to cut the steel. When we try to reinstall the forms the individual pieces have gone missing, picked up and thoughtlessly repurposed. Everything has to be fabricated anew. The wind is strong; it takes two men to steady a piece of plywood for nailing. I measure the dimensions, again; I check each cut, again. My patience is exhausted. My frustration rises. I turn sharp and willful.

The wind is strong; the rain light but steady. We begin pouring concrete on the first guardrail before the carpenters are finished with the formwork above. Dusk descends. The wind bristles, and the rain turns hard. I take command at the top of the stairs. I'm in the work line, tossing empty concrete buckets back to the mixer. From this vantage point, I can see everything. Huguener is across the building, helping carpenters form the second stair; Fanes is nowhere to be found, as usual. I prefer to be consultant rather than boss, but I have no choice. I bark at the mixing crew to keep the concrete flowing and harp on the bucket line to keep it moving. I turn my eagle eye for construction details into one looking for lazy workers and make sure every man in line is fully engaged.

We complete the first guard and stair. The finishers level the steps while the crew scour their buckets. Carpenters on the opposite side are still cutting and nailing. The world is black now; blasts of wind follow piercing rain, followed by more wind. I am useless in the dark. I leave the men to clean up and reckon the second stair will have to wait until next week.

Driving home I wallow in recriminations. I hate being so brusque. I'm here to demonstrate improved construction and help the crew comprehend its value, but I regressed to simply shouting directions. The workers did what I demanded, not because they understood, but because the white guy scolded.

The wind along Route 2 is strong; our truck swerves across the line. Thankfully there's no traffic. We almost hit two dogs staggering along the side of the road. They remind me of the family mutt from my childhood, obedient to her pen except during thunder, when disorientation eclipsed her training, and she wandered about the house. Storms affect our equilibrium and compromise our integrity.

Back at the beach I stand at the seawall. The waves are high, the wind fierce, and the rain strong. Isaac is a worthy storm; he's pushed us hard. I lost my civility, but at least Isaac will give me a rainy Saturday to lick my wounds. I tell Gama not to wake me regardless of the morning's prospects.

Most nights I enjoy rain on my roof; the water percussing on the metal resolute as Beethoven. But Isaac's wind drives the rain at a slant, producing unsettling, Schoenberg-like rhythms. I'm tired but keyed up; I need a sound sleep, yet I read past midnight and rise before six, Isaac's turbulence creates too much pressure for rest. In the gray morning, the wind dies but the rains increase. Isaac mixes wind and water, the primary ingredients of tropical storms, erratically. They never peak together, which is perhaps why Isaac never achieves full hurricane status in the Caribbean.

Lex arrives at Mirlitone around nine in a brilliant yellow slicker. He reports that the crew worked until midnight and completed the second stair. I cannot decide if I'm in awe of their achievement or consider them fools. After dawdling away the daylight they worked feverish in a dangerous stormy night. I wonder for a moment if they completed the work to spite me: *We don't need you and your efficient ways, Mr. Architect, we shoulder through nature's scourge at our own pace.* But that is a self-aggrandizing notion. Once gone, the crew forgets about the *blan* nuisance who pesters them all day.

The wind calms, but the rain picks up. Waves top the seawall. The chaconne is surrounded by a foot or more of standing water. From the veranda I have a cozy, secure view of the storm. The breeze is invigorating, the overspray refreshing. Although little more than a tin roof and a balcony floor protect me from Isaac, nothing seems the least bit dangerous.

Come on, we're all leaving. Gama shows up after noon and reports that Lex wants us to evacuate. I'm surprised, but I do not question. Seven missionaries load into two vehicles, along with Gama and Marieve and two pots of rice. No one brings a change of clothes or overnight supplies; leaving feels more like an adventure than a disaster. We lock the gates. The tire ruts in the dirt road have turned into streams; the drainage channel I often walk along is flooded; we drive through three-foot deep ravines to reach the highway. Route 2 is high but slick. We drive across the bridge. Big crowds cluster at either end, watching the river surge below. We stop on the city side to see the show. The water is mesmerizing—the usual trickle transformed into a surge of eight-to-ten-foot rapids, thick with silt, branches, roots, and occasional household objects. It tears at the banks. I wander out to mid-span, camera in hand. *Get back here!* Gama screams at me over the gale. Only then do I realize that the bridge is empty. No one dares stand in the middle, which washed away in a similar storm a few years ago.

I run back to the truck. When we arrive at MoHI's office everyone's in a jolly mood. A few sacks of rice are sandbagged across the doorway; boxes are piled on tables away from the wet floor. People squeeze in and around everything. Marieve serves hot porridge. We chat about nothing and everything, like a family digesting their Thanksgiving meal. The rain trickles away to nothing. We return to Mirlitone and walk along the beach. We wonder if Isaac is spent. I've been in the eye of a hurricane before, the eerie calm and unexpected sun. This reprieve does not feel like that, but the atmosphere is still pregnant. Isaac's eye has supposedly moved on to Cuba, but this storm is not over yet.

Mirlitone is hundreds of feet closer to the river than it was yesterday. The current eats away the soccer field. Huge trees along the bank have fallen; syrupy green water cascades over their slick

trunks. The river moves fast, it creates fantastic patterns of swirling gray and green where it slaps into the waves from the bay. The
intersection of water flowing down and waves lapping in causes dangerous eddies. Yet out in the middle of the chaos, along a
shallow smooth sand bar, two men with machetes and a wooden
dugout chop exposed limbs and fill their boat with tomorrow's
charcoal. We watch one of them, his boat full, row straight away
from the river and loop back to the far shore. I worry for the one
left behind, hacking away. One false step and he will get sucked
into the rapids. But his mate returns, and they continue mining
the valuables Isaac has bestowed.

The flat belly of dark clouds opens up to reveal puffy tops and
slivers of blue sky. The sun highlights their marshmallow upper
edges. The dividing line between river and sea, where green meets
blue, is normally tight to the river's mouth, but Isaac gives the
river the upper hand; the arc of silty debris spans the entire bay
save a thin line of clear blue on the far horizon.

Back at Mirlitone I am in bed by nine. Our premonition that
Isaac isn't finished proves true. The rains come hard, fast, and
long. With little wind, the torrent on my roof is Beethoven's Fifth
all night long. The rains pummel fierce as any flash thunder-
storm, but they aren't spent in fifteen minutes or even an hour.
The deluge lasts all night. When I finally open my eyes to a flat
gray sky and relentless pounding, it's past seven in the morning.
I have never felt so well rested. I look up at the trussed roof and
sheathing and give thanks for their stability. I wonder about my
neighbors—the ones in cracked concrete that barely withstood the
earthquake, the ones in Samaritan's Purse houses that Andy and
I built, and the ones still in tents. I can only hope they awake in
equal tranquility after such a downpour.

Gama announces no church service this morning. Marieve
brings bread and coffee to the veranda. The rain hypnotizes us.
Even though it's been falling for hours, we are compelled to watch.
By nine the rain slows; by ten it sputters. I move to the chaconne.
The world is humid and still. The water has three bands of color
this morning: It's pea green a mile or so wide around the mouth of
the river, dusty blue from east to west, with a sparkling vein of ul-
tramarine on the horizon, heralding clear water in our future. The
sea is aggressive in reclaiming the upper hand in the hierarchy of

water forms; I can actually see the green arc shrink back to the river's mouth. Nature has played out its drama, equilibrium returns. Isaac is history. He did no lasting damage to Mirlitone—it will be easy to reclaim Carissa's Hula-Hoops that blew onto the roof—but he made us take notice.

In the lazy Sunday afternoon calm, I inquire into Marieve's wedding plans. She tells me she's getting married in December, the same information she gave me months ago. But today her eyes don't dance with the news so I inquire no further. Instead, I seek out my primary cultural resource, Renee. When I mention Marieve's wedding, Renee rolls her eyes. "She's been getting married in December for years now." Renee explains Haitian marriage customs. December is the most popular month to get married, but most people have two prerequisites for a wedding: their own house and a big celebration. Many couples live together and raise a family for years, unmarried, waiting for that house and the money for the party. Marieve has been with her boyfriend for more than ten years, but he's never managed to build them a house. She is in her thirties, would like children, and her biological clock ticks.

I understand now the frustration, rather than the joy, I hear in Marieve's voice when she mentions getting married. She has cast her lot with a guy who isn't delivering, but dumping him and finding another prospect is fraught with problems. Besides, maybe she loves the guy, and love is hard to toss aside.

"When Marieve tells you she's getting married, she's asking for money," Renee adds. "She would like to get money to build their house so she can get married, but in Haiti it's the man's job to build the house, not the woman's. Marieve has been fishing for money for a long time, but we don't condone it. Her fiancé should provide."

My happiness that Marieve is getting married turns to disappointment about her bind. She is a wonderful woman and would be an awesome mother, but if her only avenue to that scenario is to marry a slacker, it could cost her much more than the price of a house.

On Monday I inspect the concrete poured during the storm. The finish is a bit rough but on the whole not too bad. We move right on to the second floor, another marathon pour that will take at least a day and a night and another day. We must be finished by Thursday. By now I know the drill. We spend Monday finishing the remaining formwork and rebar. We begin placing concrete Tuesday morning and will pour concrete for a long time.

It's 4:00 a.m. on Wednesday, the last of my concrete nights. As I survey the site, my feelings are simultaneously familiar and unique. Everything is as beautiful as the last time I walked the MoHI site during this hour, with bouquets of stars and a full moon. I crashed about ten and slept five solid hours. Now Fanes is on the mattress tucked into Renee's office. The crew slogs on, weary but resolute. They're surprised I'm still here. I like to think my presence provides motivation, but realistically their chanting and bottles of Toro do more to propel buckets through the dark.

We're going to complete the work, I can feel it, despite the particular challenges of Isaac, civic demonstrations, and power outages. We'll finish all the concrete before shutting down the jobsite when Lex and Renee leave to raise money in the United States. They need to bring back a bundle. The money from A Heart for Children is gone; MoHI is working off of bridge funding from an anonymous donor who prefers to channel the money through me. At least, that's my story. I doubt they believe it, but Lex and Renee play along with my charade. Money changes things between people, and I don't want my money to change anything between the three of us. In theory it's a no-interest loan to be paid back within a year. In reality I subscribe to Polonius's advice to Hamlet, neither a borrower nor a lender be; I don't count on ever seeing that money again.

I knew within minutes of learning about MoHI's shortfall to finish the school's structure that I would fund the gap, but it took a few days for my head to rationalize it. Fifty thousand dollars is not insignificant to me, more than half a year's salary, but I had it, and they needed it, and I suppose it's not really giving unless it hurts. If my retirement turns out to be a bit less luxurious, at least Haiti has given me an appreciation for the simple life.

The biggest thorn for me in giving money to MoHI is their Christian base. The more I live among evangelicals, the more I parry line and verse with them, the more bizarre I find their beliefs. Their interpretation of the Bible seems arbitrary. What I appreci-

ate about the Good Book is its contradictions; it defies unequiv-
ocal reading. But evangelicals impose order to mask ambiguity.
They're hierarchical and authoritative; they discourage discussion,
dissension, question, or curiosity. They remind me, sadly, of my
own traditional Catholic upbringing. Writing a check, a big one,
to an evangelical church group claws at my throat. But Haiti demands that we cross comfort lines.

Eventually, harkening back to my Catholic upbringing is how
I rationalize my decision. I was a round-faced six-year-old in a
green blazer with a gold emblem on the breast, a first-grader at
Saint Joseph's School in Toms River, New Jersey. I marched to
class each day and sat at my desk among sixty other children,
silent as a mouse, digesting what the scary-looking sisters dictat-
ed from wimpled-pinched faces. I spent three years in Catholic
school, three years of regimentation and subjugation. Those years
seem so remote from my adult self, yet they provided the roots of
my self-discipline and intellectual thirst. Catholic school taught me
rigor, rigor I have witnessed in classes at MoHI, rigor that Haiti
desperately needs.

Religious devotion is inversely proportional to intellectual curiosity. People of strong religion find their answers in their creed.
Christianity, especially of the fundamentalist persuasion, is a sim-
plistic way of viewing the world. It contains clear rules. It's easier
to navigate than one that weighs and balances every moral and
ethical dilemma. Although my Catholic education spurned independent thinking, it provided the analytical base that allowed my
independence to flourish. If that timid little boy in a green blazer
could survive Sister Katherine Andre and evolve into a person
with a broad and confident worldview, can't the little boys and
girls I see scampering around MoHI do the same? They live in
a chaotic world without prospects or expectations. They need
structure to ground them and rigor to challenge them. Many—
most—will grow into upstanding Christians, which, if they avoid
self-righteousness, is not so bad. But some, the brightest ones, will
use that structure as a springboard to transcend MoHI's doctrine
and become independent thinkers in their own right. It's a thrill-
ing, subversive idea. Catholic schools taught me the tools to escape Catholicism. I'm investing in MoHI with the hope that these
children will escape their narrow religion as well.

Since I wrote that check I've wondered how this trip to Haiti would be different than the others. We pretend the money is anonymous, but I know I'm responsible for everything going on here in a profoundly different way. It's gratifying to have work crews execute your vision in three dimensions, but being the patron of that vision satisfies at a higher level. A five with four zeroes was just a number on a spreadsheet subtracted from my retirement account. Now that number has become 160 cubic yards of concrete, a roof for eight classrooms, and two weeks' wages for hundreds of workers. That number trickles through Grand Goave, feeding and clothing its citizens in streams I will never follow. Though it is not an expenditure I can repeat, I consider it money well spent.

It's hard to believe that three months ago I had no idea where my favorite independent thinker, Jenison, was in this world. Suddenly he's everywhere. The more places he pops up the more Dickensian his story becomes, and I struggle to figure out how to be the best possible Mr. Brownlow to my deserving, twisted little Oliver.

One afternoon a young boy presents himself as I walk up the hill. He asks if I am the *blan* who loves Jenison. When I confirm he launches into a complicated story I cannot follow. I try to coax him up to Be Like Brit so Gama can interpret, but the boy, Jerry, is hesitant. Instead we retreat to MoHI where Renee translates his story. It turns out Jerry is Jenison's half-brother—same mother, deceased; different fathers, both deceased. They stay with their uncle, Pierre Richard, who works for Lex at the block factory. This makes five places that I know of where Jenison has lived in the past year. At my request Renee translates that we will speak to their uncle about sending Jenison and Jerry to school, but after the boy leaves she suggests that it may not be wise to tell a child your plans; so many things are misinterpreted. Better reveal only what comes to pass. Renee reprimands with such grace I thank her for it.

On my walk back to BLB, Jerry runs across the highway with Jenison in tow. My friend is ratty and rail thin. He gives me a detached stare as I pull his bony shoulder under my elbow. There is no longer anything endearing about this man-child long past cute. I recall those moments far along in a marriage when we look at our partner and wonder who is this person to whom we've devoted so much energy and affection, but we shoulder on because it's the right thing to do. We trust that the root of our love will thrive again. I cannot abandon Jenison just because he's grown awkward.

The next day a different boy approaches with unsolicited news. Jenison is not well; he is crazy in the head, *fou*. His report offers nothing reliable about Jenison, except I understand the streets are buzzing about this *blan* soft on a street kid. The boy tracks me all the way to MoHI—he wants money for his intelligence—but I step ahead and ignore him.

The politics of social welfare in Grand Goave demand that Lex dip his finger into the mess. When I suggest that Gama is happy to look into Jenison's plight, Lex shakes his head: *No, I will do it.* Lex's commitments are many, and he is no fan of Jenison, so I suspect little will be done.

The morning we begin the final concrete pour is also the morning the Sri Lankans run a clinic at MoHI. Sri Lanka supplies the UN peacekeepers for this part of Haiti; we are fortunate to have such humane soldiers that run regular clinics. On a break from monitoring construction I wander into the church shed where hundreds of women and children are being assessed and treated by uniformed medics. Serendipitously, the boy in the dental chair is Jenison. The translator explains that he needs two teeth pulled, but the dentist requires parental permission. I explain that Jenison has no parents but lives with his uncle. They tell me his uncle can give permission, and imply that an okay from any adult will do. I don't feel I should authorize getting Jenison's teeth yanked. I find Renee, who directs Fanes to find Pierre Richard. I tell Jenison to wait at the clinic while we get his uncle, which of course spooks the boy, and by the time Pierre Richard arrives the rascal is gone. Frail and simple Pierre Richard seems bothered by my question. *Pull the boy's teeth if that is what he needs.* Jerry, who I'm learning is quite mature, coaxes Jenison back. Jenison's visibly afraid of having his teeth pulled, so I lead him to the dental chair and hold his hand while he gets a shot of anesthesia and two rotten brown teeth removed.

I never wanted more than the two children I have, but parental feelings stir within me as the uniformed dentist from the other side of the world leans over this little black boy and inserts a dental

plier. Jenison does not move. He barely breathes. After he spits
blood into a bucket sitting on the gravel the dentist packs his
wound with gauze and tells me to keep his mouth shut for forty
minutes. *Fat chance,* I think. He hands me a script; Jenison and I
queue at the pharmacy table where another soldier makes careful
little packets of amoxicillin and aspirin; two tablets three times
a day. Another wishful gesture. Where is a boy with no pockets
going to keep pills?

I usher Jenison and Jerry into MoHI's office. I try to distract
them for forty minutes. I take down the map of the world and
show them Haiti and Boston. We count in English and Creole. Jenison takes sips of water. He tells me he has to go to the bathroom,
which I know is an excuse to escape and spit out his gauze. I managed a solid half an hour of silence from him, so I let him go.

Fanes comes in and tells me Jenison is no good, a street kid. I
tell him I know Jenison is a street kid, but he's still a human. I find
little to like in Fanes, yet I must acknowledge the man's a straight
shooter. Haiti is full of riff-raff, and Fanes doesn't yield an inch
to any of them. In that respect, he is more ideologically consistent than either Lex or Len. Though I never explicitly ask either of
them to help with Jenison, Lex already declared that Jenison cannot attend the MoHI School, and Len excluded my orphan ward
from consideration to live at Be Like Brit. They both sing the same
refrain of having to ensure the harmony of the entire institution,
but in reality, a kid with Jenison's troubles doesn't fit their agenda. He is not young, cute, or compliant. I only hope that over the
next few months neither Lex nor Len posit the question they have
asked in the past: *What can I do to repay you?* I have never asked
for anything but now that I want to take care of this kid, their
peremptory rejection stings.

When the boys return, Jenison's gauze gone, I tack the map
back up on the wall. As I reach down to find a pushpin, a familiar
hand gives me one, and I am transported back to the day I met
my friend on my first trip to Haiti after the earthquake. My hand
shakes as I push the sharp point into the dense wall; how hard his
life has been in the intervening two years, while mine has been so
easy, so rich.

Jenison insists on carrying my backpack as we climb the mountain to visit Michelle. I take it back when the terrain grows steep

and the anesthesia makes him shaky. Michelle tries to explain how Jenison is *fou*. I realize that in the United States, Jenison would be tossed on Ritalin in a heartbeat, but that doesn't mean he's crazy. We continue to Be Like Brit, where Gama gets each boy a large plate of rice and chicken and a Fanta. I would never have thought of getting the boys a soda, and even though the carbonated sugar cannot be good for Jenison's exposed gum, I appreciate Gama's knowing touch. Once again I wish I could be a little more like him. Jenison takes his first round of medicine, and we debate what to do with the rest. Eventually we decide that I will keep the pills. Gama tells Jenison and Jerry, in authoritative Creole that they must come to MoHI tonight to get the medicine.

On my final morning, after all the concrete is poured at Mission of Hope, I set up the curing tarps and direct the water boy to keep everything wet. Then I spend the rest of the day at BLB detailing the metal spiral stair, laying out medical equipment in the clinic exam rooms, and making sure Jenison gets his medicine. On my way back down the hill I run into Lex who exclaims, *We did it!* It takes me an instant to register what he's talking about because my mind has already moved on.

Architectural design is a process that begins with grand concepts and evolves into tedious minutiae. It's not always linear, architects often circle back to ensure that the part and the whole work together, but in general we work from the global to the specific. A $300 million hospital that takes three years to design starts with an analysis of potential building forms in relationship to topography and highways, prevailing winds and solar angles, until we whittle down with increasing detail and draw in fractional inches sealant joints at the wall flashing and handrail profiles that thousands of fingers will grasp over the building's lifetime. The work of completing construction documents involves hundreds of ever more detailed tasks until, all of a sudden, every item on the list is crossed off. All of our analysis and coordination are translated into piles of ink on paper or a digital disc. The inspiration ends with a whimper. I need time, and a few beers, to gain perspective on the achievement.

Lex's enthusiastic, *We did it!* reflects the construction equivalent of working through all the details at Mission of Hope. The second-floor slab is complete, forty-seven hours straight of sand and stone, cement and water by guys with buckets. Phase One of Mission of Hope's new school is fully built. In the United States completing the structure represents only 20 to 30 percent of construction; our internal systems and finishes are elaborate. But here completing the structure means we are in the final stretch. There is more to be done—the electrical conduit, plumbing and plaster—but they will come together in a typically messy Haitian way, in and around people using the building. The cooking ladies have already taken over the kitchen; it won't be long before others squat in the solid but unfinished structure.

Next month I can help to remove the forms after the concrete is strong. I can assist in pouring the ground-floor slabs, trench the drains, and install windows and doors as time and money allow, but I am no longer necessary. Lex and his guys have done that construction before, albeit on a smaller scale. My unique offering, the stuff they could not do without me, is finished. In time the satisfaction will sink in, but right now the grandeur of our feat eludes me. I appreciate Lex's exuberance, but I'm still awash in all the little attentions I've paid to this building over the past eighteen months as we took our big idea and made it real, right down to laying the last burlap curing tarp in place.

It's Thursday evening in the construction shanty, my last night this trip. There's a cosmic electrical dysfunction occurring throughout Grand Goave. For the past twenty-four hours we've had power at both Mirlitone and BLB but no lights, a typically Haitian triumph of magic over technology. As dusk settles into night, computer screens provide our sole illumination.

Gama is writing the daily report; I help him spell words like "entire." His vocabulary gets more ambitious all the time.

Jenison and Jerry perch on the cooler. We relegate loitering children there when we need to work. To my surprise, Jenison has shown up every morning, noon, and night since his teeth were pulled. He took his last pills tonight. Maybe he's been in pain; maybe he simply wants the food I provide with each dose, but with each visit the boys stay longer. Earlier they drew houses, a square base with a triangle roof and a rectangle door in the middle, exactly how kids draw houses in America, although Haitian houses look nothing like that. Now they simply watch us and giggle in the dark. They know I'm leaving tomorrow; their three squares will be less dependable. They don't have anywhere else to go, but I fancy they like it here. I like having them here.

I'm sitting next to Gilbert, a young BLB worker rich in potential. I first met Gilbert at the crew meeting before the concrete roof pour back in July when a quiet voice came from behind and translated Gama's words into my ear. When Gama was finished I turned to find a shiny young man I'd never seen before. Like everyone here, the earthquake changed Gilbert's fate. He speaks impeccable English and French, had some university training and an office position in Port-au-Prince, but returned to Grand Goave when no one was left standing to care for his aging mother. Family runs thick here. Two years later he found his way to BLB and demonstrated abilities beyond a standard laborer. Now Gilbert is Gama's clerk; he tracks each worker by trade, task, and location, providing the necessary data to measure productivity and generate payroll. Every day Gilbert draws a lined chart. I asked him if he would like to learn how to use a computer to avoid a fresh sheet every day. He leapt at the opportunity; tonight's our first lesson.

Gilbert proves a model student. He is already familiar with a keyboard. Still, explaining rudimentary concepts like *document*, *file*, *row*, and *cell* proves a challenge; computer basics that are second nature to me are utterly foreign to him. We use one of his hand-drawn charts to create a facsimile of his daily work. He's good at data entry; I show him how to copy and edit. The waning twilight outlines the hill rising beyond our shanty. Jenison flashes me a smile. I'm thankful the void from his yanked teeth is in the back.

Night falls; our eyes strain in the monitors' glow. Gama finishes his report, I teach Gilbert the *save* command, and Jenison and Jerry run off down the road. When we step outside a silver dollar full moon floats over the mountain, and pixilated stars span the galaxy; the billions upon billions of rewards we receive for living in a land of dark nights. "Do you see the same moon in Boston that we see here?" I'm startled by Gilbert's question, perplexed by a well-educated Haitian's knowledge gaps yet enchanted by his childlike query.

I take his hand in mine and hold it in front of his face, seeking an answer that will address both his quest for comprehension as well as connection. I wrap his fingers into a fist. "You are the earth." I lift my hands away and make my own right- and left-handed fists. "Here is the moon; here is the sun." I rotate my hands to demonstrate the interplay of sun, earth, and moon. "We all see the same moon, but how much we see depends on how sunlight strikes the moon's surface and reflects it back to earth." I explain how three spherical bodies, one rotating around another and another, create geometries that produce a full moon only once a month. Half-moons and slivers form as the angles change, and the moon disappears completely when the sun offers nothing to reflect.

I'm not an astronomer, but I get the gist. Gilbert seems satisfied with the essential information. This guy is hungry for more than Grand Goave can offer. If we had lights, if I could remain another day, he would gobble up more computer lessons, and more stories of the moon. But we are in the dark, and I must be gone. So I promise more lessons before the moon cycles through and displays itself full again.

Reentry to the United States is always hard for me, much harder than returning to Haiti. I am baffled by our hurried brusqueness, yet I'm instantly hurried and brusque myself. On Saturday I find a wonderful little book, *The Moon Seems to Change*, at the Harvard Coop. It's aimed at five-to-nine-year-olds, but offers the right level of graphics and description to give Gilbert a better idea why the moon comes and goes. I dine out with a friend, enjoy a lavish dessert that satisfies my sweet tooth as no Haitian food ever can. We attend the premier of *Marie Antoinette* at the American Repertory Theater, a scathing comic diatribe of social foibles.

We walk out of the theater into the gentle September night, and I stop short. I begin to cry. My friend thinks perhaps I've gone *fou*. Nothing so dramatic is happening. It's just the moon. My breath stops, my tears fall. The glorious orb hangs over Harvard's steeples in full splendor, the same moon that's shining on Grand Goave's shacks, linking our disparate worlds.

Plaster

September–October 2012

Jenison and Jerry hang out at Be Like Brit all the time now. They show up around ten in the morning; I tell the gate guard to keep them outside until lunch, but they usually manage to finagle their way in by eleven. Once on site, they make drawings and play with the water bubbler in the construction shanty while I try to do my own work. At noon we all eat; I pay Gama to make sure they each get at least one meal a day. Jerry's capacity is enormous; the boy inhales his huge plate of food and finishes up my leftovers as well. One day they raid the snack table before lunch when I'm not paying attention. Later, they cannot finish their meal. Their eyes glaze in confusion at the food that will not fit in their stomachs. Having more than they need, perhaps for the first time, is unsettling.

After lunch the three of us usually go to a quiet place and practice Creole. They howl at my pronunciation. They contort their mouths and exaggerate the guttural sounds they want me to mimic, and then laugh at the sounds I actually make. Jenison sings and I dance; I sing and he dances. He's much better than me; his bones turn into fluid curves. Jerry refuses to dance but is a great singer. Turns out we all know "We Are the World." It's corny but fitting.

After our lunch break, we always walk down to MoHI to see the progress of the work. They latch their arms around my waist. Jenison carries my camera. He snaps random images of the road, and the sky and snapshots of me. Everyone on the hill stares at us. Wizened Haitian faces scowl at such undeserving youth landing this plumb connection: meals and crayons and dancing, even rumors that I will send them to school. I'm uncomfortable with this display of favoritism, but it is only human nature that Jenison flaunts his elevated station; just last month these same people denigrated him as a street orphan.

Lex and Renee are in the States on their annual fund-raising swing. Huguener is overseeing the MoHI work, removing forms and plastering the classroom ceilings. I visit daily, but nothing requires much supervision.

One afternoon, Huguener informs me that he's found a school in town that will accept Jenison and Jerry for the fall. Huguener, and I are scheduled to visit the director and teachers on Friday. For the first time I believe they understand the game plan. They declare that they want to go to school. They shout *I love you!* at an embarrassing volume. They even differentiate between *Mwen re-men*, the pedestrian Creole that covers the full gamut of affection, and *Je t'aime*, the French, with its deeper meaning.

We usually finish our work at MoHI by 3:00 p.m., including time to splash at the water spigot, run up and over the school's stair, and hop over the picnic tables. Time for me to return to BLB. I give them a hug and they scramble across Route 2. I trudge back up the hill, content in the anticipation that I will see them again the next day.

One of their favorite pastimes in the construction shanty is to draw. Jerry is Joan Miro, fantastic forms all jumbled on the same plane. Jenison is more Grant Wood, archetypical shapes with precise draftsmanship. One morning, Jenison writes BLB in bold letters across the top of his universal house. I figure he knows the alphabet, so I ask him to sign his work. His quizzical look tells me I've assumed too much; he does not know how to write. Jerry comes to his aid and directs his brother letter by letter. D-I-E-U-N-I-S-O-N. "What is that?" I ask. "That's his name, Dieunison," Jerry replies.

I stare at the word. No matter how deep I get here, I will never know Haiti, where accepted truths turn to illusion in an instant. I have known this boy more than two years, grown attached to him, yet I never even knew his actual name.

Dieunison. Son of God. If this rascal is the son of god, the world is in for one heck of a second coming.

One afternoon after leaving the boys, as I ascend the road back to work at BLB, a pitch black baby wrapped in a white sheet lies in the alley where her mother used to moan. Now that her baby is born the mother is more social; she smiles at me as I pass and allows other women to share her breeze. Neighborhood children peek under the newborn's wrap and tickle her. The little girl has an incongruous, prophetic name: Sandy.

Now that the base building at Be Like Brit is complete, construction activity shoots off in a dozen simultaneous directions. Workers are in every room installing rough plaster, finish plaster, floors, tile, doors, hardware, outlets, sinks, bunk beds, and wardrobes. Everywhere there is painting, painting, painting. Instead of eighty men focused on a single objective—our next concrete pour—we are fifty men scattered across the site doing disparate tasks. We've gone from singing close harmony to wild cacophony. It's harder to manage, so I adopt my usual response to any problem and develop a spreadsheet that Gama and I can use to monitor the status of each room's finish and make sure all work is in forward motion.

Similar complexities invade my personal life. I've been here long enough to know many people; even more people know me. After months of being an object of aloof respect, I am now, due to my support of Dieunison and Jerry, a fair target for anyone willing to plead his case. I am inundated with personal requests for aid. Social work is a vocation to which I am particularly ill suited.

On Thursday a trio of young men—Martel, Manaus, and Nicky—climbs the hill to see me. The recent high school graduates, who speak passable English, have found Louisiana State University School of International Development on the Internet and announce they want to go to college there. Will I help them get a scholarship? I spend an hour directing them toward more relevant concerns. I describe passports and visas; I show them websites that offer scholarships to deserving Haitians, and I focus on the TOEFL exam; their English is nowhere near college level.

They barely hear a word I say beyond the Haitian penchant to misinterpret *I will help you* as *I will give you*, despite the words *help* and *give* sounding as different in Creole (*ede, bay*) as they do in English. The boys are giddy, ready to pack their bags. Meanwhile

I print a dozen pages of sample TOEFL questions, tell them to answer as best they can and I will review their responses. Such work is of no interest to the scholars compared to dreaming of their American future. They tag after me the entire walk home. I lose patience with their begging, which merely inflates *give me one dollar* to *give me one scholarship*. I regret offering to help them in the first place and want to shout at them that the appropriate request for people without money in this world is *give me one job*.

I arrive at Mirlitone without the psychic boost I usually receive from my walk. There is no food. I shrug, recall my policy of taking what comes my way, and head upstairs when Angela appears and announces she has supper for me in her room. "What ever happened to serving meals under the chaconne?" She and I have had this ugly conversation before. Mirlitone rules are that all food is served and eaten under the chaconne to keep vermin out of the sleeping rooms. But Angela and Gama make exception for themselves. In the past, when few people were around, Angela asked Marieve to spread our meals on the veranda until I objected, citing animal concerns. Now I grasp her new tack, circumventing the animal issue by keeping the food in her room. "I don't mind getting food for you." Angela is always looking for ways to demonstrate service. Problem is, I don't want Angela to serve me; I don't want her to know whether I have seconds or if I eat all of my bread. I am not her husband. It is an irrational irritation, but nonetheless real. I hold my tongue as she hands me my plate, which I take to the chaconne and eat alone.

Friday morning I commandeer Francky and the mule for our ten o'clock meeting at Jerry and Dieunison's school. We fetch Huguener, who makes us late by demanding we drive to his house so he can change clothes; Huguener is a dandy. I like the feel of the Maranatha School—very clean, more spacious than MoHI, with big basins for hand washing and instructions for avoiding cholera. There's a small balcony with a single room up a flight of stairs, director Maxi's office. He is the antithesis of Lex. He commands the room by his silence, whispers when he does speak, and rarely looks me in the eye. A globe sits on a portion of his tiny desk; educational posters hang from his walls; books fill his shelf, so I decide I like him, as if my opinion matters. The children's teachers, Harry and Naomie, carry the conversational load. We discuss the boys' home life, school lunches, homework, expectations for attendance, and performance. The teachers offer to take the boys for after-school sessions since they have little home support. Everyone is proper; all business is fully complete when I finally bring up money. I brought $500 in cash with me this trip. The academic in me finds satisfaction that the first money I ever spend in Grand Goave is $203 for school tuition. When I think we're finished, Harry mentions that he and Naomie would like consideration for the extra work they will be doing. It takes me a moment to digest his meaning. Fifty dollars a month for each boy, he replies quickly when I ask how much, the math being well settled in his head. I am swift at math myself and realize that paying the teachers under the table for a year runs many times the cost of tuition. I agree to the borderline bribe, but I up the ante. "These boys are going to be difficult. I am happy to pay you every month for your extra effort, but only as long as they demonstrate real progress."

I spend the afternoon teaching the computer to Gilbert and Pantyack, another worker keen to learn. We make spreadsheets to monitor inventory of paint and tile. The idea that a specific cell contains only certain information is difficult; showing them how to make equations is torture. I strive to be patient but would rather just do it myself. Pantyack also dreams of going to college in America, so I share my newfound expertise on TOEFL exams and scholarships. While checking construction progress, Leoness, one of my favorite workers, asks if I can send his five children to school. I am sure Leoness's need is real, that his children are likely more deserving than the two rascals I've taken under my wing. Perhaps I could affect more good here if I just stayed in Boston, worked full-time again, and forwarded my salary. I could send fifty, maybe seventy children to school. But I am not so selfless; I decline Leoness's request.

I leave BLB piqued by so many outstretched palms. I walk home at a quick clip with a deliberate scowl, yet it seems every person along the road approaches me. Children want their pictures taken, kite-flying boys each want one dollar, an old man asks for food, the three scholars shuffle after me with questions, and MoHI's shapely housekeeper sashays for favors. I avert my eyes from every comer, but they do not stop. I want nothing more than to be left alone, but on Friday evening along Route 2 a *blan* with a reputation for helping street kids is a magnet.

I reach the thickest cluster of people. A leering man gestures me into his *tap-tap*. I step into the road to deflect his overture. As I shift back to the shoulder another man comes toward me, a solid guy with an oblong face. He grabs my wrist and pulls me to his *moto*. He holds my forearm and pinches my muscle into my ulna to show he means business, though not enough to bruise. I am shocked rather than afraid. I was mugged once, in Brooklyn back in the 1980s, before Brooklyn went artisanal. When the street thug stuck his knife in my back, indignation trumped fear, and I turned belligerent. Thirty years later the exact same sensation fills me. *Let go of me!* I scream. Time stops. Each moment is a minute, an hour. I am hyper-aware, simultaneously registering my surroundings from every angle. The man keeps pulling. He does not let go. Dozens of black faces surround me, none that I know. *Let go of me! Let go of me!* My eyes rivet on the man clenching my arm. I am in danger of being robbed or worse, abducted, but my mind refuses to focus on the immediate threat. It zooms away from this danger, like an aerial camera over Grand Goave. I see the bread seller clamoring for gourdes, the little girl begging for a photo, the hungry old man, Edna flaunting her breasts, Manaus fishing for scholarships, Job begging for water, his mother shaking her hips at me, Pantyack's spreadsheet, the tile boss, the masons, the carpenters, the painters, Francky, Len, Gama, Angela, Huguener, Dieunison, Jerry, Harry, Naomie, even the distinguished director Maxi. *Let go of me!* My voice is low and firm, determined. I do not scream. We trace a circle, he drawing me close to his *moto*, me pulling the broadest arc of resistance. This place is tugging me in every direction. I cannot breathe, I cannot think, I cannot find the space to be me.

Finally a man steps out of the crowd and forces the attacker to release his grip. I don't know if the *moto* man was determined or *fou* or toying with me. No one would get away with absconding Lex's regular volunteer along Grand Goave's main street in broad daylight; he would be found out, tortured, maybe burned. But I do not suffer his violence lightly. I stand my ground; I sneer at the assembled crowd. Time resumes its inevitable march. I renounce him with a cold stare and continue over the river.

My arm tingles for twenty or thirty minutes; I'm not hurt, but the pressure of his grip persists. I take the narrowest path home so I will encounter the fewest people. I already have more faces than I can handle rattling in my head. When I reach the isolated stretch between the shacks and the sea my cloudy mind begins to clear. Then I worry about what lies ahead. If my supper is cloistered behind Angela's door again I am in no state to resolve the issue in a polite way.

I close Mirlitone's gate behind me, look toward the buffet table under the chaconne and make out the profile of a food basket. Marieve has put out at least some food in the chaconne, where it belongs. I sit down and eat, happy for this modicum of control. Marieve sits in a rocking chair on the edge of the space and listens to gospel music. Theo sits on the steps and munches boiled potatoes and plantains. They do not intrude into the cocoon I spin around me. The food is a tonic simply because I get to choose it myself and eat it in solitude. With so much of Grand Goave grabbing at me, I must nourish myself any way I can.

When my children were young, I loved parent-teacher conferences. Abby, Andy, and I would walk to their school together after dinner and sit at a low table with their teacher and aide on one side, their mother would join me on the other. Everyone praised our children's excellent progress. Our collective presence demonstrated how many adults cared for them.

That memory feeds my fantasy today: Gama, Huguener, and I, Pierre Richard, director Maxi, Naomie, and Harry all sitting in a circle with Dieunison and Jerry, explaining the benefits that school will offer them, encouraging them to excel, affirming our love and commitment to these boys. It's a warm tableau, yet I know it's an illusion. I do not know what will corrupt my vision, only that too many things can go wrong for such a saccharine scene to play out in reality.

I've been tenacious setting this up. I tell Gama I want him to attend; sending Huguener in his stead is not acceptable. We tell the boys to be at their uncle's house at 9:30 a.m. I badger Gama to leave BLB early. We get to MoHI, and I shadow Huguener until he joins us. The route to Pierre Richard's is a labyrinth of dirt road turns. A group of boys play soccer in a clearing, running and laughing, lithe and carefree. I wonder how we will entice Dieunison and Jerry to forego such tangible pleasures for something as abstract as a better future. Pierre Richard is waiting for us in a clean knit shirt, but where are the boys? He doesn't know. We call BLB and MoHI, Francky jumps in the mule to find them. We continue to their school for our 10:00 a.m. meeting; perhaps the boys are there. There's no sign of them when we arrive. The teachers are also absent. Director Maxi is present, taciturn as ever. Huguener and the director speak French in clipped, accusatory tones. Without four key players our meeting is a bust. Huguener calls Harry; he will be here in ten minutes. They lapse into Creole; at least now Pierre Richard can understand what is going on. I read only body language; it conveys none of the warmth I imagined. Harry shows up; Dieunison and Jerry never do. We review the adults' expectations, school start times, lunch, homework, standards of behavior. Pierre Richard appears to be more cooperative than I expected. Everything is settled, if we ignore the fact that the objects of our meeting have gone AWOL.

I tell Gama the boys get no lunch today; they need to suffer consequences for their action. He flashes a surprised smile and high-fives me when he realizes that *blan* does not equate with soft. The boys do not appear before lunch; sure sign of their guilt. Dieunison shows after noon. I meet him at the gate and escort him to the shanty, sit him on the cooler chest, and ask questions in a quiet tone. For a guy whose temper flames at minor infractions, I am very composed when the stakes are real. "Where were you supposed to be this morning?" Dieunison squirms. I name each adult who was present; Gilbert translates how much they want to help Dieunison, and how disappointing it is to us when he runs away. The boy's protests are feeble.

"Nothing is free. If you want lunch and drawings and taking photos and treats, then you have to do your part, which is going to school. If you do not go to school, you will not get the rest." I explain he will receive no lunch for two days and is banished from the site. The look on his face confirms he understands, but I make

Gilbert repeat it in Creole. I tell him we can resume on Friday. "If you behave we will get your supplies and uniforms and you can still start school on Monday. But you must uphold your part."

This is my first opportunity to put into practice at a microscopic scale my nascent theory of international development, that while it's important to assist the less fortunate, expectations must be set in return. Over the past decade two major theories have framed the discussion about the efficacy of international aid. Columbia University economist Jeffrey Sachs's *The End of Poverty* argues that the challenges of the Third World are so grave, an infusion of resources from wealthy nations is essential to jump-start development (he estimates 0.7 percent of wealthy nations' GNP would be an effective target). Robert Calderisi of the World Bank counters in *The Trouble with Africa* that pure economic development projects are the key to real progress. Guided by my own favorite maxim from Pearl S. Buck's *The Good Earth*, "when confronted with two options, I choose the third," as well as personal experience observing people's motivations, I don't believe either of these approaches is viable. I prefer a compromise position. Call it aid with strings.

Direct aid addresses immediate problems but creates expectations that thwart developing self-sufficiency. Haiti has more NGOs per person than any country on earth. They have helped Haiti to a degree, as evidenced by the rise in education and nutrition levels and the fall in infant mortality, but they foster a culture of dependency that undermines the work ethic. So many people here have been handed so many things for so long, they see no correlation between effort and reward.

However, I believe that any economic assistance that includes the word *loan* is a nonstarter. Lending money to countries with little or no ability to pay it back simply bankrupts them.

Aid with strings posits that no one receives anything without giving something in return, yet it does not presume repaying loans; what we demand in return need not be economically balanced. We give a child a meal; we require them to attend a lesson. We give a family a sack of rice in exchange for a bag of picked up trash. Ideally, the work provided in kind can be relevant, but even if it's not, we cement the fundamentals of a transactional world. Idealists may argue against such raw capitalism, but people cannot rise above subsistence until they understand and engage in trade. Haiti cannot shed its culture of dependency until Haitians accept the quid pro quo that drives the developed world.

Aid with strings would be difficult for Haitians, but it would be much, much more difficult for governments and aid organizations. When the United States tosses our extra rice and flour at Haiti, we reduce our surplus and undermine their local farming. If every sack of rice is tied to some measure that we monitor, weigh, and eventually make relevant enough to diminish the need for sacks of rice altogether, our aid policy would have to focus on pulling Haiti up rather than tossing our leftovers out. It would require more strategy and purpose on our part, with the objective of eliminating the aid business altogether as Haiti becomes a viable member of the world's economic community.

It's easy for Americans to give out fish; we have so many more than we need. But teaching Haiti how to fish requires a complete rethinking of aid's purpose. Right now, the US has no incentive to help Haiti stand on its own. We depend on Haiti for nothing and feel virtuous in giving the country what we want. This keeps Haiti in a state of perpetual need. If we redirect our focus from giving to training with the objective of enabling Haiti to stand on its own, we will need to invest many more resources, for it takes coordination and follow-up to tie a sack of rice to an expectation rather than simply throwing it off the back of a truck. And if we're successful, we will wind up creating a competitor. It's much easier to maintain a dependent than to do the right thing, so I suspect the US will continue to follow our established pattern, intervening from disaster to disaster, feeding our desire to be viewed as generous, while failing our neighbor.

I am motivated to test my ideas on my two beloved subjects. Dieunison and Jerry have demonstrated they can survive what Haiti throws at them. I'm offering them an opportunity for a greater stake in the world. Time will tell how well I do my part and whether they do theirs.

The first day the boys are banished from the site, I am also pulled away. Most people would be thrilled at the prospect of a day off and a $10,000 shopping spree. But when that day off is a trip to Port-au-Prince in an aging box truck and the shopping spree is for mattresses, paint, tile, stoves, propane bottles, two-by-twelves, fans, and water bubblers, enthusiasm wanes. I prepare by creating a comprehensive list with proposed target prices and exact quantities for every type of tile, paint color, and lumber size we need. I also bring an unread *New York Times Magazine*, a sketchpad, and my netbook for the inevitable downtime that is the hallmark of any Haitian excursion.

Gama and I get the crews on task at BLB and take to the road with Pastor Akine behind the wheel. We reach the mattress factory on the far side of Port-au-Prince before eleven. The factory owner speaks English, and they have what we need in stock. We negotiate a volume discount, and get the truck loaded. We snatch phenomenal street food for lunch and get to MSC Plus by noon. Like stateside superstores, MSC Plus has many people wandering around in shirts with company logos, but few employees who actually help. We cannot find a cart, though dozens sit in the corner filled with unshelved merchandise. I ask Gama to get an employee to empty one for us. He gives me a fearful look but reluctantly does my bidding. Over the next three hours Gama's calm, acquiescent nature melts into comatose passivity. We need dozens of things; many require assistance from the warehouse, yet he will not ask anyone to help. He wanders the aisles aimlessly. I take the task in hand. I study the list. Things that will fit in our cart are easy; I write down SKU numbers for what we have to order. We pace the tile aisle for over an hour; nothing the interior design group selected is available. Indecisive Gama and colorblind Paul are left to select thousands of dollars worth of tile. In the end his reticence is more stubborn than my visual defect, so I make the call—how wrong can we go with white?

By 3:00 p.m. we are through checkout. Our basket is full. One guy puts our paint on a pallet; another wheels out the stove. Pastor Akine brings the truck around, and we wedge our purchases between the mattresses. We drive to the loading dock for our tile and lumber. Gama says it will be awhile, so I take out my magazine. An hour later, an hour and a half later, we haven't moved. I am amazed at my patience, though it hardly matters whether I sit here or in the truck, I have given the day over to Port-au-Prince. The truck gets loaded around five. I remind Gama to check the receipt and make sure we have everything. We are the last customers of the day.

"We need to hurry, Pastor Akine is in a rush," Gama says as we turn into standstill five o'clock traffic. I did not plan to recount the shortcomings of our lackadaisical shopping spree, but Gama's comment is too comical to dismiss. Besides, if my job is to help Haitians understand what holds them back, that applies to management as well as labor. I explain that, if we needed to get through MSC Plus faster, Gama was the person capable of making that happen. "You speak both Creole and English; you are the customer spending thousands of dollars; you are the boss of the project." Gama protests, "But every guy says 'that is not my job,'" as if wanting to weasel out of his own job just now. "Then you go above them; you go to the manager or the service counter and tell them you want someone to complete your order right away. You are paying, you deserve service." Such aggressive action is inconceivable to Gama. He looks out the window and whispers, "You are right," his customary, conciliatory way of avoiding disagreement. Gama defers without analysis or conveying any interest in improvement.

Crawling through Port-au-Prince streets with the sun laser-beaming into our foreheads, I recall a story Gama told me from when he was living in Massachusetts and attending Wachusett Community College. In a discussion course students were asked to reveal character attributes they wanted to improve. "When they came to me, I said I am fine just the way I am." On first hearing, I was charmed by this man of certainty, but now, months later, I see how the story reflects Gama's lack of curiosity, his aversion to critical thinking, his inability to measure potential—as if identifying opportunities for improvement were akin to admitting defects.

It pains me to witness people here crumble in the face of new situations; Haitian bravado crinkles into thin skin at the slightest bluff. With the glaring exception of Lex, who thrives on what he does not know, Haitians are immobilized by anything unfamiliar. Masons refuse to start a row of block in the center, even though it's both easier and better; Dieunison feigns excitement about school, but when time comes to actually meet his teacher he flees; carpenters throw up hundreds of feet of staging around the building in a day, yet are baffled when asked to apply the same skills to a wood stud partition. People here do the same thing the same way every day, but in a land disinclined to analysis, they never consider how applying their actions in new ways could expand their skills. They remind me of the first grader who learns how to spell *cow* and *rat* but who doesn't understand that within those two words lie all the tools needed to spell *cat*.

Within his comfort zone at the BLB site, Gama possesses extraordinary insight. He understands it's easier to teach new methods to laborers than to bosses; laborers do not own a set of skills they must protect. Yet in Port-au-Prince, Gama retreats to being a typical Haitian boss. He sits in the shade for two hours, biding his time, hoping nothing will go wrong, rather than being a pro-active manager who makes sure things go right.

After two days the boys are back on site, and I'm enjoying our time together. Until I do something so stupid one might think this is my first trip here.

Our routine of lunch and snacks and drawing and games and walking down to MoHI has spun out of control. With Dieunison and Jerry in the shanty I hardly feel I can expel Franson, a docile favorite of Len's who loiters on site every day. At three to one I am seriously outnumbered. The snack table, which seemed bottomless given the Gengel penchant for junk food, is beginning to wear thin. The peanut butter crackers, Goldfish, and granola bars are all gone. Since I restrict the boys to two choices each, they avoid insignificant items like lollipops and Twizzlers. Today they make puzzling selections, Cup-a-Soup mix and a scoop of Gatorade, before settling into drawings cluttered with boats and Haitian flags, as if the last nation on earth to use dugout canoes is about to launch an armada.

When it comes time to walk down to MoHI I don't realize that Dieunison still has a Cup-a-Soup in his hand. Less than ten steps beyond the gate three other boys swarm us moaning *grangou* and angling for his food. In bringing the shanty's bounty onto the public road, I've created chaos. I gave the soup to Dieunison; I cannot very well take it back. But he just had a huge lunch, and I realize he's banking the soup in case dinner turns up short. Meanwhile his friends are hungry. I try to explain the virtue of sharing, but it's a hard concept for a ruffian, especially in a foreign tongue. I'm disgusted with myself for having such limited Creole after all this time and frustrated by Dieunison's selfishness, until I ask the other boys if they had lunch. Every one of them did. I am the one who's been duped. Telling a *blan* you're *grangou* is a ritual, same as *give me one dollar*, it has nothing to do with the actual condition of one's stomach. I give up negotiating the Cup-a-Soup and vow never to let a snack leave the shanty again.

The rest of the walk continues, downhill. The boys argue and push, giggle at my accent, and yank at my camera. Whatever love I have for two Haitians is sliced too thin to spread over six. By the time we arrive at MoHI to plan their shopping trip for school supplies with Huguener, we're all tired of each other. I don't complain when the boys escape across Route 2. I check construction at the school and chat with Huguener until they decide to return. The prospect of tomorrow's shopping rejuvenates them, and they buoyantly accompany me back up the hill.

We are only three on the return, there is no way to ever shake Franson, but Christlove and Mackinlove, the two boys who used to live at MoHI and now live with their mother in a two-room house that BLB volunteers built halfway up the hill, meet us at the BLB turnoff. Within a minute Mackinlove clips Dieunison with a stick, hard, on the back of the legs. Crying ensues. I storm toward Mackinlove, who crumbles onto the ground in tears before I'm even close enough to put a hand on him, which I'd never do anyway. I leave him there, turn, and stare up the hill. This is going to be one long climb. I have to do something—right now—to smooth the discord. I grab Jerry by one shoulder and Franson by the other. I teach them how to walk like Dorothy and the scarecrow, the tin man and the lion along the yellow brick road in *The Wizard of Oz*. We never get to the line "*lions and tigers and bears, oh, my!*" but as long as we chant *rive, gauche, rive, gauche* we long-leg it up the hill with both precision and hilarity.

Once the rhythm is set, my mind wanders back to Mackinlove, traipsing behind us, envious yet too wounded to join in. Mackinlove was the first child star of the Be Like Brit juggernaut, the cover boy of their fund-raising book. Eighteen months later he is past his peak; Christlove is cuter now, their cousin Job is also in many photos. Mackinlove has developed a wicked temper but no guts;

this is not the first time I've seen him act vicious and then wither the moment he's taken to task. He hit Dieunison out of jealousy for my favoritism. Dieunison's elevation diminishes Mackinlove, who knows nothing but violence to assuage his frustration.

The children that Len and I and other *blan* anoint here taste exhilaration. We stimulate but also agitate; we broaden their experience while rendering them discontent with what they have. Children who were so docile two years ago are now more energetic and curious but also more quarrelsome and attention seeking. In short, the presence of so many Americans has made these children more like Americans. Perhaps this is what Lex meant when he said, many months ago, "Wherever Paul goes, there is trouble." Wherever I go, I raise expectations, and like everything else in this world, that is both good and bad.

I remember those halcyon days of sitting around the main conference room at TRO JB's office, reviewing sketches of elaborate ironwork railings with curlicued *B*'s to ornament the orphanage. At the end stages of construction, all of that is fantasy. We have a budget crunch and a surplus of wood—over eight hundred sheets of cut-up plywood and hundreds of two-by-fours left over from all the concrete formwork. Despite a desire not to use wood in a country prone to rot, we are now using it to build the courtyard stairs, the secondary partitions, furniture, and guardrails. These elements won't last the life of the building, but they don't compromise its integrity and can be updated over time.

We have twenty-one guardrails around the courtyard's second floor, each ten feet, six inches long. Although we have a lot of wood, we don't have many pieces that long, and I want each top rail to be continuous. First thing I do is ask Williere, the furniture maker, how many two-by-fours we have that are long enough to create continuous handrails. "None" he replies. I doubt this, so we go find a few, and I design a guardrail with one long top and a series of shorter horizontal and vertical elements, plywood infill, and a trio of stars. It has design integrity, if not elegance, and can be built with what we have on hand. I review the drawing with Williere and mark it on the column face at full scale. When I return two hours later he's made a pretty good facsimile of the idea, using four long two-by-fours. Miraculous how a guy who said we had none this morning found plenty to save a few cuts. I explain that we have to save the longest pieces for top rails and cut shorter the pieces as I drew them or we will not have enough long two-by-fours to make every guardrail the same. He shoots me an inscrutable look, dubious of such advance planning.

Although I like to give the crews autonomy in how they work, I realize the only way to get this built the way I want is to become Williere's shadow. I spend three hours with him, measuring, cutting, nailing, making sure that the mock-up reflects not only what I want but materials we have available. This is a challenge because, as a furniture maker, Williere thinks of freestanding objects, but the guardrail has to be built incrementally out from the columns. He is a pleasant fellow, much brighter than most of the crew, who knows how to find the centerline of a board and, when I set a dimension on one side of the rail, understands its counterpart. Williere is skilled with a saw; his cuts are accurate. We work well together.

Considering that the materials in the guardrail have already been used three or four times, supported concrete for months and been exposed to Haiti's severe weather, it's a haggard piece of construction. But we'll prime and paint it up in a bright color and the children can peer through its stars. Maybe there is elaborate ironwork in the orphanage's future, but this will get us off to a safe and satisfactory start.

By the end of my second week, my social work caseload is trending in a positive direction. Manaus, one of the scholar trio, walks me home, sober in the reality that he has neither the knowledge base nor the registration fee to take the TOEFL exam. Our conversation is grounded in what he can do here and now to obtain a job. I suggest he call Len, who always needs good English speakers. Manaus is nervous about approaching Boss Len, an admission I take as a positive sign, since Haitians rarely reveal shortcomings or doubt. I encourage him to be confident, reminding him he has nothing to lose. The worst Len can do is say no, but there is a real chance Len will say maybe or even yes.

Angela comes off the veranda to eat with us in the chaconne. One evening she apologizes for the rants I hear through the walls in our close quarters. I tell her, "The stuff I am not supposed to hear, I pretend not to hear." Those few words soothe the friction between us. Angela and I are more alike than not, each struggling to fit in this land that is not an easy match for our personalities. She has it tougher than I do, without the release valve of two weeks in the States every month.

Computer sessions with Gilbert are often interrupted by other tasks, and configuring equations on spreadsheets is a particular challenge for him. But he's made amazing progress. We want the payroll computerized this week. I do the formatting but Gilbert inputs all the laborers' data himself. He does an excellent job, is justifiably proud, and payroll runs smooth.

I become more gracious in turning people away. I cannot meet every request nor would I even want to, but I look each person in the eye when I tell them *no*; I shake their hand and put my arm around their shoulder. I don't give them what they ask, but I try to give them respect.

Huguener takes Dieunison and Jerry to the Saturday market; I stay on site because everything would cost twice as much with a *blan* in tow. They arrive at the shanty after noon, each with a solid new backpack, a pair of school shoes, sneakers, four pairs of socks, underwear, belts, soap, toothpaste, even a mirror. Their uniforms will be ready this afternoon; school starts on Monday. They each give me a hug; Dieunison kisses my chest. The easy comradery that made us buddies is more complicated now that their good fortune flows from me, but I still feel genuine affection from these boys.

Gama and I tally up their expenses. My $500 is gone; I am already in arrears. My days of living in Haiti without money are over. I have responsibilities here now; next month I will bring more cash.

Len arrives on Sunday with Cherylann and a small entourage. The BLB group is staying on site for the first time; the apartment is finished with two bathrooms, a tiled kitchen, a stove, power, and running water. Williere built five tables out of leftover plywood. We arrange them in the upstairs community room overlooking the bay. We spend the afternoon discussing progress and determining next steps. Dinner is paté and passion fruit juice as we watch the sun set behind towering cumulus clouds.

We roll down the hill to Sunday evening service; Angela's voice rings out over all the others. A dozen of us pile into the back of the BLB pickup under a constellation-filled sky. Jerry appears out of nowhere; we strike knuckles and wish each other well on tomorrow's respective adventures. Nothing's better than the wind blowing sharp on my face as I clutch the sides of an open truck driving down Route 2 on a starry night. Haiti at its best.

I'm up at 5:00 a.m. on Monday. Traffic is heavy all the way to Port-au-Prince. Young girls in braided pigtails wearing white blouses, khaki skirts, and shiny leather shoes with lace anklets stand beside gaunt boys in collared shirts and fresh-pressed slacks fastened with oversize belts. They wait for buses to carry them to their first day of school—more schoolchildren than I've ever seen. A good sign for Haiti. Way back, beyond the image in my rearview mirror, I can only hope that two more young boys are brushed and shined and on their way to school as well.

Plumbing
October–November 2012

"It's times like this when Haiti deserves its position at the bottom rung of the world." The temporary bulb strung across the ceiling casts my body in a giant shadow that lurches across the floor as I pace the office that Gama and I now share in the new building. My temper ricochets off the walls. "How can adults just leave children to fend for themselves?"

Gama listens patiently, but I intuit he's keyed into my frustration. "You cannot understand how self-centered people are in this country until you live here and observe it, and even then, it is hard to accept." His quiet words of truth offer no comfort. Though I don't need comfort as much as those two boys sitting in the next room do. It's 8:00 p.m. on my first night back and they have no proper place to sleep tonight.

Despite my worry, Jerry and Dieunison have gone to school every day. Huguener and Gama kept tabs on them and they're making progress. They arrived at BLB about three this afternoon and announced their tutor was sick. We can't verify their claim; maybe they skipped out to see me again. In any event we celebrated my return by spending the afternoon together. They ate leftover spaghetti and made drawings. I created an intense collage of black lines; an unsettling Rorschach. I brought them new clothes; we carried them down the hill to drop at Pierre Richard's after visiting MoHI. Halfway down the boys pointed to a shack "*Pierre Richard habit la.*" I was confused. "Do you live there, too?" "*Non, nos habit calle granmere.*" As usual I understood enough to know that their

199

equilibrium was skew but not enough to fully grasp the detail.

We detoured to visit Michelle. She sat on a chair next to a man I didn't know, taking in the afternoon view. *Is Pierre Richard here? No. Do the boys live with him? No.* She was placid, seemingly unconcerned by the latest domestic upheaval, yet withholding. Michelle looked defeated, disengaged from the world on this perfect afternoon. Poverty had finally ground down the industrious carpenter I knew from our Samaritan's Purse days.

Dieunison, Jerry, and I didn't linger; I could get a full translation at MoHI. As we descended, the man called Jerry back. Dieunison and I continued on. In a few moments we heard the man upbraid Jerry, fierce and loud. Even my rudimentary knowledge of Creole could decipher that Jerry was being scolded to keep *blan* out of their business. The man galled me, yet another so-called adult claiming authority over these boys without taking any responsibility.

Renee untangled the tale. Pierre Richard broke up with his girlfriend and moved to a shack on the hill. The girlfriend remains at her house in town. The boys moved into their grandmother's place, where they share a room, but the grandmother is in Port-au-Prince. The girlfriend doesn't feed them; they get what they can from school and from Gama. I didn't like them living alone, but the boys appeared unconcerned. Destitution has sharpened Dieunison's wit. The Artful Dodger in him joked: *We have been living by ourselves forever!* Sadly, he spoke the truth.

By the time we sorted things out it was evening. I couldn't just let the boys disappear into the twilight, so we trudged with our bundle of clothes back up the hill, and they sat quiet while I finished MoHI's electrical conduit estimate. Fortunately, three other volunteers are staying in BLB's apartment so Len has a full-time cook who made all of us dinner, *diri et sus pwa* with grilled chicken. But the food did not satisfy.

Now I've finished my daily report and am venting my frustration to Gama, desperate for understanding. Intellectually I know that Haiti is full of kids their age turned out on the street, but when it comes to Dieunison and Jerry I cannot simply shrug off Haitian indifference; the whole lot of grown-ups who have abandoned them disgusts me.

Gama's words calm me, but my stomach still gnaws from stress and discomfort rather than from actual hunger. I retrieve two chocolate bars from my backpack, give one to Gama and split the other between Jerry and Dieunison. Giving the sweets away satisfies my craving better than consuming them myself. After our work is complete we pile into the pickup and drop the boys along Route 2. I hate leaving them to seek their empty house alone, though they don't seem to mind; especially since we promise them dinner again tomorrow night.

Clouds spread across the vast sky; they begin to spurt, and eventually the drizzle turns into the deluge that becomes Hurricane Sandy. At BLB we become a rare thing in Haiti—a family of men. The boys arrive every afternoon, at first around three—insisting that their tutor is still sick—then earlier when school lets out for the storm, then by lunch when the storm closes everything down. Alan, Dave, and Tom, the three plumbers installing fixtures at BLB, work right through the weather; Gilbert, who is now cook and translator in addition to computer expert and inventory guru, remains 24/7 as well. I never thought anyone could be as pleasant as Gama until I met Gilbert; they are mutually delightful. Gama and I stay on site from sunrise past sunset, busy with our work and surrogate parenting the boys. Francky and Toto are here as well because, well, they're just always around.

There is a rhythm to these rainy days: morning bread and coffee, work until noon, hot meal, work until five, shower and chat, dinner at six, then disperse to wherever we sleep; a rhythm quite foreign to Dieunison and Jerry. They spend most of their time in the kitchen. They do their homework and draw; I teach them table football, they teach us hip-hop steps. They are patient while we work and happy when we show them attention. Their manners at meals are improving; they have gained the assurance that comes with knowing there will be another meal after this one. Still Jerry finishes off everyone's leftovers; his capacity is remarkable. They pick up their plates without being asked and help me wash and dry the dishes. Alan and Dave each have only daughters; they relish the physical play of boys.

Sometimes I catch Jerry or Dieunison observing us as we go about our tasks; constantly recalculating what it means to be a man. They have never seen men act predictable and responsible. They have never seen a man cook, as Gilbert does, or clean the tables, as we all do. We spend a stormy week doing useful work with warm camaraderie and mutual respect. For my two young friends, this storm is a revelation.

Unfortunately, the storm does not have such positive consequences for others. Hurricane Sandy is on her third day of delivering heavy rain to Grand Goave. Unlike Isaac, who shuffled through his fierce gales and heavy rains in two days, Sandy's swirling clouds refuse to spin away. Perhaps she lingers to visit her tiny namesake at the bottom of our hill. Perhaps she wants us to reconsider the wisdom of constructing a building so heavy it cannot move when an arc might serve us better. Perhaps she wants to demonstrate the destructive power of the slow-moving tortoise over the quick-fleeing hare. Sandy has already done more damage than Isaac, and the skies show no sign of clearing.

This morning five people in Grand Goave died from Hurricane Sandy. A landslide down the mountain next to Be Like Brit buried a tent where a mother and her four children slept in one bed; smothered beneath the canvas and the mud. When Francky and Gilbert ran to the scene I considered joining but thought better of it. The few corpses I've seen in my sheltered life have all been neatly composed in coffins, this sight was sure to be grizzlier.

According to the World Bank, the average life expectancy for a baby born in Haiti in 2012 is 60.6 years, but that optimistic statistic doesn't jibe with anyone's experience here. Making it past sixty in Haiti is not the norm; it's a rare achievement. People who are thriving and vigorous one day are gone the next. Haitians mourn untimely deaths with loud flamboyance then quickly return to their daily rhythms. If people lingered in grief, grief here would be perpetual.

In the United States I might hear of a few people who die during the course of a year; most of them after a full life. On every monthly visit to Haiti I learn about someone who has died. Here's a representative list from 2012. I imagine anyone else in this fragile country could give a similar accounting.

Dieunison's mother died at the beginning of the year. She was reportedly a Voodoo priestess, as was her mother before her. I've never heard anyone mention her cause of death, though she could not have been very old.

In February an elderly woman was hit by a motorcycle near

MoHI's gate. Gama, who is a paramedic, rushed to the scene and delivered her to the hospital, but the woman did not survive.

In March, Gama's cousin died, a thirty-three-year-old woman with a husband and three children. She had a short, fatal illness though I never heard a diagnosis.

Marieve's cousin died in childbirth in April. She is survived by a husband, young son, and twin daughters, one of whom was born blind.

In May, Pepe's father-in-law died. He, at least, had a long life.

Three local youths died in a horrendous wreck when their small car was run into a ditch by an out-of-control truck in June. The truck's chassis ploughed right over the car, crushing and killing the boys on the spot.

In July, Lex's sister-in-law died at age forty-two.

August was a month when horror visited children. A six-year-old Hands and Feet orphan drowned in the Caribbean. After searching for hours, the matrons gave up when night fell. The girl's body was discovered the next day, her arms and legs were missing. The same month Kylene, a MoHI Sunday singer, lost her third baby. It was her fourth pregnancy. The baby was full term, yet born dead.

I hoped that September would break the pattern, but all kinds of odd disease flourished. Toto had a wound on his arm that blistered and needed treatment at the hospital; he missed three weeks of work. Ble, the painter, got a cut on his leg that festered into an ugly infection. He limped around the site for days with his pant leg rolled up so fresh air could help scab over the wound's oozing pus, but with so much plaster dust in the air his leg healed slowly. Fanes came down with a stomach bug, the front-end version of what plagued me but in a more severe form. He could not keep any food down, lost sixty pounds, and moved to Les Cayes where his family could care for him. Two days after I returned to the States, Fanes died. Was it dysentery? Worms? An evil curse? Whatever took this healthy man in his middle forties was likely something that could have been diagnosed and treated in any industrialized nation.

When I return this month a banner in the crew's lunch tent honors Boss Fanes, but in truth, I have not heard his name mentioned even once. Two weeks after his passing, life without Fanes is the new normal; everyone has moved on.

There is no time to grieve for Fanes or for the drowned girl or for Pepe's father-in-law, or for Dieunison's mother because today we have a new tragedy, five bodies lying together wrapped in a USAID tarp. Lex prays over them while a crowd of Haitians in ponchos and ripped garbage bags witnesses their passing before Hurricane Sandy even departs our shores.

At least half the people I know who died this year could have been saved by elementary public health measures—clean water, safe houses, vehicle inspections, maternity care, lifeguards. We take these things for granted in the United States and other developed countries. But for nine million Haitians, and a billion other people around the planet, these simple safeguards do not exist. So people continue to die from landslides and labor, dysentery and drowning, and as long as we allow these conditions to prevail for our fellow humans, our society is much less developed than we pretend.

If I were Elizabeth Gilbert and this were *Eat, Pray, Love*, by this late date in the narrative *amour* would have seeped into the plot, touched my heart, and delivered the deepest meaning to my search. Perhaps love would be exotic: a strong-shouldered, silent black man takes me into his arms, I yield completely to his island charms, and we build our own breezy, though sturdy, chaconne by the sea. Perhaps love would be redemptive: a tender young missionary from Ohio reveals the eternal truth of the man/woman bond, I lapse back to being straight, and we move to Cleveland to minister to the urban poor. Perhaps love would be reflexive: a fellow volunteer and I shack up after hard days of sweat and toil; we anchor Haiti to stable ground and then retire to his cabin in Oregon. But I am not Elizabeth Gilbert, and this narrative has no such tidy capitulation. I'm a crusty gay guy closing in on twenty years of being single, and I'm likely to remain that way. I have many good reasons to be in Haiti, but love has never been one of them. Still, I cannot stow my sexuality in a Miami airport locker while I am on Hispaniola; it is a perpetual carry-on that influences my life here.

You would think all the guys here are gay. Gama laughs and shakes his head about the workers holding hands. Gama does not like guys holding hands; Lex detests it. They have lived in the United States where men holding hands makes a statement. Whether provocative or sexual or political, it is never innocent. But I've come to enjoy the arm press of a calloused palm against mine. When a man takes my hand I accept; sometimes I even initiate the gesture. I appreciate the bond of fraternity it represents and have stopped worrying that the touch holds different meanings on each side of the grasp.

There is a guy at Be Like Brit who sets off my gaydar; he's definitely a member of the tribe. He is too suave, courtly toward women, crisp in his clothes, and inept at conjuring imaginary girlfriends to pass for a traditional Haitian male. We developed an instant camaraderie. Although we have Creole/English language barriers, our shared inclinations provide a language all our own. When we lunch together the conversation leaps beyond recitations of family trees and personal histories; our commonality allows us to express aspirations that transcend everyday life here.

I'm frustrated by not being fully myself with this fellow, not offering him a glimpse of the freedoms men like us enjoy in the United States, but I say nothing. I will not even reveal his name. For he has never been outside of Haiti, has never been to Port-au-Prince; his entire life will be spent in Grand Goave. He lives alone, a rare condition for a Haitian man. Other crew members accept his difference with unspoken *d'accord*. Still, he never takes another man's hand, and he's never offered his to me. Even as we intuit the bond between us, the bounds of Haitian society prohibit its physical expression. We limit ourselves to the satisfactions our mutual sensibility affords. My friend does not seem frustrated by his situation. Like most Haitians, he's disinclined toward self-analysis. He may not even realize he's gay. Haitians do not suffer Americans' penchant for giving everyone and everything a label or a diagnosis. People just *are*. Life here is too difficult to bother acknowledging personal differences with anything more than a shrug.

I lead a celibate life here, both in practice and in spirit. That might not prove satisfactory for years on end, but I enjoy the reprieve from being a gay American, a hyper-sexualized group within a hyper-sexualized culture. Haiti does not bombard me with beefcake and the corresponding insufficiency my middle-aged body feels in its reflection. This is not to imply that Haiti is Victorian. The shapely women and sculpted men in this torpid climate ooze sexuality, but their sexuality is so relentlessly hetero it barely registers on me. Every once in a while a pretty woman throws me a come-hither look so blatant that even I can interpret its meaning. I assume she is clueless or desperate or both.

Freed from the possibility of physical expression, I enjoy the opportunity to ponder love at a more meaningful level. When I signed on to come here regularly, I understood there would be both challenges and joys in working with Lex on a daily basis. I knew I loved him, as I have loved a handful of other men in my life. Not gay men, not realistic partners, but straight guys worshipped from a distance. I have a consistent history of filling my fantasies with unattainable objects, thereby confirming my own unworthiness for love. Not surprisingly, these are unsatisfying relationships. Actually, they're not relationships at all. But I knew that if I came here either my crush on Lex would crumble, or we would have to shape it into something more meaningful than arm's-length adoration. Which we have done. I have learned how to relax in his presence, to express my opinion, to ease off my pounding heart and occasionally tell a joke. We will never be fishing buddies; we don't have that much in common, and it will always be easier for me to have a casual chat with Renee. Sometimes Lex's stubborn insistence on things clearly impossible is so annoying I tune him out only to slip into the idle pleasure of simply gazing at his fine, fine face. But more often than not I am his balancing partner, and for me to carry that off with a guy who still yanks my heart is no small achievement.

I believe that loving someone is a blessing, and receiving his or her love in return is a miracle. I reason that a life of many blessings can be worthy, even if my miracle never occurs. I feel blessed to love Lex, even as I appreciate that Renee is his miracle. I am proud of myself for moving beyond dumbstruck idolatry; Lex and I have reached a place of mutual blessing; our connection is more complementary than I've ever achieved with a fantasy attraction. When Lex says, *Paul, we love you man*, which he still does from time to time, he understands that his words carry a deeper weight than he did when he first mouthed them over a year ago. And though I've never had the strength to say those same words back to him, perhaps someday I can.

Perhaps someday I will learn how to send and receive blessings from all sorts of directions, and one can never know when a miracle might result, for by definition miracles defy prediction or logical explanation. I'm aging, but I'm still too young to forfeit the possibility that there might be somebody out there, my miracle man, who will join in my adventures. Or better still, who might prove sufficient to bring my searching closer to home, someone to entice me to grow old together gracefully. I will not find him in Haiti, but Haiti has given me an opportunity to step back from the folly of my love life in America and move in a more fitting direction.

After we dry out from the hurricane we realize that returning Jerry and Dieunison to Pierre Richard is futile; the man is either incapable or unwilling to mind his nephews. The boys are too old to go to an orphanage yet too young to be on their own if we want them to avoid becoming street thugs. Lex and Renee have become more invested in this pair, in part due to my strong attachment but also because the boys show promise. Regular meals are a great civilizing force.

Every day, we float new schemes for how to care for them, numerous as soap bubbles and just as ephemeral. By Monday a tentative plan takes shape. Lex has a small two-room building near the block factory; it was intended as an administrative office but has never been used. Jerry and Dieunison can live in one room, and we will find an adult to live in the other, prepare their meals and do their laundry.

Lex decides to make improvements to the building and asks me to fund them. My wish to send these kids to school has ballooned beyond paying tuition to include uniforms and tutors, casual clothes, books, meals, and now beds, linens, cooks, and laundresses. I balk at paying for improvements to a house already far better than most in Haiti. Lex makes the improvements anyway; asking me for money was his easiest option, but the man always has some plan B.

Finding the right person to tend the boys proves difficult. The woman needs to be old enough to command respect, but most adult women have children of their own. We float a few options but nothing clicks until Huguener, who shares a house with other guys, offers to move in. In exchange for having his own room, he will look out for Dieunison and Jerry, and we will hire someone separate to handle meals and laundry.

Our goal is to move the boys in on Thursday, the day before I leave, though since we are still formulating our plan, we relay very little to them. All week Dieunison and Jerry enjoy Gilbert's cooking and the wonders of the snack cabinet. They spend hours doing their homework, drawing, and conniving mischief at BLB. My Friday departure looms. They show up at lunch on Thursday—no school on All Saints' Day. We plan to go to tutoring together, but Jerry climbs into the snack cabinet, fills his pockets and escapes; come tutoring time only Dieunison remains. Francky, Dieunison, and I drive the Mule all over town in search of the older brother, but Jerry's turned invisible. We deposit Dieunison at tutoring and drive back to BLB. It's dark by the time Gama and I wrap up the details of my last day, Skype with Len, and update the room-status spreadsheet; Jerry and Dieunison do not show for dinner.

"Do you mind if we look for the boys?" It's after 8:00 p.m., and I know Angela wants him home, but I take advantage of Gama's giving nature. We call Huguener. The three of us retrace the circuitous route to Pierre Richard's former house. The BLB truck barely fits between the narrow walls, right, left, right, until we emerge into an open space surrounded by shacks. The dark is ripe with movement; I hear people all around. A few cell phones cast thin shafts of light toward the ground, yet figures move with a nighttime ease I will never attain.

Huguener speaks with a young man, then a couple. He beckons me to follow along a path between two houses. We turn left against two walls, we squeeze around a tree trunk, I watch my step as the ground gives out under roots; we take a right between two more walls, shimmy sideways to a final turn, and then Huguener stops. "Here it is." He flips his cell phone to illuminate an opening between a pair of concrete block walls. "This is where the boys live."

I suspected that the boys' room at their grandmother's house might be lacking in amenities. I'd asked Gama whether they might have a bed or a chair; he thought not. I've seen enough shacks here to know that two boys living on their own would be in skimpy quarters, but what the cell light reveals is the absolute worst, flimsiest excuse for shelter I can imagine. It is not a room in a house. It is not a room at all; there is no house. It is a sty, a scrap of dirt no more than six feet by eight feet with walls on three sides and a tin roof so low even the boys cannot stand up straight within. There is not a sheet, not a blanket, nor any personal effect save the backpacks I got them for school. I picture them asleep in this hovel, the dirt caking to their hair, the grit working into their shorts, any animal free to shuttle in and peck at them. I am astonished how much effort it must take to present themselves every day after waking from this patch of soil; Jerry and Dieunison always smell fresh; their hair is always clean, and their skin always glistens. I am humbled by how they greet the day with such good spirits and never once fret about returning to this hovel each night.

We retreat. The boys are not there, and there is no reason to linger. I wonder how long Gama and Huguener are willing to pursue the search. Fortunately, Jerry appears. My pique at him for stealing sweets and skipping tutoring evaporates. I fault myself for doing nothing to prepare the boys for life after I leave; for all Jerry knows he may not have a sure meal until I return. He fetches Dieunison and the five of us huddle in the privacy of our F-150 king cab; anything I say in the open field would spread across town faster than a power line could transmit.

I tell them they will get a good meal every day while I'm gone. I tell them we will get someone to wash their clothes every weekend. I tell them that if they go to school, I will take care of the rest. Gama translates. I do not tell them they are moving; nothing is firm in Haiti until it's complete. After we're finished, we hug. We leave them to their neighborhood, to their lean-to, to the life they know and accept. I remind Gama and Huguener that they are not young children, that I want the idea of moving presented as an option, not a requirement. The boys will flee if they feel trapped; they've lived with nothing for so long, having nothing doesn't frighten them.

We have failed in our objective to get Jerry and Dieunison a secure and sanitary place to live before I leave. As I suspected, aid with strings is proving more difficult for the donor than the recipients, but before I return I will hound everyone from afar to accomplish our objective.

Paint

November–December 2012

When I get off the plane in PAP, instead of being directed downstairs to the shuttle and tin-roofed customs barn, I walk straight into the new terminal where an agent processes me quickly and directs me to a two-story baggage-claim area complete with stainless steel carousels. I welcome these new amenities as a symbol of closure. I have arrived at the new Haiti, and everything is looking up.

Well, maybe not everything.

The new terminal is immeasurably better than the old chaos; the gauntlet is gone and the main entrance connects to a large, well-ordered parking area. Still, I'm stuck behind a gussied up Haitian at customs. She paws through her immense purse, oblivious to others, until she finds her customs slip and presents it as ceremoniously as a god bestows a gift.

The boulevards of Port-au-Prince are spanking clean with uniformed women sweeping the gutters. Saplings have been planted in the medians. But Ricardo and I get stuck behind a vintage Toyota van kerplunking along on only three inflated tires.

We pass a soccer team practicing on a legitimate field complete with uniforms, coaches, and referees. The field just happens to abut a tent city.

Giant billboards stretch ever farther out Route 2. There are local signs for hotels and discos, restaurants, and construction materials, even a distillery in Leogane. The signposts also provide a convenient support for lean-to shacks.

The plaster finish at Mission of Hope School looks terrific; we hope to open in January. But we will do so without electricity;

MoHI has not been able to raise the funds to purchase panels, conduit, and light fixtures.

Electricity has arrived at Be Like Brit; the lines snake up and across the road. The security light at the main gate burns all night. Unfortunately the beacon obscures our starry nights.

Huguener is supervising a new project for Hands and Feet orphanage, and Gilbert generates spreadsheets as easily as he cooks up *legumes*. But Martel and Maneus prove to be lazy; they're fired from BLB and return to dreaming of America in the shade.

My breath comes up short every time I take in the majestic view from the orphanage. But I cannot enjoy my walks home; Grand Goave is too unsafe due to a protracted manifestation (the local euphemism for a riot) against the mayor. Every morning Route 2 is littered with lingering bonfires and trucks blocking the road.

Ble and Toto are back at work, their wounds well healed. But the monthly march of death continues; the protestors shoot a bus driver point blank, and one of Lex's teachers from St. Etienne goes missing. His body later shows up in a Port-au-Prince morgue.

The boys' tutor gives them each a positive report. Dieunison has developed beautiful cursive, which is how I learn that Jerry's name is actually spelled Dieurie. Still nearly every week Dieunison manages to create some new form of trouble and gets sent home from school.

Dieunison and Dieurie have moved into their house with Huguener. Syltan cooks a meal for them every day and does their laundry. My rascals have taken to treating her like a maid so I must scold their haughtiness.

Completion is in sight for both projects; Dieunison and Dieurie are hardly the same boys they were three months ago. But I'm exhausted and long for an extended period back home. Haiti has worn me down.

Every detail of Haiti seems precious this trip; I don't know when I will return. I witness the everyday rhythms with new vigor, from Mirlitone's star-filled nights to the humble sweeping Gama and I observe in the emerging dawn.

At 5:30 a.m. roosters are long past awake; dogs and pigs meander along the road as we drive to work. The few men with jobs are already up and gone, but folks with no agenda are just beginning to stir. Shadows pass in and out of shacks; dressing, splashing their faces with whatever water's left in last night's basin. The women of the house are the first ones about their chores, and the first chore is to sweep the front yard, the packed earth that connects the house to the street.

Haitian brooms are charming, if ineffective, pieces of folk craft. The pole is a sturdy branch about four feet long and an inch or so in diameter, tied off at one end with hundreds of narrow fronds, bunching out unruly as a cheerleader's pom-pom. Some women sweep only a narrow path from road to entrance; others clear a broad open plane that provides the inhabitants a full view of the passing world. Unless the weather is foul, the front yard is where the family dwells until nightfall; interior spaces are only used to escape storms and catch sleep. The day's opening ritual is to tidy up the parlor.

As we drive in the dim light women stand with their feet apart, sway their hips counter to the rhythm of their arms and sweep away whatever the wind cast down during the night. It's a trance-like motion without rhythmic variation; back and forth they shift across their property, half-sleeping forms of arms and torso, legs and broom, zombie-like movements long ago chiseled into motor memory.

For a year I've witnessed these women, yet every morning I am transfixed by their quiet, futile dance. They sweep dirt from dirt. They raise dust, push it away, and more dust rises in its place. Are they fools, scratching at Haiti's tenuous soil? Are they noble in their quest to create a place of hygiene and order in a land that defies either? Or are they trapped in a Sisyphean cycle of endless sweeping that will never achieve their desired objective of a clean world?

This dawn motion reveals contradictory human truths. We are creatures of habit, of pattern. We do what we know, not always because it's best for us, but because it gives us comfort. Sweeping dirt provides the illusion of making things neat. If we sweep every day, long enough and hard enough, we convince ourselves that our sweeping makes a difference. By sweeping their yards the women claim them; they own them in a more tactile way than any deed can bestow, just as anyone who cultivates a patch of land possesses it and becomes possessed by it.

Witnessing this useless exercise of sweeping dirt energizes me. It prods me to create enough hard surface here to ensure that people can eat and sleep and learn and play without mud packing their heels or spiders climbing their legs. I don't wish to replicate the brutal blacktop that smothers so much of our country. I simply want to help these women achieve a beneficial result for their effort.

The women stand upright. Their sweeping is a dignified act, an act of caring, an act that says, *I matter and my family matters.* But it is also an act of defiance, defiance against the trials of this land. Sweeping dirt denies the reality of natural disaster and physical deprivation; it ignores political instability and economic hardship; it rejects every calamity grinding down on these poor people. Sweeping dirt asserts that these women, like mothers the world over, will do everything in their power to create a sanctuary for their family. The will to improve our lot in this life is an elemental aspect of being human, even when our lot amounts to no more than a patch of dirt.

The order and clarity I absorb from these women in the wee hours of the morning reminds me of a similar quest for order I sought at this same hour of the day many years ago. In graduate school, being awake at 5:30 a.m. was the result of an all-nighter rather than an early rise. Fifteen of us drew and built models in a large room as our caffeine-spiked moods shifted from giddy to somber, ecstatic to moribund. During coffee and Coke breaks we debated architecture's grand truths: would we design renowned landmarks, or would we lend our hand to strengthen the fabric of great cities. We understood these to be different, sometimes opposing, callings. Great cities possess a collective form that transcends any particular structure, whereas signature buildings must be unique. Notoriety interrupts the prevailing order. Some of my peers emulated the rising starchitect Frank Gehry; I embraced incrementalist Giancarlo de Carlo as my mentor. But one thing we all agreed upon during those long nights was the rule of thirds, the ineffable truth that because architecture is an art burdened by the pesky realities of construction and function, not every endeavor will succeed.

One third of all buildings an architect designs will fall short. The confluence of a narrow-minded client, a poor site, and/or a skimpy budget will lead to failure despite his best efforts. One third will be wonderful; success occurs with only modest effort on the architect's part. The remaining third will teeter between success and failure; these are the projects where the architect's talent and energy influence the result. The best architects design each project as if it were in the last category; we like to think we make a difference. Yet every architect has designed some bad buildings, and we've all enjoyed successes out of proportion to our talent and effort.

My three projects in Haiti conform precisely to the rule of thirds. Forward in Health—remember them, the group that got me involved in Haiti—is an architectural disaster. After my fateful visit with Hal I was never invited back to Les Cayes. John and Paula Mulqueen eventually abandoned building with local tradesmen and contracted an American company to complete the clinic with a shotcrete (concrete-spraying) system. I coordinated layouts with the fabricators, but the project slipped away from me. Whenever John called I was quick to respond, but now I'm just another name on their mailing list. They underestimated the challenges of building in Haiti, and when those challenges grew more daunting after the earthquake they took a simpler route to meet their objective of creating clinic space. I hope the building meets their needs, but as architecture, the project is a failure.

Be Like Brit is notable despite its architect; Len wouldn't have it any other way. Building in Haiti is difficult, but the Gengels' motivation and resources blessed the orphanage with a better chance of success than most projects. The final building addresses all three of our objectives, though not equally well. It's a stunning tribute to Brit, it's provided an engrossing outlet for the Gengels' grief, and it will function adequately as an orphanage. The edifice we created on the hill is showier than an orphanage ought to be; a collection of cottages resting lightly along the slope with a central court or a chaconne would have created a more domestic environment for parentless children, but an informal organization would have diminished the memorial aspect of the building. The completed structure possesses clarity worthy of good architecture. It's a fitting memorial and will be a satisfactory orphanage, yet it could easily suit other purposes as well. Centuries from now it will be an amazing ruin, for whatever happens, this building cannot wash away.

The MoHI School rests in that middle third of architectural success. It is a building that belongs to Grand Goave yet subscribes to Vitruvius's dictums of firmness, commodity, and delight. The structure is strong without equal, every wall is locked to every column without a single unfilled cavity; it suits its purpose in a straightforward manner, yet contains architectural touch points that are both more subtle and more appropriate than those in the orphanage. The majestic stair is functional and inspiring; it marks the school as a public building worth reckoning. Yet it's too soon to call the building a success. We have built only half of it; we don't know when the rest will come. Right now it's squat; at its finished height the building will be regal. The Haitian penchant for glomming appendages onto the sides and tops of things could mar its integrity, but its bones are good. If Lex demonstrates care and restraint, the building will be a stunner.

During conception, a building belongs to me: a singular vision percolating through the right side of my brain. I share it through drawings that flow from my imagination and then modify that perfection to accommodate my clients' feedback and the realities of mass and gravity. As construction proceeds, my ownership seeps away until by the time the first orphan or schoolchild enters the building, I no longer own any of it. The contribution of my hand vanishes; its evolution is beyond my control. Since I've never been an overprotective parent, I have no trouble letting it go. Still, any architect will tell you that his best project will be the next one; it is still pure.

I would love to live in a world of 100 percent success where every building is perfectly aligned in its form and function. But that is an unrealistic expectation. So I try as hard as I can. I shrug off the elements that miss the mark and savor the ones that pierce the target.

This trip is about odds and ends and reflections. One cool evening Lex and Renee and I sit under the chaconne with nothing to do but enjoy one another's company. I ask Renee what single thing would most help Haiti. *Bring jobs to a country with 70 percent unemployment*, she says without hesitation. Lex points out why that's so much harder than it seems: *First, the government is too unstable to entice international corporations. Second, the red tape feeds corruption and everyone sticks his finger where there's money. Third, our work force is not disciplined enough to produce a consistent product on a regular basis.*

Lex's words remind me of a lecture I attended last summer, Daron Acemoglu reading from *Why Nations Fail* at the Harvard Book Store. I was curious how deep Mr. Acemoglu would get in his presentation before uttering the word *Haiti* and didn't have to wait long; Haiti was the very first country he described as a failed nation. It is the poster child of problem countries: poor, corrupt, debt-ridden, and ungovernable. The portrayal is fully deserved, yet I also know it's incomplete.

Mr. Acemoglu posits that successful countries support inclusive institutions that enable the majority of citizens to contribute to society. This enhances both individual and collective well-being. The flip side is failed nations, where extractive institutions run by elites deny citizens personal or collective benefits. This scenario, authoritarian regimes imposing their will on the populace for personal gain, describes Haiti at pretty much any point in its three-hundred-year history.

Why Nations Fail supports Lex's first two explanations of Haiti's economic limitations by tying a tight knot between economic and political stability. It's hard to pick the loose thread that might reverse Haiti's persistent downward spiral. Companies will not invest in a nation without a stable government, and a stable government is difficult to establish in a country where revolving-door rulers devote most of their energy to fending off the next coup. Governments fixated on their own survival value control above all else; they cannot embrace Mr. Acemoglu's advice that loosening economic reins actually provides the best chance for long-term stability.

Lex's third point—Haiti's challenge to create consistent, high-quality work—interests me most. I've witnessed Haitians work incredibly hard one day and turn unfathomably lazy the next. This variability wreaks havoc on our American fixation on schedule and productivity. Fortunately, Laurent Dubois's brilliant *Haiti:*

The Aftershocks of History offers a useful perspective on this point. Although Mr. Dubois does not use the terms *inclusive* versus *extractive*, he describes exploitation as the defining pattern of Haiti's history; plantation slaves overthrow their owners for the opportunity to tend their own plots only to be obstructed by two hundred years of mulatto elites, presidential generals, US Marines, and international corporations trying to boot heel them into export-producing laborers. The central government, always changing, always in debt, always seeking tariff revenue, always controlling through subjugation and fear, re-creates variations of a plantation-style economy to generate sugar or coffee for export. Meanwhile, the peasants, whose memory of slavery is strong despite two centuries of independence, are as wary of the central government as they were of their French owners. They establish *lacou*, group settlements with prescribed patterns of collective work, informal land ownership, and community marriage designed to distance, and even thwart, the central government.

Learning about Haitians' historical craving for local autonomy coupled with their well-founded distrust of national government gives me insight into the mentality of so many Haitian workers. When a laborer believes his work is directly beneficial to him, his effort is Herculean. But the moment he gets a whiff of working for the Man, however defined, his effort slows to a crawl. In the United States we dilute such conflicts; everything has a dollar value. We earn so much per hour or per week or per widget; so long as the worker reaps a benefit, he doesn't much care if the Man skims a reward as well. But that logic holds no sway here. The Man, whether a French planter or a UN peacekeeper, is the sworn enemy of the peasant, and the peasant will elect to suffer in pride rather than allow any of his sweat to enrich the enemy.

Haiti has been kicking and screaming against outsiders for three hundred years, and I'm convinced it will kick and scream for three hundred more before capitulating to order imposed by others. The global economy offers no successful model that fits Haiti, not the US, China, India, Germany, or even Rwanda. Truly successful industry in Haiti will have to adapt to Haitian terms, ones that bolster local initiative and downplay centralization. The model will never reach the efficiency of the vertically integrated

conglomerates prevalent in the US or China, it may not even bring
Haiti fully into the twenty-first century. But decentralized efforts
offer the best hope for Haiti's economic development.

Haitians are differently motivated than any other people I've
ever met. Toiling for a giant enterprise is a nonstarter; money
alone does not trigger motivation. Any viable Haitian economic
model must acknowledge that. At BLB and MoHI, we achieved
greatest productivity when we worked with a shared purpose
directly rooted to everyone's personal interest. The best way to
get things done was to align my objective with their objective.
Sometimes that meant reminding the men ours was a community
effort; sometimes it meant pitching in to erase the line between
labor and management; often it meant doing consciously silly
things, since nothing motivates Haitians more than trumping the
blan. If we can develop an economic system that flourishes in that
sweet spot, Haiti will prosper in its own unique way.

Which brings me back to my pervasive question: *What am I doing here?* The only honest answer is, *not enough.* I'm happy to be
here, and Haiti's happy to have me, but in truth, architects are
not Haiti's biggest need. Haiti needs both people with broader vision and those with more specific skills. We need a new breed of
master planner, one with a decentralized view; we need lawyers
and bankers and diplomats, even politicians, who can conceive
of a Haitian order in which the people, the *lacou*, inform the government rather than the other way around. And we need people
with truly basic skills—plumbers, carpenters, masons, and civil
engineers—to introduce the rudimentary aspects of public health
and construction safety we take for granted in the United States.
Universal clean water and sanitation would save more lives than
all the itinerant medical missionaries ever will; enforced building
codes would provide safe housing for more children than our orphanage can shelter. The longer I work here, the less architecture
I do. Most of my time is spent teaching and supervising construction; the more fundamental my mentoring, the more useful and
lasting my contribution.

It's Saturday afternoon, the end of the workweek. Len arrives
tomorrow with Cherylann and ten others. I will hand over a punch
list of outstanding work; he will remain for two weeks to install

finish plumbing, electrical fixtures, and complete the building. Our progress has been significant, but when I look around my eyes see only what is yet undone. I wanted the main courtyards finished, the tile floors grouted, the guardrails painted, the altar complete. I wanted Len and Cherylann to step through the front door and be enfolded in perfection. But we didn't achieve that; we're at 95 percent and holding. I don't know how to motivate these men to put the polish on my vision.

The carpentry crew is installing the final balusters on the main stair. They look good; vertically level and well spaced. There's a tarp on the tile floor; a guy on a ladder above us is painting the guardrail we finished yesterday. Polisca, a carpenter, steps without looking and kicks over a can of paint. I hear the sound and hustle from my perch at an upper baluster. A thick blue circle, the size of a large pancake, spreads out on the tile. Six guys watch it ooze across the porcelain surface.

"Don't just stand there, clean it up." I run into the kitchen and grab a roll of paper towels; when I return the guys are still peering at the blob. I fall to my knees, right the can and set it back on the tarp. The paint lid slipped across another tile, thin arcs of blue streak the surface. "Move the lid, on the tarp." No one acts unless I tell him. I rip open the towels and begin soaking up the paint, working from the outside in.

Faneus arrives with a trowel and skims up the thickest goop. Gama appears and offers to get gasoline. The worst of the paint is gone, though blue is etched in every crevice. Francky laughs. "Don't laugh at me." My voice is sharp. Francky turns on his heels and leaves. I wish the others would leave as well.

Gama arrives with gasoline. We daub our towels with the strong vapors and tackle the serious business of lifting the blue pigment. Fierce, mindless, manual labor can induce the deepest meditation. With my fingers focused on a few square inches my mind runs free. Francky's laughter rings in my ears. I've heard it time and again, a Haitian response to behavior they cannot comprehend. I've heard it when I complained about rebar installed with slack tolerance, when the diagonals of a rectangle didn't justify, when we didn't pull the plastic covering on temporary houses taut enough. It's the sound of people baffled by the quality I demand. It's not that Francky thinks spilt paint is funny so much as he cannot fathom why it matters so much. I must admit, as I kneel on the floor with raw knuckles, it is an apt question.

Why do I care so much about a few blue scratches on beige tile? They will probably wear away as orphans scurry up the stairs, or even if they don't, even if the paint binds to the tile forever, does it really matter? Somewhere back at MIT or in Catholic school or even before, the quaint notion that anything you do, you do right, was screwed so tight into my head that I pay more attention to a spot of blue paint than I do to my fellow humans. My fists clench the gasoline-soaked towels as I work into every crevice. The workers drift away. I am alone battling against the blue; I will not stop until it is vanquished.

Though my eyes are fixed on paint fragments, I am surrounded by a piece of great construction, construction built by Haitian hands. Yet I never sense they take as much pride in their achievement as I do. They should. The remarkable work is due to their effort. But they were just happy to have a job. When the *blan* makes a fuss they build it his way, when he turns his back they retreat to familiar methods. They tolerate the *blan*, but they do not understand him, and they certainly don't want to emulate him.

I scrub until all blue shadows evaporate. I lean back on my heels. I'm tired; I want to go home. I stand up. We have finished more than most thought possible even as we fell short of everything I hoped. But the day is ending; the workers linger in the shade, awaiting their pay. The crew will do no more, and neither will I.

On my last Sunday in Grand Goave I ask Lex and Renee if I can say a few words during church service. They agree. Gama translates.

"*Bonjou, zami mwen.*

"I have asked Pastor Lex and Renee to inscribe this Bible verse on the wall of your new school. The Gospel according to Luke, chapter 6, verse 48: *He is like a man building a house, who dug down deep and laid the foundation on rock. When a flood came, the torrent struck that house but could not shake it, because it was well built.*

"I have spent the past year living among you, working with you to create a house well built. It is a large house, with many rooms, and even though it is not complete, we have built enough that is strong and good and we can begin to use it. Over time we will finish this part, then add more rooms. The building will never be completely finished. It will change and grow old with us; for it is so sturdy it will outlive the youngest person here today.

"Every person in this church is a person with strong beliefs. We hold many beliefs in common. We believe in man's ability to improve his lot here on earth. We believe that when we work together we can create something greater than when we labor alone. We believe in constructing our buildings strong.

"Some of our beliefs are different. You believe that Jesus Christ is the Son of God. That is a powerful belief. It is a belief that brings you peace and brings you strength; it helps you overcome difficulties in life and be strong in the face of adversity.

"There are as many ways to worship god as there are different countries and different cultures. There are Buddhists and Christians and Hindus and Muslims and Jews. And within each of these religions there are many sects. Among Christians alone there are Methodists and Baptists and Catholics and Fundamentalists and Evangelicals and Lutherans. And among evangelicals there are many, many churches, each with inspired leaders.

"You are lucky here at Mission of Hope because you have Lex Edme, a truly inspired leader. He is a man of great faith as well as a man of great action. He is firm in what he believes, he is unwavering in his devotion to Jesus, and he guides this congregation with a clear vision.

"But Lex is not just a man of faith; he is a man of wisdom. In his wisdom he knows that this congregation, this community, this Mission of Hope cannot reach its full potential by itself. In order to provide the people of Grand Goave the opportunities you deserve, Lex reaches out to other Christians, to other religions, even to those who practice no religion. There is so much to be done here, and so much worth doing, and Lex knows the world is full of people with talent and energy who want to lend their hand here.

"I have known Lex for many years now. I love him very much. I am thankful for the opportunity he gave me to come to Grand Goave and work among you. You are some of the finest people I have ever met and you have allowed me to do some of the finest work I have ever done. Not every pastor has the strength and courage to invite a nonbeliever into his fold, but Lex is a man of strength and courage, and Mission of Hope has a new school because of his vision.

"I do not know when I will return to Grand Goave, but I will return. We will complete your building together. I hope it will be a place where your faith in Jesus Christ can grow stronger and stronger. But remember, it was built by people with many different ideas about god. May your faith be solid as the foundation Luke tells us about in his gospel. May you also remember that the reason our foundation is so strong is because we all built it together.

"Thank you very much. God bless you all."

The following morning, as the plane climbs out of Port-au-Prince, I should be full of recollection, but I'm not. Len and crew arrived on Sunday afternoon; we worked into the night reviewing all that remained to be done, distributing light and plumbing fixtures to their respective rooms, scribing the remaining cabinets to be built on walls. Len, being Len, insisted on more photos and glad-handing this morning, so we left late, ran into prodigious traffic and landed in a pothole that required four Haitians to bail us out. I managed to get to the airport on time, barely, but it hasn't been a morning conducive to reflection.

We cross the northern tip of Haiti, the countless Bahaman islands spread out beneath us. I read a back issue of *New York Times Magazine*, an article about a survivalist. The opening page sports an aerial photo of a huge fat man with a wife and six children laying on their lawn surrounded by the hundreds of possessions they believe will see them through disaster: stocks of grain, freeze-dried meals, sealed drums of water, battery packs, and, of course, guns. The article describes his plan to defend his family and his stuff against those less prepared when disaster strikes. Statistically, the morbidly obese man is more likely to die of cardiac disease and leave his young children Social Security dependents than to ever need his survival rations.

Welcome back to the United States, a nation that celebrates the dual illusions of individualism and consumerism to such extremes we actually believe that in the face of disaster what will save us is our stuff rather than our neighbor. I'm disgusted by the smug family, so confident in their possessions, so wrong in their belief that security can be achieved through accumulation. Instead of working to alleviate the political turmoil, climate change, and wars that trigger disaster, they bunker themselves against fellow humans and mistake hoarding for virtue. They remind me of the missionaries who come to Haiti to convert souls rather than teach skills, their incessant focus on an imagined future obscures their ability to fully participate in the present.

During my time in Haiti my own country weathered another presidential election, but no sooner was a winner proclaimed than we started arguing again, for we have become a nation where bickering has replaced conversation, grandstanding has replaced debate, and we define ourselves by our differences rather than our similarities. If Haiti is a country of teenagers, the United States is a nation of spoiled brats. We have forgotten that our beautiful country with its bountiful resources and enlightened form of government requires a diligent, educated, involved citizenry to remain strong. Instead of engaging a rapidly globalized world, we are slipping in education, in competitiveness, and in stature. We are the only superpower left standing and the only one stupid enough to deplete our advantages by waging war after war to no real purpose and for no real gain. When Rome burned, Nero at least made beautiful music; all we make is partisan noise.

According to the ideological divisions so precious to the United States, people like Len Gengel, Lex Edme, and Paul Fallon have no business knowing one another, let alone working together. We presume a black evangelical preacher, a conservative developer, and a gay architect share no common ground. But that assumption is not only wrong, it denies the inspired solutions that can only come from diverse collaboration. Haiti is such a desperate place that strange bedfellows are barely acknowledged; anyone willing to roll up his sleeves against the overwhelming need is welcome. In combining our talents, we not only created two impressive buildings, but we also surpassed what any one of us alone could achieve. In a land that understands what it takes to survive more acutely than any overfed American can pretend to know, we learned to depend upon one another.

The plane begins its descent into Miami. I never tire of seeing the sun glisten off the condominium towers on the barrier islands, the cars rolling over the causeways, the grid of Miami streets claimed from swamp, the miles of pastel houses with tile roofs and sparkling blue swimming pools. At descending altitude the United States appears to be an orderly expanse of fine-tuned harmony. I wonder if my next adventure might not be here, in the homeland I love so much I feel compelled to criticize its shortcomings. I pull my seatback upright, push my tray-table into place, eager to see what lies ahead.

Haiti is behind me, though I'm not entirely finished with it. I still have its dirt under my fingernails; we still need to build the school's trusses, and I'm responsible for two boys there. When I told Dieunison and Dieurie it would be some time before I return, Dieunison pleaded to get zipped into my duffel. But the boys belong in Grand Goave; it's their home.

Every moment I spent on that magic island was a restless search for meaning. I never found a rational explanation for how or why this tragic nation limps along; the clearest truth I found is scribed on those boys' faces. They have nothing, they expect nothing, they can survive on nothing, yet they thirst for more. In their short lives they have encountered as many setbacks as are in Haiti's history, yet the rudimentary miracles of regular meals, a durable roof, and the chance to learn awaken their potential.

Perhaps I might work in Haiti again, but I do not presume it. I understand that the confluence of such good people doing such good work is a stroke of fate that may not repeat and cannot be forced. Haiti beckoned me, and I answered her call. I am a better man for it, and I hope that Haiti has reaped some benefit from my effort. What beckons me next is for fate to decide. My task is simply to remain open to possibilities I cannot yet imagine.